D0205258

CRITICAL LEGAL STUDIES

STUDIES IN MORAL, POLITICAL, AND LEGAL PHILOSOPHY

General Editor: Marshall Cohen

CRITICAL LEGAL STUDIES

A Liberal Critique

Andrew Altman

PRINCETON UNIVERSITY PRESS
PRINCETON, NEW JERSEY

Published by Princeton University Press, 41 William Street,
Princeton, New Jersey 08540
In the United Kingdom: Princeton University Press, Oxford

Library of Congress Cataloging-in-Publication Data

Altman, Andrew, 1950–
Critical legal studies : a liberal critique / Andrew Altman.
p. cm. — (Studies in moral, political, and legal philosophy)
Includes index.
ISBN 0-691-07839-4
1. Critical legal studies. I. Title. II. Series.
K230.A447L38 1989
340.11—dc20 89-10429

Publication of this book has been aided by
the Whitney Darrow Fund of Princeton University Press

This book has been composed in Linotron Palatino

Princeton University Press books are printed on acid-free paper, and meet the guidelines for permanence and durability of the Committee on Production Guidelines for Book Longevity of the Council on Library Resources

Printed in the United States of America
by Princeton University Press,
Princeton, New Jersey
1 3 5 7 9 10 8 6 4 2

For my parents

CONTENTS

ACKNOWLEDGMENTS

A large number of persons and institutions have aided the writing of this book. Had it not been for my attendance in 1983 at a summer seminar for college teachers sponsored by the National Endowment for the Humanities, the book would never have come to be. Led by Joel Grossman at the University of Wisconsin-Madison, this seminar focused on the role of courts in American society. It was there that I first became acquainted with Critical Legal Studies and began to develop the understanding of law and legal institutions that I would need to write a book in legal philosophy. That summer I also had the good fortune to meet David Trubek, who along with Duncan Kennedy, proved to be instrumental in helping me obtain a Liberal Arts Fellowship in Law at Harvard Law School for the 1984–1985 academic year. I spent that year learning more about Critical Legal Studies, legal philosophy, and American legal doctrine. I am indebted to Harold Berman, Lewis Sargentich, Morton Horwitz, Duncan Kennedy, and Frank Michelman for discussing with me their ideas about law and philosophy and to the John Dewey Foundation for providing me with generous financial assistance during that year.

The George Washington University has been exceedingly generous in providing me with time and financial support for my research and writing; research grants from the university during the summers of 1987 and 1988 and a sabbatical leave for the fall of 1988 greatly aided the process of research and writing.

Jeffrey Lea expertly typed drafts of the first three chapters. Kathryn Fadem ably assisted me in the final preparation of the manuscript. Mark Tushnet, Fred Kellogg, Paul Schollmeier, and Robert Park read and commented helpfully on early versions of some chapters. I owe a special debt to John Fellas, whom I first met during my year at Harvard and who has been a constant source of encouragement and ideas. John carefully read through my drafts and discussed them with me at great length. The final product is substantially improved as a result of his help.

CRITICAL LEGAL STUDIES

INTRODUCTION

Over the course of the last decade, a group of legal scholars has generated an important body of literature that challenges some of the most cherished ideals of modern Western legal and political thought. This literature is part of a trend in legal scholarship known as the *Critical Legal Studies* movement (hereafter, CLS). The major theoretical aim of the movement is to provide a critique of liberal legal and political philosophy, and at the focal point of the critique, lies the concept of the rule of law. CLS scholars argue that the liberal embrace of the rule of law is actually incompatible with other essential principles of liberal political thinking. They thus charge that liberalism is logically incoherent and that the liberal commitment to the rule of law is implicated in this incoherence. CLS scholars argue as well that the rule of law does not exist in contemporary liberal states because the legal doctrines of those states are riddled with contradictions and inconsistencies. Moreover, some CLS thinkers contend that the rule of law cannot possibly serve the ends for which liberal theory embraces it. Law cannot perform the liberal task of constraining power and protecting people from intolerance and oppression, so even if the rule of law did exist, it could not accomplish its liberal goals.

This book is a critical examination of these CLS positions. It defends liberalism by exposing the flaws and the limitations of the principal CLS arguments. An important part of my critique of CLS is based on the idea that there are two incompatible strands of thinking within the CLS literature—one radical, one more moderate. The radical strand rests on indefensible conceptions of language and social reality. The moderate strand rests on conceptions that are largely defensible but from which nothing follows that significantly damages the essential elements of liberalism. Despite these serious shortcomings of CLS, the confrontation with its literature does provide a valuable service for liberal thought: It helps to provide liberalism with a clearer and stronger account of its essential commitments, fundamental premises, key arguments, and limitations.

After the initial chapter outlining the CLS-liberalism debate, the book proceeds in the second chapter to lay out the fundamentals of liberal legal and political philosophy. The chapter has two main aims: to present an account of the idea of the rule of law and to locate the role of that idea within the wider context of liberal political philosophy. In the course of pursuing those aims, the chapter examines and seeks to resolve a central debate within contemporary liberal legal philosophy: the dispute between Dworkin and Hart. The chapter interprets the dispute as one over competing liberal conceptions of the rule of law. From its examination of that dispute, the chapter develops a liberal account of the rule of law that remedies some of the inadequacies found in the work of Hart and Dworkin.

The third chapter, beginning a detailed examination of the CLS attack on liberalism, examines the CLS thesis that the principle of the rule of law is incompatible with other central principles of liberal political philosophy. The chapter presents and criticizes the three main lines of argument in the CLS literature for the thesis. Two of these lines are part of the moderate strand of CLS thinking; the other belongs to the radical strand. I argue that the moderate arguments fail to subvert liberalism because they are guilty of serious non sequiturs and rest on confusions about the meaning of liberal claims. Particularly pervasive in the CLS literature are confusions about the meaning of the liberal claim that the state ought to be neutral on questions of the "good." In order to untangle these confusions, I distinguish four forms of liberal neutrality and show how the apparent inconsistencies of liberal theory disappear when those distinctions are kept in mind. In addition, I contend that the radical line of CLS argument depends upon an incoherent and indefensible conception of linguistic meaning and defend an alternative approach to meaning that is consistent with liberal principles.

The fourth chapter is devoted to the CLS charge that the legal doctrines of liberal states such as the United States and Canada are riddled with contradictions and inconsistencies. In the CLS literature, this charge is conjoined to the premise that the rule of law, as liberalism understands it, is incompatible with the existence of contradictions and inconsistencies in legal doctrine. CLS thinkers thus conclude that there is a fatal incompatibility between actual liberal law and the liberal commitment to the rule of law.

In the fourth chapter, I distinguish three theses associated with the charge of doctrinal contradiction and examine the arguments for each. The first thesis holds that legal doctrine is a patchwork of norms deriving from starkly incompatible ethical viewpoints. The main lines of argument for the patchwork thesis are criticized as resting on a mistaken view of the kind of logical connection that exists between legal doctrines and the ethical viewpoints that underlie them. Moreover, CLS reasoning for the patchwork thesis confuses giving a historical account of the development of the law with providing a rational reconstruction of it.

The second thesis holds that the structure of legal doctrine can be seen in radically different ways, leading to conflicting results for individual legal cases. I show that there are two interpretations of this thesis to be found in the literature—one connected to the radical wing of CLS, the other to the moderate wing. The radical version holds that the structure of legal doctrine is, in effect, in the eyes of the beholder and that there is no sense in which there is an objective structure to the law. I argue that under the radical interpretation, the thesis rests on a highly questionable social ontology. A detailed and critical examination of that ontology is reserved for the final chapter. The moderate version concedes that there is an objective structure to the law but argues that the structure can be drastically changed over time by lawyers who try to extend the scope of doctrines that are at present of only marginal significance within the law. Under the moderate interpretation, the thesis is acceptable and important, but I show that it is also perfectly consistent with liberal thinking.

The third thesis holds that the principles that underlie legal rules are not consistently applied to all of the cases over which they claim moral authority; the principles are truncated short of the full range over which their proponents would have them exercise jurisdiction. I argue that this truncation thesis is sound and important as applied to Anglo-American legal doctrine but that nothing in liberalism's understanding of the rule of law is incompatible with the soundness of the thesis. In fact, the moral pluralism characteristic of the liberal state leads one to expect that the truncation thesis will accurately portray the legal doctrines of a liberal state. Truncation is the outcome of the processes of compromise and accommodation that are essential to the functioning of the liberal political order.

The fifth and final chapter examines the CLS claim that law cannot accomplish the liberal purpose of constraining power and protecting people from intolerance and oppression. The claim is shown to rest on a view about the ontology of social reality that revolves around the idea that social structures have no objective existence. The chapter shows that this idea underlies the radical arguments examined in the previous two chapters. I criticize the idea and its related ontology, showing the sense in which social structures are objective and explaining how law can constrain power. This phase of my argument completes the criticism of the radical views of the CLS movement. In addition, the chapter demonstrates that there is a more moderate view of social ontology in the CLS literature but that such a view actually supports the liberal claim that law can effectively constrain power and protect people. This phase of my argument completes the task of showing that the ideas of the moderate wing of the movement are compatible with liberalism.

The issues raised in the final chapter reveal an important limitation of the liberal reliance on law to protect people from intolerance and oppression. Liberal thinkers have often exaggerated the ability of law to constrain power and thereby to protect people, and they have similarly underestimated the degree of assistance that the law needs from other cultural practices and institutions. CLS thinkers point to the many occasions when laws designed to protect have failed to accomplish that end. Yet I argue that liberalism can accommodate these CLS points. It must be a form of liberalism that acknowledges that law is one among many cultural institutions that serve to shape the moral quality of our lives. However, such a liberalism may still cogently maintain that law can make a vital contribution to the task of protecting people from the evils of intolerance and oppression.

No one who reads this book should labor under the impression that it provides an exhaustive account of CLS. It examines CLS mainly from the perspective of the issues that have occupied Anglo-American legal philosophy over the last several decades. There are undoubtedly other viewpoints from which CLS can be fruitfully approached: social-scientific, legal, and other philosophical approaches. The reader should not expect this book to examine every important aspect of the CLS movement. However, the reader should expect to find a clear and systematic account of the philosophical significance of CLS and some strong, if not conclusive, rejoinders to the main CLS attacks on liberalism.

ONE

CRITICAL LEGAL STUDIES v. LIBERALISM

The Players

This book presents a sustained encounter between two players on the scene of contemporary legal thought: CLS and liberalism. The players are antagonists. So deeply has the antagonism run that too rarely has one side been willing to engage the other in a serious and sustained debate over the deepest issues that divide them. Thus, Ronald Dworkin, perhaps the leading figure in contemporary liberal legal theory, has declared that CLS's principal arguments "have so far been spectacular and even embarrassing failures."[1] It is not surprising, then, to find that Dworkin has devoted only a few pages to CLS in the more than eight hundred pages of his last two books.

CLS theorists have been no more generous in their assessment of Dworkin and his fellow liberals. Elizabeth Mensch dismisses both Dworkin and John Rawls in a few lines of a footnote. Of the latter, Mensch writes that he "somewhat whimsically, has simply resurrected seventeenth-century social contract theory in an effort to universalize liberal thought." A few lines later, Dworkin is disposed of with the claim that he "simply vacillates between an implicit reliance on natural law theory and reliance on the inherent legitimacy of the judicial tradition."[2] Alan Freeman and John Schlegel write about liberal theorists in the same vein, dismissing Rawls, Ackerman, and Locke in less than half of a law-review page.[3] It is not strange that no serious engagement with the liberal

[1] Ronald Dworkin, *Law's Empire* (Cambridge: Harvard University Press, 1986), p. 274.

[2] Elizabeth Mensch, "The History of Mainstream Legal Thought," in *The Politics of Law*, ed. D. Kairys (New York: Pantheon Books, 1982), pp. 18–19.

[3] Alan Freeman and John Schlegel, "Sex, Power, and Silliness: An Essay on Ackerman's *Reconstructing American Law*," *Cardozo Law Review* 6 (1985): 855.

tradition has been forthcoming in the wake of such dismissals of its leading spokespersons.[4]

In general, then, liberal theorists and their CLS critics have been highly dismissive of one another's work. There are, to be sure, some exceptions. On the liberal side, Lawrence Solum and John Stick have written illuminating pieces in which they have taken the CLS view seriously and subjected it to thoughtful criticism.[5] On the critical side, Roberto Unger has significantly modified his views over the years in order to incorporate into his thinking more and more of the ideas of liberalism.[6] The fact remains, however,

[4] In Mark Tushnet's recent CLS critique of constitutional law, there is a prima facie puzzling divergence from the standard CLS attitude toward liberal theory. Referring to the liberal tradition, Tushnet writes: "Most systematic political thinkers have had a more subtle understanding of the problems than those I will describe as inherent in the tradition." He goes on to use the phrase "amateur political theory" to describe the sort of liberalism which is at the focus of his critical account. Tushnet, *Red, White, and Blue: A Critical Analysis of Constitutional Law* (Cambridge: Harvard University Press, 1988), p. 5 n. 9; see also p. 13 n. 35.

These remarks are puzzling if Tushnet intends to make a contribution to the theoretical debate about liberalism, since one would expect that a convincing CLS critique of liberal thought would tackle its most sophisticated and systematic defenders, not its amateurs. Of course, Tushnet's work is largely historical and aims to analyze the most widely held versions of liberal ideas rather than the philosophically strongest versions. However, the work is not entirely historical and does seek to contribute to the theoretical debate between CLS and liberalism.

I believe that Tushnet's remarks about the amateur status of the liberal ideas on which his critical account focuses stem from a realization that has yet to strike most other CLS authors. The realization is that the picture of liberalism on which CLS has based its attack does not do justice to the ideas propounded by liberalism's most sophisticated theorists. This realization is, as I show in later chapters, exactly right. But Tushnet fails to take the next logical step: to concede explicitly that the CLS attack on liberalism is rendered highly problematic by its failure to come to grips with the most sophisticated liberal theorists. Instead, he argues that the attack succeeds against the amateurs of the liberal tradition! To be fair to Tushnet, it must be conceded that he levels devastating criticisms at some liberal constitutional theorists who are anything but amateurs in the law—e.g., Ely. But those criticisms are limited to the domain of constitutional theory and do not reach the basic philosophical underpinnings of liberalism.

[5] Lawrence Solum, "On the Indeterminacy Crisis: Critiquing Critical Dogma," *University of Chicago Law Review* 54 (1987): 462–503; John Stick, "Can Nihilism Be Pragmatic?" *Harvard Law Review* 100 (1986): 332–401. However, these careful liberal responses to CLS are quite atypical. Cornel West describes the overall trend in recent liberal commentary on CLS in this way: "In the recent wave of commentary, unfortunately, hostile gut reactions have replaced guarded respectful responses; passionate political and cultural evaluations have supplanted balanced intellectual assessments." West, "CLS and a Liberal Critic," *Yale Law Journal* 97 (1988): 757–58. I agree with West that most recent liberal commentary has exhibited an excess of hostility and a dearth of careful analysis, but I do not think that the earlier liberal commentary was any better on that score. An example of recent intemperate liberal polemics against CLS can be found in William Ewald, "Unger's Philosophy: A Critical Legal Study," *Yale Law Journal* 97 (1988): 665–756.

[6] William Ewald is, at best, misleading when he claims that the arguments in Unger's recent work build upon those in his first book, *Knowledge and Politics*. See

that the literature contains no comprehensive, systematic, and closely argued exploration of the deepest issues in legal and political philosophy that divide the two sides.

This book is the outcome of an effort to fill that lacuna. It proceeds on the premise that CLS and liberal theorists are wrong in their mutually dismissive attitudes. Each side can profit by taking a more careful and systematic look at the other side's claims. This is not to suggest that minds will change drastically as a result. It is to suggest that both liberals and critics can gain a better grasp of their own position, its strengths and its weaknesses, its essential elements and its adventitious ones, through a serious confrontation with the ideas of their antagonists.

I make no pretense of writing this book from a perspective neutral between liberal theory and that of CLS. My perspective is committed to the basic elements of liberal legal philosophy. My aim is to show that the CLS critique of liberal legal thought fails to inflict any serious damage, that liberal thought contains the resources required for meeting successfully the challenge posed by CLS. Yet I also aim to show that the confrontation with CLS provides liberal legal theory with a clearer and stronger account of its essential principles, its central arguments, and its limitations.

In this initial chapter, I sketch the outlines of the controversy between CLS and liberalism. Each viewpoint is treated in a highly preliminary manner. The more complete treatment and assessment are reserved for subsequent chapters.

The Rule of Law

The CLS movement is a trend in legal scholarship that has developed over the last decade or so in a large number of law-review articles and in a few key books. Its ideas have proved to be unusually controversial, leading the dean at a major American law school to declare that adherents to CLS are not fit to teach in law schools.[7] The controversy stems in large part from the movement's challenge to some of the most cherished ideals of modern liberal thought. In particular, CLS represents a challenge to a principle

---

Ewald, "Unger's Philosophy," 729. Ewald fails to recognize that there have been some drastic changes in Unger's thinking that bring him quite close to the liberal camp on a number of important issues. I discuss some of the important changes in Unger's views in the final chapter of this book.

[7] Paul Carrington, "Of Law and the River," *Journal of Legal Education* 34 (1984): 227.

central to liberal legal thought—the rule of law. The central contention of CLS is that the rule of law is a myth.

Undoubtedly, I have put this contention in a form that is too crude and calls for clarification and qualification. Yet it is an appropriate first approximation of the heart of the CLS view and serves to draw the main battle line along which CLS has chosen to wage its campaign against liberal legal philosophy. Its critique of liberal legal thought largely stands or falls with the success of its attack on the idea of the rule of law as it is understood by liberal thought.

There can be no doubt that a vital element of liberal legal philosophy is the principle that a society ought to operate under the rule of law. Its commitment to the rule of law originates with the birth of modern liberalism in the seventeenth century and remains as strong as ever in contemporary liberal theory. And the terms in which the rule of law is endorsed by liberals have remained remarkably constant throughout rather substantial changes in certain aspects of liberal theory and some rather deep disagreements among liberals themselves. In his *Second Treatise of Government*, Locke expressed his commitment in these words:

> [F]reedom of men under government is to have a standing rule to live by, common to every one of that society and made by the legislative power erected in it, a liberty to follow my own will in all things where the rule prescribes not, and not to be subject to the inconstant, uncertain, unknown, arbitrary will of another man.[8]

Locke went on to argue that

> the legislative or supreme authority cannot assume to itself a power to rule by extemporary, arbitrary decrees, but is bound to dispense justice and to decide the rights of the subject by promulgated, standing laws, and known authorized judges.[9]

And the importance of the rule of law to Locke's thinking is concisely formulated in his *Letter Concerning Toleration*: "There are two sorts of contests amongst men; the one managed by law, the other by force: and these are of that nature, that where the one ends, the other always begins."[10]

Several centuries later, Hobhouse argued for the reconstruction

[8] John Locke, *Second Treatise of Government* (Indianapolis: Bobbs-Merrill, 1952), p. 15.

[9] Ibid., p. 77.

[10] John Locke, *A Letter Concerning Toleration* (Indianapolis: Hackett, 1983), p. 49.

of liberal theory, implicitly and explicitly rejecting significant elements of Locke's early version. Hobhouse argued that the state should adopt economic policies calculated to reduce the vast inequalities generated by the operation of the market. He called for social control over basic economic resources and rejected what he regarded as traditional liberalism's excessive reliance on private ownership and the market mechanism. Yet the ringing endorsement of the rule of law remains the same:

> [T]he first condition of free government is government not by the arbitrary determination of the ruler, but by fixed rules of law, to which the ruler himself is subject.[11]

A few decades after Hobhouse's classic reformulation of liberalism, Hayek repudiated the tendency toward socialism and state economic planning that Hobhouse's liberalism embodied, which was gaining wide acceptance in Western liberal democracies. Yet Hayek too endorsed the principle of the rule of law and even proceeded to claim that socialist economic policies were to be rejected because they were necessarily inconsistent with it:

> Nothing distinguishes more clearly conditions in a free country from those in a country under arbitrary government than the observance in the former of the great principles known as the Rule of Law. Stripped of all technicalities, this means that government in all its actions is bound by rules fixed and announced beforehand—rules which make it possible to foresee with fair certainty how the authority will use its coercive powers in given circumstances and to plan one's individual affairs on the basis of this knowledge.[12]

In recent years, Joseph Raz has rejected Hayek's argument against socialistic economic policies, suggesting that Hayek exaggerated the importance of punctiliously observing the rule of law. But it is manifest that Raz himself places great value on its observance and stands squarely in the liberal tradition when he declares that "it is clear that deliberate disregard for the rule of law violates human dignity."[13]

Finally, we may cite the two most influential American legal phi-

[11] L. T. Hobhouse, *Liberalism* (New York: Oxford University Press, 1964), p. 17.

[12] Friedrich Hayek, *The Road to Serfdom* (Chicago: University of Chicago Press, 1944), p. 72.

[13] Joseph Raz, *The Authority of Law* (New York: Oxford University Press, 1979), p. 221.

losophers of the last half century, Lon Fuller and Ronald Dworkin. The work of these important liberal thinkers embodies a strong commitment to the rule of law. Fuller writes:

> Surely the very essence of the Rule of Law is that in acting upon the citizen (by putting him in jail, for example, or declaring invalid a deed under which he claims title to property) a government will faithfully apply rules previously declared as those to be followed by the citizen and determinative of his rights and duties. . . . Applying rules faithfully implies, in turn, that rules will take the form of general declarations. . . . [T]he basic principle of the Rule of Law [is] that the acts of a legal authority toward the citizen must be legitimated by being brought within the terms of a previous declaration of general rules.[14]

And Dworkin describes the rule of law in its most general form in this way:

> [T]he most abstract and fundamental point of legal practice is to guide and constrain the power of government. . . . Law insists that force not be used or withheld, no matter how useful that would be to ends in view, no matter how beneficial or noble these ends, except as licensed or required by individual rights and responsibilities flowing from past political decisions about when collective force is justified.
>
> The law of a community on this account is the scheme of rights and responsibilities that meet that complex standard: they license coercion because they flow from past decisions of the right sort.[15]

In citing this line of liberal thinkers from Locke through Dworkin, I do not mean to suggest that they all have precisely the same conception of the rule of law. There are important differences, which we shall have the opportunity to explore in the next chapter. Yet there is a remarkable similarity of conceptions and commitments, given the immense span of years and the wide divergence on issues in political philosophy that otherwise divide these thinkers.

The rule of law plays such a central and abiding role in the theories of liberal thinkers because they judge it to be an indispens-

[14] Lon Fuller, *The Morality of Law*, rev. ed. (New Haven: Yale University Press, 1964), pp. 209–10, 214.

[15] Dworkin, *Law's Empire*, p. 93.

able institutional mechanism for securing the dominant value cherished by their tradition—individual liberty—and those values that are intertwined with it, such as toleration, individuality, privacy, and private property. The liberal believes that in the absence of the rule of law, there would be no way to secure in practice the individual liberty that he cherishes in theory. The law is an indispensable mechanism for regulating public and private power in a way that effectively helps to prevent the oppression and domination of the individual by other individuals and by institutions. Law as such is not sufficient to accomplish this purpose, and every liberal will also concede that oppressive laws are not only a logical possibility but a historical reality as well. But liberal legal thought holds that the rule of law is, in the world of the modern nation-state at least, a necessary condition for securing a sufficiently wide zone of individual liberty. Moreover, it is a necessary condition that in practice, takes us a significant way toward the goal of preventing the oppression or domination of the individual. The rule of law can do this, according to liberal thought, because the law has the power to constrain, confine, and regulate the exercise of social and political power.

The CLS *Attack*

There are three main prongs to the CLS attack on the liberal embrace of the rule of law, three main elements to the CLS charge that the rule of law, as liberal theory conceptualizes it, is a myth. Each of these is examined in detail in chapters 3, 4, and 5, respectively. But a preliminary characterization of them is possible at this stage.

The first prong hinges on the claim that the rule of law is not possible in a social situation where the kind of individual freedom endorsed by the liberal view reigns. Such a situation would be characterized by a pluralism of fundamentally incompatible moral and political viewpoints. The establishment of the rule of law under the conditions of pluralism would require some mode of legal reasoning that could be sharply distinguished from moral and political deliberation and choice. There would have to be a sharp distinction, so the argument goes, between law, on one side, and both morals and politics, on the other. Without such a distinction, judges and other individuals who wield public power could impose their own views of the moral or political good on others under the cover of law. Such impositions, however, would destroy the rule of law and the liberal freedom it is meant to protect.

Thus, the liberal view requires that legal reasoning—that is, reasoning about what rights persons have under the law and why—be clearly distinguished from reasoning about political or ethical values. Legal reasoning is not to be confused with deciding which party to a case has the best moral or political argument. Yet it is precisely this kind of legal reasoning that is impossible in a setting of moral and political pluralism, according to CLS. The law-politics distinction collapses, and legal reasoning becomes tantamount to deciding which party has the best moral or political argument. Karl Klare puts the CLS position concisely: "This [liberal] claim about legal reasoning—that it is autonomous from political and ethical choice—is a falsehood."[16]

Duncan Kennedy is even more blunt, but the essential point is the same:

> Teachers teach nonsense when they persuade students that legal reasoning is distinct, *as a method for reaching correct results,* from ethical or political discourse in general. . . . There is never a "correct legal solution" that is other than the correct ethical or political solution to that legal problem.[17]

The second prong of the CLS attack on the rule of law revolves around the claim that the legal doctrines of contemporary liberal states are riddled by contradictions. The contradictions consist of the presence of pairs of fundamentally incompatible norms serving as authoritative elements of legal doctrine in virtually all departments of law. These contradictions are thought to defeat the notion that the rule of law actually reigns in those societies that most contemporary liberal philosophers regard as leading examples of political societies operating under the rule of law. Kennedy contends that the contradictions are tied to the fact that legal doctrine does not give us a coherent way to talk about the rights of individuals under the law: "Rights discourse is internally inconsistent, vacuous, or circular. Legal thought can generate plausible rights justifications for almost any result."[18] Klare echoes Kennedy's claim: "Legal reasoning is a texture of openness, indeterminacy, and contradiction."[19]

[16] Karl Klare, "The Law School Curriculum in the 1980s: What's Left?" *Journal of Legal Education* 32 (1982): 340.

[17] Duncan Kennedy, "Legal Education as Training for Hierarchy," in Kairys, *Politics of Law*, p. 47.

[18] Ibid., p. 48.

[19] Klare, "Law School Curriculum," p. 340.

As Klare and Kennedy suggest, the CLS view is that the consequence of these doctrinal contradictions is pervasive legal indeterminacy—that is, the widespread inability of the authoritative rules and doctrines to dictate a determinate outcome to legal cases. The contradictions enable lawyers and judges to argue equally well for either side of most legal cases, depending on which of two contradictory legal norms they choose to rely upon. Moreover, the existence of indeterminacy is tied to the collapse of the distinction between law and politics. Judges can and do covertly rely on moral and political considerations in deciding which of two incompatible legal norms they will base their decisions upon. In existing liberal states, we have not the rule of law but the rule of politics. Joseph Singer sums up this phase of the CLS attack on the rule of law nicely:

> While traditional legal theorists acknowledge the inevitability and desirability of some indeterminacy, traditional legal theory requires a relatively large amount of determinacy as a fundamental premise of the rule of law. Our legal system, however, has never satisfied this goal.[20]

Closely associated with the first two prongs of the CLS attack on the rule of law is the thesis that the very idea of the rule of law serves as an instrument of oppression and domination. David Kairys expresses the general idea in a manner characteristic of much CLS writing:

> The law is a major vehicle for the maintenance of existing social and power relations. . . . The law's perceived legitimacy confers a broader legitimacy on a social system . . . characterized by domination. This perceived legitimacy of the law is primarily based . . . on the distorted notion of government by law, not people.[21]

In the CLS view, then, the idea that our political society operates under the rule of law serves to perpetuate illegitimate relations of power. Exposing the rule of law as a myth is thought of in the CLS movement as an essential part of a strategy designed to undermine those relations of power.

I do not provide in this book any detailed exploration of the CLS premise that illegitimate relations of power pervade contem-

[20] Joseph Singer, "The Player and the Cards: Nihilism and Legal Theory," *Yale Law Journal* 94 (1984): 13.

[21] David Kairys, "Introduction," in *Politics of Law*, pp. 5–6.

porary liberal democratic societies. Any such exploration would take us far afield from the issues in legal philosophy that form the focus of the book and would carry us too deep into the complexities of normative political philosophy. Although I find it impossible and undesirable to avoid entirely issues of normative political theory, the center of gravity of the book lies in the area of legal philosophy. However, to the extent that I defend the possibility and reality of the rule of law, my argument undercuts the CLS notion that relations of power in our society, illegitimate or not, are sustained by the belief in a fiction.

The third prong of the CLS attack focuses on the idea that law is capable of constraining the exercise of social and political power. The contention is made that to think of law as capable of such constraint is to adopt a form of fetishism—to be guilty of regarding a human creation as though it were an independent power capable of controlling those who in fact have created and sustained it. This form of fetishism disempowers human beings; it places them in thrall to forces over which they can and should be the masters. In this CLS view, then, the idea of the rule of law must be criticized as part of a general attack on ideas that disempower humans.

The Totalitarian Charge

In light of the CLS attack on the rule of law, it should not be surprising that the movement has generated an unusual degree of controversy and opposition among legal theorists. There is, however, another source of controversy. The CLS literature is often construed by its opponents as strongly inclined toward a total rejection of liberal values. The attack on law is seen as one phase of a more general totalitarian tilt against the individual freedoms associated with the tradition of liberal political philosophy.[22] I do not believe that a fair examination of the CLS literature can support such an interpretation. It is, at best, a gross caricature. Many CLS authors often do argue that liberal values present only one side of the human story, that there are things people do and should cherish that are either omitted or distorted in the liberal picture. Solidarity and community are the values most often invoked in this regard. However, it is a mistake to infer some sort of totalitarian tilt in CLS from its talk of solidarity, community, and so forth; its

[22] One of the most recent liberal attacks on CLS intimating that the movement has totalitarian or fascist overtones is Ewald, "Unger's Philosophy," pp. 733, 741–53.

thinkers are strongly committed to the essential individual freedoms that liberals have fought to secure against their absolutist, fascist, and totalitarian foes. The words of three prominent CLS authors testify to this conclusion.

First, consider the single most important text in the CLS literature, Roberto Unger's *Knowledge and Politics*. This work has been interpreted as a total rejection of liberal values. It is true that Unger repeatedly insists that what is needed is a "total criticism" of liberalism rather than the "partial criticisms" which many thinkers have offered hitherto.[23] However, Unger does not equate "total criticism" with "total rejection."[24] As Unger uses the term, a *total criticism* of liberalism is one that sees liberalism as a whole, as a single, interconnected system of principles and postulates about human psychology, morality, law, and politics. Unger explicitly states that the liberal value of individual freedom is a part of the liberal system that must be cherished and preserved. And in allusion to the great English liberals—including Locke, Bentham, and Mill—Unger declares:

> Many of the liberal thinkers were devoted to freedom. . . . If for no other reason than for this devotion, they will rank forever as heroes and teachers of the human race, and all the sins of England will be forgiven because of her services to liberty.[25]

Unger's purpose is not to reject the liberal devotion to individual liberty but to claim that there are other aspects of human life that ought to be cherished for which liberal theory does not adequately account. It may be wrong that liberalism cannot adequately account for community, solidarity and the like. But it is instructive that liberal philosophers do not reject the importance of those values; rather, they argue that liberal theory can adequately account for them.[26] The propensity of liberal theorists to make such arguments testifies to the fallacy of inferring that CLS is guilty of a totalitarian tilt against individual freedoms because it insists on ac-

[23] Roberto Unger, *Knowledge and Politics* (New York: Free Press, 1975), pp. 1–3, 10, 15, 17–18.

[24] Karsten Harries appears to misinterpret Unger on this point. See Harries, "The Contradictions of Liberal Thought," *Yale Law Journal* 85 (1975–1976): 842.

[25] Unger, *Knowledge and Politics*, p. 277.

[26] See, e.g., Joel Feinberg, "Liberalism, Community, and Tradition," *Tikkun* 3 (May/June 1988): 38–40, 116–20. Feinberg declares that "liberals should begin by acknowledging the bedrock importance of community to human nature and well-being" (39).

knowledging the central importance of community and solidarity in human life.

Another CLS author, Mark Tushnet, echoes Unger's view that liberal values are not to be rejected but are to be seen as part of a fuller account of what humans do and should cherish. For Tushnet, it is the civic republican tradition in modern political thought that provides the needed supplement. He claims that "just as the republican tradition correctly emphasizes our mutual dependence, the liberal tradition correctly emphasizes our individuality and the threats we pose to one another."[27] And Duncan Kennedy is also not hesitant to embrace liberal freedom. In a discussion of the liberal conception of individual rights, Kennedy claims, "Embedded in the rights notion is a liberating accomplishment of our culture: the affirmation of free human subjectivity against the constraints of group life, along with the paradoxical countervision of a group life that creates and nurtures individuals capable of freedom."[28]

These statements by three of the leading critics hardly evidence a commitment to the totalitarian repudiation of individual liberty. To be sure, liberal theorists will see a threat to liberty in the CLS effort to brand the rule of law a myth. But that view hinges on a particular answer to one of the points of contention between the two groups. CLS does not deny the importance of individual liberty, contrary to the claims of those who intimate that the movement is tainted by totalitarianism. Rather, CLS denies that the rule of law does, or could, protect such liberty and so asserts that other social mechanisms must be invented for such protection. I will argue that the CLS position is unsound, but my argument is wholly consistent with recognizing that individual liberty holds a key place in CLS thinking.

Conflict within CLS

It would be a mistake to complete this overview of the CLS-liberalism debate without introducing some of the disagreements that divide the CLS movement. The movement is by no means monolithic, and there are fundamental differences that divide it into various wings. I am especially concerned with two incompatible strands of thinking that run through the CLS literature, one of

[27] Tushnet, *Red, White, and Blue*, p. 23.

[28] Duncan Kennedy, "Critical Labor Law Theory: A Comment," *Industrial Relations Law Journal* 4 (1981): 506.

which may be characterized as *radical*, the other as *moderate*.[29] The radical strand combines a position on the meanings of legal terms and norms that can loosely be described as *deconstructionist* with the idea that there is no objective structure to the law or any social institution. The position on meaning holds that the words that constitute legal norms and doctrines have no stable or fixed meanings, but are rather "empty vessels" into which the individual may pour whatever meaning he or she chooses.[30] This view is conjoined to the position that it is an illusion to see the law, or any other element of social reality, as having a structure independent of any individual's perception of it. Tushnet expresses the radical position on the structure of legal doctrine in the course of endorsing a certain strand of thinking in the American legal realist movement:

> The materials of legal doctrine are almost measureless, and the acceptable techniques of legal reasoning—distinguishing on the basis of the facts, analogizing to other areas of law where cognate problems arise, and the like—are so flexible that they allow us to assemble diverse precedents into whatever pattern we choose.[31]

The moderate strand of CLS rejects the deconstructionist position on meaning and the view that law and social reality have no objective structure. It holds instead that words do have a settled core of meaning but that the interpretations required to render legal decisions are inescapably responsive to the individual's moral and political beliefs. It holds that our law does have an objective structure but that this structure is a function of a certain controversial and inadequate ethical perspective. Unger gives the most consistent and systematic expression to the moderate strand in CLS. He has never even flirted with deconstructionism, and the social theory that he has recently developed involves a clear rejection of the view that social reality and law are not constituted by objective

[29] Solum's distinction between a strong and a weak interpretation of the CLS claim that the law is indeterminate parallels in some measure my distinction between radical and moderate strands in CLS thinking. However, I attempt to go beyond Solum's account by showing that the different CLS versions of the indeterminacy thesis stem from starkly incompatible conceptions of language and social reality and exploring in some detail the soundness and the political implications of those conceptions. See Solum, "On the Indeterminacy Crisis," 470.

[30] Clare Dalton describes legal categories as "empty vessels" in "An Essay in the Deconstruction of Contract Doctrine," *Yale Law Journal* 94 (1985): 1002; see also, in the same article, 1008–10.

[31] Tushnet, *Red, White and Blue*, pp. 191–92.

structures. Unger describes the kinds of explanations offered by his social theory by claiming that they

> assign central importance to the distinction between routine deals or quarrels and the recalcitrant institutional and imaginative frameworks in which they ordinarily occur. . . . In the contemporary Western democracies the social framework includes legal rules that use property rights as the instrument of economic decentralization [and] constitutional arrangements that provide for representation while discouraging militancy.[32]

Unger's idea of a social and legal framework that shapes and guides routine activities and is resistant to change rests on a rejection of the radical premise that social reality and law do not consist of structures independent of the way any particular individual chooses to think about them.

These important differences between the radical and moderate wings of CLS lead to differences in argument when it comes to the three main elements of the attack on the rule of law as the liberal conceptualizes it. The radical wing attacks on the basis of its deconstructionism and its view that law has no objective structure. The moderate wing attacks on the basis of its claims about legal interpretation and the relation of the existing structure of law to a certain (allegedly) deficient ethical viewpoint.

My strategy in defending liberal legal philosophy can now be concisely stated, albeit in a slightly oversimplified form. On the one hand, the strategy aims to show that the radical arguments of CLS rest on flawed theoretical premises regarding language and law: The deconstructionist position on meaning and the idea that law and social reality have no objective structure are both indefensible. On the other hand, my strategy aims to show that the theoretical premises of the moderate wing are basically sound but do not entail any serious deficiency in the liberal conception of the rule of law. There are indeed certain forms of liberal theory whose conceptions of the rule of law are arguably inconsistent with the ideas of the moderate wing, but that is only to say that certain forms of liberal theory are weaker and more vulnerable to criticism than others. The basic ideas of the moderate wing, to the extent

[32] Roberto Unger, *Social Theory: Its Situation and Its Task* (New York: Cambridge University Press, 1987), p. 3. Unger's theory of social frameworks is inconsistent with the third element in the CLS attack on the rule of law. The implications of this inconsistency are explored in the last chapter.

that they are sound, are fully consistent with stronger liberal conceptions of the rule of law.[33]

The initial task in this liberal critique of CLS, then, is to examine various versions of liberal legal theory with the aim of stating a sufficiently strong version. This can best be carried out, I believe, by presenting the ideas of some of the main theorists in modern and contemporary liberal legal philosophy and examining the debates between such theorists. Let us turn now to those ideas and debates.

[33] There are ways of criticizing CLS that take a quite different tack from the one taken in this book. For example, some commentators have argued that CLS undercuts its own avowed aim of transforming society because it focuses too heavily on legal doctrines and philosophical theories about law, and not enough on actual social behavior and thought. I do not expound or examine these criticisms because my interest is precisely questions of philosophical theory and legal doctrine, but this is not meant to deny the importance or cogency of such criticisms. For a good statement of this kind of criticism, see Frank Munger and Carroll Seron, "Critical Legal Studies v. Critical Legal Theory," *Law and Policy* 6 (1984): 280. For a somewhat different version of the idea that CLS undercuts its own political program, see Donald Brosnan, "Serious but Not Critical," *Southern California Law Review* 60 (1987): 264–65, 356, 375, 392.

TWO

LIBERALISM AND LEGALITY

The Rule of Law: A Generic Liberal Model

The principle that societies should operate under the rule of law has been embraced by legal and political thinkers for over two millennia. It is one of the few principles of political philosophy upon which the ancients and the moderns agree. The defense of the principle of legality—that is, the rule of law—is to be found not only in Locke, Bentham, Constant, and the other modern liberal theorists but in Plato and Aristotle as well. Plato blames the unjust conviction of Socrates on a democratic Athens that flouted the rule of law.[1] The political society of Plato's *Laws* is one in which the rule of law reigns.[2] And Aristotle is as insistent as Plato that in practice, the best form of political society is one that is under the rule of law.[3]

The grounds upon which modern liberal thinkers have embraced the principle of legality are, however, significantly different from those of Plato and Aristotle. It is true that for both ancients and moderns, a political society operates under the rule of law when both public and private power are regulated and constrained by law. It is also true that both ancients and moderns see the rule of law as an indispensable mechanism for preventing political corruption—the use of public power for private ends. And for both ancients and moderns, the rule of law involves equality under law: There is to be a single set of authoritative norms that apply equally

[1] Plato, *Crito*, in *The Collected Dialogues of Plato*, ed. Edith Hamilton and Huntington Cairns (Princeton: Princeton University Press, 1961), p. 54b–c.

[2] Plato, *The Laws of Plato*, trans. Thomas Pangle (New York: Basic Books, 1980), p. 715d. The standard interpretation of *The Republic* construes it as suggesting that the philosopher-king is not subject to the constraints of the rule of law. I accept such an interpretation, but it is clear in Plato's later dialogues, such as *The Laws*, that he believes that the rule of law is essential to any mode of political life in our imperfect world.

[3] See Aristotle, *The Politics of Aristotle*, trans. Benjamin Jowett (Oxford: Clarendon Press, 1885), p. 1287a.

to all citizens.[4] Yet for the ancients, the ultimate aim of political society, and thus of the law, was the inculcation of virtue in its citizens. The virtues were understood as qualities that were constitutive of, or enabling conditions for, the best human life, and the ancients had a relatively restrictive conception of such a life. Participation in political affairs and philosophical contemplation were major ingredients. Economic activity had little if any role in the good life, and manual labor had none at all. Plato and Aristotle saw the law as one means for inculcating in citizens the virtues that would be needed to live well as human beings. And they, like many other ancient thinkers and statesmen, believed that for all practical purposes, a political society must operate under the rule of law in order to succeed in its prime task of inculcating virtue.

The modern liberal defense of the rule of law severs the connection between law and personal virtue. The notion that the supreme aim of political society is to promote some restrictive conception of the best human life is rejected. A liberal political society is one in which there is a sharp distinction between the state and society. Society is the domain of interaction within and between groups, each organized around a distinctive set of interlocking beliefs, dispositions, and values. The interacting groups have competing conceptions of the good, the virtuous, the divine, the sacred, the right, the just, and the beautiful. The state is the institutional power that is to stand above these diverse groups and regulate their interaction. Citizens do not necessarily see the state as a wholly alien power, yet neither can they embrace it as the full embodiment of their normative vision of the world. It is in their particular social groups that citizens find an objective embodiment of their normative visions. The value of the state resides principally in protecting social groups from one another and preserving the freedom of the individual to mold a normative vision and to join others with a similar vision in pursuing it.

In the modern liberal view, the rule of law serves two important principles of political morality: fair notice and legal accountability. The former principle requires that the state establish a well-defined zone of freedom within which each person can arrive at his

[4] The ancients, of course, had a decidedly more restricted idea than modern thinkers of which human beings were worthy of the status of citizenship in the polis. But the idea of equality under law for all citizens was clearly articulated and endorsed in Greek political life by the end of the sixth century B.C. See Chester Starr, *Individual and Community: The Rise of the Polis* (New York: Oxford University Press, 1986), p. 90.

or her own conception of the best human life and pursue that conception. With a zone of freedom thus demarcated, people will have fair notice of when and how the state will intervene in their lives. The principle of legal accountability requires that any deployment of power by the organs of the state be authorized by a preexisting system of authoritative legal norms. Those who wield public power are held accountable not merely to their own sense of the public good but to a system of norms that simultaneously authorizes and confines their powers.

The ideas of fair notice and legal accountability are logically distinct. It is conceptually possible for an organ of the political community to give citizens fair notice of its intended actions, yet for those actions to be beyond what the organ is legally authorized to do. It is also conceptually possible for an organ of the political community to create ill-defined zones of freedom, thus failing to provide fair notice, yet to act within its legal authority. The generic liberal model of the rule of law insists that both fair notice and legal accountability be satisfied.

From the liberal point of view, fair notice and legal accountability are important because of their connections to individual freedom, the freedom of the individual to mold and live out a normative conception of human life. Rawls writes lucidly of the connection between fair notice and freedom; Neumann, of the connection between legal accountability and freedom. First, Rawls:

> Now the connection of the rule of law with liberty is clear enough. . . . [I]f the precept of no crime without a law is violated, say by statutes being vague and imprecise, what we are at liberty to do is likewise vague and imprecise. The boundaries of our liberty are uncertain. And to the extent that this is so, liberty is restricted by a reasonable fear of its exercise. . . . The principle of legality has a firm foundation, then, in the agreement of rational persons to establish for themselves the greatest equal liberty. To be confident in the possession and exercise of these freedoms, the citizens of a well-ordered society will normally want the rule of law maintained.[5]

Neumann describes the connection between the legal accountability of public power and individual freedom in the liberal state under the rule of law:

[5] John Rawls, *A Theory of Justice* (Cambridge: Harvard University Press, 1971), pp. 239–40.

> [T]he state may intervene with the individual's liberty—but first it must prove that it may do so. This proof can be adduced solely by reference to "law" and it must, as a rule, be submitted to specific organs of the state: courts or administrative tribunals. . . . [T]he "law" by which the state proves its right to intervene with individual rights can only be positive law. . . . The liberal legal tradition rests, therefore, upon a very simple statement: individual rights may be interfered with by the state only if the state can prove its claim by reference to a general law.[6]

From the perspective of the modern liberal, then, the crucial difference between a political society operating under the rule of law and one not so operating revolves around individual freedom. The rule of law is regarded as an indispensable element in any political society that will secure a sufficiently wide area of individual freedom. This is not to say that liberal legal theory holds that the rule of law will, by itself, guarantee a sufficient zone of liberal freedom. Political societies can, of course, have oppressive laws. But it is to say that the liberal believes that in the absence of the rule of law, liberal freedoms can exist, if at all, only in an unacceptably precarious condition. The rule of law is, in practice, a necessary condition for making such freedoms as broad and as secure as they ought to be.

Both ancient and modern political thinkers have understood the rule of law to consist of the constraint and regulation of public and private power by law. But regulating power to secure individual freedom demands a system of regulation quite different from a system whose regulation is aimed at inculcating personal virtue. For this reason, liberal thinkers have integrated into their conception of the rule of law features that are not found in the accounts of Plato and Aristotle but seem especially important if the rule of law is to secure individual freedom. Of course, if one goes too far in expanding the idea of the rule of law in this direction, the result is, in effect, to build all of the principles of liberal political morality into the idea of the rule of law, thus guaranteeing as a conceptual matter that the rule of law will secure a sufficiently wide zone of liberal freedom. The reason that it would be unwise to carry things that far is that it would leave us unable to say that a given state is

[6] Franz Neumann, *The Democratic and the Authoritarian State* (Glencoe, Ill.: Free Press, 1957), pp. 163–64, 166.

under the rule of law but that, because of the oppressive character of its laws, the state stifles liberal freedoms.[7]

A more moderate tack is to integrate some relatively formal requirements that bear on the matter of individual freedom into the idea of the rule of law. Indeed, Rawls has done just this in the preceding quotation. The clarity of legal norms is related to the degree of freedom they afford. The relation is not so strong that clear legal rules guarantee a broad zone of freedom. But one can argue, as Rawls does, that other things being equal, a clear rule provides a greater area of freedom than a vague or indefinite one. Because of this connection, Rawls introduces into the idea of the rule of law the requirement that the norms regulating power under the rule of law must be clear in meaning.

In a typical liberal account of the rule of law, then, the norms that reign must have certain features. The account will require the norms to be (1) general in scope, (2) made public, (3) applied prospectively, (4) clear in meaning, (5) duly enacted (i.e., enacted in conformity with existing authoritative laws), (6) possible to obey, (7) stable (i.e., remaining in force for a reasonable period of time), and (8) enforced in a manner consonant with their meaning.[8]

This liberal conception of the rule of law is characteristically expanded to incorporate the idea that certain general sorts of institutional arrangements are required if the rule of law is to be established and secured. The arrangements include an independent judiciary to interpret and apply the authoritative norms; access to the courts by the population; and the guarantee of a hearing, fairly conducted, in which the relevant parties to any case can present their sides of the story.[9] Such arrangements are designed to secure the rule of law by insuring *due process* of law.

Moreover, the arrangements secure the liberal principle that there must be a distinction between law and politics in any political society that operates under the rule of law. The political realm of the liberal state is that in which competing conceptions of what is good and right for the community clash and, through a process of compromise and accommodation, produce settlements which are embodied in legal rules. The realm of law is that in which the

[7] Cf. Joseph Raz, *The Authority of Law* (New York: Oxford University Press, 1979), pp. 210–11.

[8] See Lon L. Fuller, *The Morality of Law*, rev. ed. (New Haven: Yale University Press, 1969), chap. 2.

[9] See, e.g., Raz, *Authority of Law*, pp. 216–17.

rules generated by the political process are interpreted and applied.

In the generic liberal model, the law-politics distinction means that the process of interpreting (or applying) the law should be insulated from any assessment of the substantive merits of the contending normative views in the political arena whose clash produces the law. The meaning of a settlement reached in the political arena is not to be viewed as a function of which contending normative view was more sound and which less. The function of the political process is to provide a procedure for coming to settlements over disputed matters that is fair to the different groups that make up society with their different normative conceptions. The function of the legal process is to construe and enforce the meaning of those settlements, with no reference to the merits of the positions held by those groups. Only in this way will the results of the political process be respected. Only in this way will the meaning of the settlements—and thus the boundary between freedom and obligation, between authorized and arbitrary power—be discernible in a noncontroversial manner. Everyone will be able to agree on what those boundaries are, because their perceived locations will not hinge on conflicting assessments of the moral and political positions that contend with one another in the political arena.

Virtually every contemporary thinker of note who defends this version of the rule of law will concede that in practice it is impossible to insulate the legal process completely from judgments about the relative merits of the views that compete in the political arena. But the generic liberal model concludes with two important claims about the infiltration of such political and moral judgments into the legal process. First, it is something to be regretted, an aspect of the inevitable imperfection of the world. Second, it can be kept to a minimum, reduced to a merely marginal phenomenon in a process that for the most part operates (or can operate) uninfluenced by such judgments.

One Problem with the Generic Model

A number of problems might be raised regarding the generic liberal model of the rule of law. For current purposes, though, one is most important. It revolves around the fact that the legal systems of contemporary liberal democracies seem to violate the conditions laid down by the account. Contemporary law incorporates many vague and open-ended terms, such as *due process*, *unconscionability*, and *good faith*. The authoritative interpretation of such terms often seems to rely on controversial conceptions of justice and goodness, apparently violating the law-politics distinction in more than a marginal way. In addition, courts engage in substantial reconstruction of legal doctrines in areas such as tort and contract on the basis of controversial political and moral principles. Finally, the discretion of administrative and regulatory agencies in carrying out the vague mandates given to them by the legislature is extensive. Such agencies both enact rules having the force of law and adjudicate disputes arising from those rules—in apparent violation of such fundamental due process principles as the demand for an independent judicial body to hear and resolve disputes. In light of these developments in the legal culture of twentieth-century liberal democracies, it seems that the generic liberal model of the rule of law has been rendered obsolete.

Liberal thinkers have not been blind to the significance of the features of the twentieth-century legal landscape that appear to render obsolete the old liberal wisdom. Nearly half a century ago, Hayek observed the emergence of those features and condemned them for destroying the rule of law. Hayek took to heart the generic liberal view that the virtue of law lay in its clear-cut demarcation of the boundaries of individual freedom, and he judged harshly the drift of liberal democracies toward state economic planning and away from their traditional wisdom:

> In fact, as planning becomes more and more extensive, it becomes regularly necessary to qualify legal provisions increasingly by reference to what is "fair" or "reasonable"; this means that it becomes necessary to leave the decision of the concrete case more and more to the discretion of the judge or authority in question. One could write a history of the decline of the Rule of Law, the disappearance of the *Rechtstaat*, in terms of the progressive introduction of these vague formulas into legislation and jurisdiction, and of the increasing arbitrariness and uncertainty of, and the consequent disrespect for, the law and the judicature, which in these circumstances could not but become an instrument of policy.[10]

[10] Friedrich Hayek, *The Road to Serfdom* (Chicago: University of Chicago Press, 1944), p. 78. See also Hayek, *The Constitution of Liberty* (Chicago: University of Chicago Press, 1960), pp. 234–47. Hayek was by no means the first thinker to recognize or criticize the trend of twentieth-century legal systems away from the generic liberal model of the rule of law. Franz Neumann and Otto Kirchheimer analyzed and

Many liberal thinkers, however, have taken a different approach in responding to the features of the twentieth-century legal landscape. They have been unwilling to join Hayek's condemnation of contemporary liberal democracies and have sought to show how such states can be said to conform to the principle of the rule of law. One line of thinking concedes the existence of significant (though not extensive) areas of public and private action that are not closely regulated by the rule of law. But this concession is tempered by three collateral points. First, in any system of rules there will necessarily be significant areas of indeterminacy because of the very nature of human language and social rules. Second, the area of legal indeterminacy in contemporary liberal states is significant but peripheral in the overall operation of the law. Third, some significant degree of legal indeterminacy and government discretion to promote the public good is desirable because it gives the organs of the political community a valuable flexibility in responding to the problems and needs of the community.

In light of these points, this line of liberal thinking argues that a sound theoretical model of the rule of law must have more room for indeterminacy than the generic model would allow. It would be a mistake to demand, as the generic model does, that indeterminacy be reduced to the smallest degree humanly possible and an equally serious mistake to build one's theoretical model around such a demand so that any significant departure from it appears to do damage to the rule of law. This line of liberal thinking contends that a sound model would leave liberal states significant flexibility in responding to social problems, though not so much as to destroy vital liberal freedoms. Not every departure from legal determinacy damages the rule of law, and a theoretical model is needed which does not make demands for the reduction of indeterminacy and government discretion that are as stringent as the demands of the generic model.

H.L.A. Hart is the most influential of contemporary theorists who have developed this line of liberal thinking. Hart's theory

---

criticized the trend in Weimar Germany. Unlike Hayek, though, Neumann and Kirchheimer were socialists. They believed that the requirements of liberal legality should and would be *aufgehoben* in a socialist state. See Franz Neumann and Otto Kirchheimer, *Social Democracy and the Rule of Law* (London: Allen and Unwin, 1987), and Franz Neumann, *The Rule of Law* (Leamington Spa, U.K.: Berg, 1986). Other early discussions of the implications for the rule of law of the rise of the administrative-regulatory state are Lord Hewart of Bury, *The New Despotism* (New York: Cosmopolitan, 1929), and John Dickinson, *Administrative Justice and the Supremacy of Law in the United States* (New York: Russell and Russell, 1927).

provides a detailed account of how the rule of law involves the regulation of public and private power, at the same time showing how gaps inevitably arise in such a regime of legal regulation and arguing that such gaps are a good thing. He contends that "we should not cherish, even as an ideal, the conception of a rule so detailed that the question whether it applied or not to a particular case was always settled in advance. . . ."[11] And what Hart claims about a single rule he applies as well to an entire legal system. Because of human limitations in foreseeing future situations which the law will have to confront, it is better to have some play in the system that allows officials to adapt legal norms to unexpected situations than to subordinate the officials entirely to a rigidly determinate system of law.

A very different line of liberal thinking is found in the work of Ronald Dworkin. In cases where Hart sees the law as "running out" and individuals and the state thus operating free from the strict regulation of law, Dworkin sees the law as continuing to confine and regulate public and private power. He is not willing to concede the existence of a significant degree of legal indeterminacy in contemporary liberal democracies.[12] And contrary to the generic liberal model, Dworkin has argued that moral and political judgments can and do play a legitimate role in the legal process. Accordingly, he has undertaken to develop a liberal model of the rule of law that differs from both the generic model and Hart's model.

The dispute between Hart and Dworkin has continued for two decades now and has been widely discussed in the literature. I have no intention of providing a detailed account of that debate. My examination will be limited to those aspects that are particularly pertinent for the goal of constructing a liberal critique of CLS. Two issues are especially important in this regard. The first revolves around the question of whether the legal authority of a

[11] H.L.A. Hart, *The Concept of Law* (New York: Oxford University Press, 1961), p. 125.

[12] Some commentators have argued that the latest version of Dworkin's theory, in *Law's Empire*, is not committed to Dworkin's earlier thesis that virtually every case in our legal system has a single objective right answer. For example, Michelman argues that the theory of *Law's Empire* makes the quite distinct claim that in our legal culture, judges typically have the subjective experience of there being a single right answer to the cases which they are called upon to decide. Dworkin does make this latter "subjective right answer" claim in *Law's Empire*, but I believe that he also makes the former "objective right answer" claim as well. When Dworkin raises the objective claim on pp. viii–ix of *Law's Empire*, he is clearly not rejecting it, and much of the section on skepticism (pp. 76–86) is devoted to a defense of the objective claim against a certain kind of skeptical attack. See Ronald Dworkin, *Law's Empire* (Cambridge: Harvard University Press, 1986), and Frank Michelman, "Traces of Self-Government," *Harvard Law Review* 100 (1986): 70–71.

norm is ultimately solely a matter of convention. The second focuses on the question of whether there is a significant degree of indeterminacy in our legal system. To a large extent, Hart's theory is a defense of affirmative answers to both of these questions, while Dworkin's is a defense of negative ones. I will be defending Hart's answers, but I will also argue that Dworkin's theory provides some important insights into our legal culture that are either incompatible with Hart's account or receive insufficient attention from it. After examining the two theories, I will return to the immediate issue that prompted our consideration of Hart and Dworkin—the suggestion of Hayek and others that the rule of law, as the liberal should understand it, no longer exists in contemporary liberal democracies.

Hart: Law and Social Rules

Hart's model of the rule of law is based largely on his account of *social rules*. This is because he regards the law as ultimately a matter of convention alone. For Hart, the legal authority of any norm depends ultimately on the social rules that are accepted within the relevant population. Let us examine his account of social rules and his analysis of law in terms of such rules.

Hart argues that social rules are constituted by both behavior and thought. It is what most of the people in some relevant population do and think that constitute a given social rule. Against the behaviorist orientation of legal realism, Hart insists on the "internal" aspect of social rules. To claim that rules have such an aspect is to imply that the existence of a behavioral regularity in which most people in population P do X is not sufficient to establish that there is a social practice (or social rule) of doing X in P. In addition to the convergent behavioral regularity, Hart claims:

> What is necessary is that there should be a critical reflective attitude to certain patterns of behavior as a common standard, and that this should display itself in criticism (including self-criticism), demands for conformity, and in acknowledgements that such criticism and demands are justified.[13]

Thus, where most people in the relevant population do X and agree in adopting a critical reflective attitude toward such conduct, then there is a social rule requiring the performance of X.

Hart integrates this account of the ontology of social rules into

[13] Hart, *Concept of Law*, p. 56.

his theory of law. Law is a system of social rules constituted by behavior and thought in essentially the same way that other social rules are constituted. What differentiates a society under the rule of law is that its system combines *primary* and *secondary* rules. Primary rules impose on people in the relevant population the duty to act, or refrain from acting, in certain ways. All societies have such primary rules, even societies that lack any legal system. Law enters the picture when secondary rules are added. The secondary rules provide means for identifying, enforcing, and changing the primary rules. Of particular importance among the secondary rules are the rules of *recognition* and *adjudication*. The rule of recognition incorporates the criteria that must be satisfied by any primary rule for it to count as a valid legal rule. The rules of adjudication authorize certain persons to render authoritative decisions about whether the primary rules have been violated and set up procedures for making such decisions. It is helpful to think of these procedural rules of adjudication as containing (though not exhausted by) criteria for determining how the set of valid legal rules is to be applied to the particular case at hand in order to yield a decision.

In Hart's account of law, it is the behavior and thought of officials that constitute these vital secondary rules. Thus, the rule of recognition is constituted by the convergent behavior of legal officials in identifying the valid primary rules and by the critical reflective attitude such officials adopt toward the criteria they commonly use in making such identifications. The set of criteria for identifying valid primary rules *is* the set that legal officials conventionally employ and toward which they adopt a critical reflective attitude. Similarly, the rules of adjudication are constituted by the procedures that officials conventionally employ in deciding particular cases and by the critical attitude they share regarding such conventional procedures.[14]

Nonetheless, legal officials do not always agree on the answers to legal questions. In a significant number of cases, there is rather extensive disagreement. Hart insists that in such cases, there is no unique correct legal answer. The law is indeterminate with respect to such cases. Suppose a judge who conscientiously consults the authoritative materials comes to the conclusion that the plaintiff is legally entitled to win a certain case. Hart tells us that

[14] Hart also insists that for there to be law, there must be general compliance in the society at large with the primary rules that officials identify using the rule of recognition. See Hart, *Concept of Law*, p. 113.

> no purpose is served by insisting that if a brother judge arrives after the same conscientious process at a different conclusion there is a unique right answer which would show which of the two judges, if either, is right.[15]

Hart's position on the connection between legal disagreement and legal indeterminacy rests on his account of the nature of social rules. The most basic argument that can be reconstructed from his theory goes something like this:[16] Suppose that there is extensive disagreement between legal officials about the correct legal decision in a certain case. The disagreement might arise because some officials count a certain norm as part of the law, but others identify a contrary norm as valid. Or it might occur because, though they all agree on the relevant valid norms, they disagree over how the norms are to be applied to the case at hand. In either event, the argument goes, given that the law is a system of social rules, it must be indeterminate with respect to the case. The law must have a gap here because there is a gap in what legal officials conventionally agree to in identifying and applying the law, and, as a system of social rules, the law is nothing more than what such officials commonly agree to. The law is not a system of norms existing in some Platonic heaven but is simply the system that legal officials conventionally identify and apply. Extensive legal disagreement entails no conventionally accepted criteria sufficiently robust to decide a case, and no conventionally accepted criteria sufficiently robust to decide a case entails indeterminacy in the law with respect to that case.

Hart's familiar argument for legal indeterminacy based upon the open-texture of the general terms in a language is, in a sense, a special case of this social-convention argument for indeterminacy.[17] The meaning and extension of terms are constituted by the

[15] H.L.A. Hart, *Essays in Jurisprudence and Philosophy* (New York: Oxford University Press, 1983), p. 140.

[16] My reconstruction of Hart's argument has been aided substantially by Dworkin, *Taking Rights Seriously*, pp. 49–58.

[17] In his more recent writings, Hart has pointed to weaknesses in his argument for indeterminacy based on the open-texture of language. He confesses that he eventually recognized that

> the question whether a *rule* applies or does not apply to some particular situation of fact is not the same as the question whether according to the settled conventions of language this is determined or left open by the words of that rule. For a legal system often has other resources besides the words used in the formulations of its rules which serve to determine their content or meaning in particular cases. (*Essays in Jurisprudence and Philosophy*, pp. 7–8)

social rules governing those terms. Semantic rules are social rules, nothing more than the criteria that the relevant linguistic population conventionally attaches to various words. When there is extensive disagreement within the relevant population over the extension of some general term—for example, *cruel and unusual punishment*—it follows, or so the argument goes, that the semantic rule governing the term must be indeterminate and fail to cover the case under dispute. For semantic rules are social rules and so extend only as far as the conventional agreements of the linguistic community.[18]

One of the important implications of Hart's theory is that when judges decide controversial (or "hard") cases, they are *creating* the law rather than applying it. This "judicial legislation" is not the

---

The key point to keep in mind here is that these other resources are themselves social rules, such as rules that stipulate special meanings for legal terms or conventions that stipulate that the clear purpose of a rule dictates its meaning for a case. Because these additional resources are also social rules, Hart's basic argument for indeterminacy, resting on the idea of law as a system of social rules, survives his current criticism of the argument based on open-texture.

[18] David Brink has recently claimed that Hart's view rests on a defective semantic theory which holds that the meaning and reference of terms are fixed by the conventions of usage within a given linguistic community. Brink cogently argues that such a theory cannot provide a plausible account of a term such as *mass* as it is used in physics. The theory has the implausible implication that physicists who dissent from the currently conventional beliefs about mass could not even coherently formulate their alternative views, since the conventional beliefs dictate the very meaning and reference of the term. The conventionalist theory also implausibly implies that if there were no conventionally agreed upon use of the term due to deep disagreement among physicists about the nature of mass, disputed questions about mass would have no determinate answer. Brink suggests that legal terms are similar to the terms of natural science in this regard: dissent from their conventional usage is coherent, and the absence of a firm convention regarding their use in a certain case does not entail that there are no determinate answers to questions about their application to the case. See David Brink, "Legal Theory, Legal Interpretation, and Judicial Review," *Philosophy and Public Affairs* 17 (1988): 106–16.

The major flaw in Brink's argument is that he fails to take account of the ontological difference between nature and law. The terms of natural science refer to a mind-independent realm; the nature of mass is completely independent of what humans say or think or agree to. It is quite different with law, however. The terms of law refer to a socially constructed reality that would not exist without human action, thought, and choice. Hart's argument about legal indeterminacy proceeds from the premise that this socially constructed reality extends only as far as the conventional agreements that create it. While Brink is correct to argue that a conventionalist semantics of the sort which he examines leads to patently implausible consequences when applied to terms that refer to the mind-independent reality of the natural world, he is wrong to assume that he can use that argument to discredit by analogy Hart's conventionalist account of the terms that refer to the socially constructed world of the law.

result of some ethical lapse on the part of the judiciary but stems from the purely conventional character of law. Where the conventions that constitute the law are silent, judges cannot apply the law to decide a case. If judges are to decide controversial cases, they have no choice but to exercise their discretion and legislate for such cases.

Dworkin: The Soundest Theory of Law?

Dworkin contends that judges in our legal system think about and decide cases in a way inconsistent with the view that the law consists solely of what legal officials can agree on.[19] The rules and doctrines that are conventionally agreed to and their conventional meanings are certainly part of the law; they constitute the *settled law*. But, Dworkin argues, judges characteristically dig deeper than the settled law, deeper than those conventional agreements in deciding certain sorts of cases, "hard cases." In order to decide these controversial cases, judges typically search for the principles belonging to what Dworkin has called "the soundest theory of the law."[20] They base their decisions on the principles that they regard as part of that theory.

The soundest theory of the law is the most defensible ethical and political theory that coheres with and justifies the norms and decisions belonging to the settled law. The coherence does not have to be perfect, for Dworkin concedes that some of the settled legal norms and decisions may be characterized as mistakes. But there must be coherence with a substantial portion of the settled law. If there is more than one theory that fits enough of the settled law—and Dworkin thinks that there will often be more than one

[19] In the most recent presentation of his theory of law in *Law's Empire*, Dworkin defends his jurisprudence in part on the basis of a general theory of interpretation. This has led Dworkin to change some of his terminology and to provide additional and somewhat different arguments for his key jurisprudential positions. Although I do introduce the general theory of interpretation at one point in my examination of Dworkin's jurisprudential claims, for the most part I focus on those of his arguments that can be formulated independently of that theory. I agree with Soper's assessment that the theory is not especially helpful in shedding light on the main jurisprudential issues with which Dworkin is concerned. See Philip Soper, "Dworkin's Domain," *Harvard Law Review* 100 (1987): 1168, 1173. Dworkin's best arguments are not founded on his general theory of interpretation. For this reason, I rely heavily on his previous argumentation and terminology. For example, I use the term *soundest theory of the law*. In Dworkin's newer terminology, the equivalent expression would be *best constructive interpretation of the law*.

[20] Dworkin, *Taking Rights Seriously*, pp. 66–68.

in hard cases—then the soundest theory is the one that scores the highest on some measure of both fit and ethical adequacy.

The identity and weight of the principles belonging to the soundest theory are likely to be a matter of controversy among legal professionals. This is because each person's judgments about the soundest theory will be a function of his or her moral and political beliefs. In a society with a pluralism of normative beliefs, there will invariably be disagreement over what the principles of the soundest theory are and how much weight they carry. Dworkin does not blink this implication of his theory: "Different judges belong to different and rival political traditions, and the cutting edges of different judges' interpretations will be honed by different ideologies."[21] The upshot is that "legal judgments are pervasively contestable."[22]

Because of the controversial nature of the soundest theory, the judgments that courts render about legal rights in hard cases are bound to be controversial. However, Dworkin argues, this does not entail that the law is really indeterminate in those cases or that the judge is really making the law rather than applying it. The law is determinate even in hard cases; the correct legal outcome is determined by the principles of the soundest theory of the settled law. From the fact that there is controversy over precisely what the soundest theory entails for a particular case, it does not follow that the soundest theory is silent on that case. It simply follows that people do not agree on what it is saying, and Dworkin insists that it is saying something sufficiently definite to decide the case. Because the law is determined in part by what the soundest theory says, and not solely by what legal officials can agree to, there can be and are legally determinate answers to cases over which officials disagree.

Dworkin concedes the bare logical possibility that there may be some hard cases in which the considerations for and against the plaintiff are so evenly matched that the soundest theory must declare a tie.[23] In such a case the law would be indeterminate. But Dworkin doubts that one is likely to run across a significant number of such cases in any system of law as richly textured as ours. Virtually all cases have legally determinate answers dictated by the soundest theory in combination with the settled law.

We are now in position to understand Dworkin's conception of

[21] Dworkin, *Law's Empire*, p. 88.
[22] Ibid., p. 411
[23] Dworkin, *Taking Rights Seriously*, p. 286.

the rule of law. A political community is under the rule of law, in his view, when any proposed deployment of force by the organs of the community will be allowed to proceed only if it is authorized by the settled law and its soundest theory. Because the nature of the soundest theory will be a matter of political controversy, no sharp distinction can be made between law and politics under the Dworkinite rule of law. Decisions according to law will often be politically controversial and hinge on disputed judgments of political morality. But, Dworkin contends, while a political community that operates under such a rule of law cannot promise always to provide legal decisions that are noncontroversial, it can promise that the law will be regarded by officials as the embodiment of a coherent scheme of normative principles rather than a miscellaneous hodgepodge of rules and decisions. Moreover, such a community can also promise that it will treat its citizens in accordance with the demands of such a scheme of principles. Dworkin understands integrity as the value that requires the principled treatment of people. Thus, he claims that a political community that abides by his conception of the rule of law will display integrity in the treatment of its citizens. Such integrity, he contends, cannot be promised and provided by those political societies that reduce the law to the norms and meanings that are conventionally agreed to by legal officials.

Dworkin goes on to suggest that the political community of the United States (and presumably of the other liberal democratic states) actually operates under the rule of law as his theory of law conceptualizes it. He suggests that other models of the rule of law, such as Hart's, can be cogently criticized for failing to conform to our legal practices and institutions. Dworkin contends that no such criticism can accurately be leveled at his model. It not only shows how law secures the vital value of integrity but also provides a descriptively accurate portrait of our legal culture.

Assessing Dworkin and Hart

In this section, I examine two of the main issues of contention between Dworkin and Hart: whether legal authority is at bottom purely a matter of convention and whether there is a significant degree of indeterminacy in our law. Although I come down on Hart's side on both of these issues, I also argue that Dworkin's theory provides some important insights into our law that are consistent with acknowledging the purely conventional character of legal authority and the existence of a significant degree of legal indeterminacy.

Convention and Legal Authority

Dworkin argues that the way in which judges commonly reason about hard cases shows that Hart is wrong in suggesting that the legal authority of a norm depends on convention alone. Legal reasoning about hard cases reveals a nonconventional element of the law. The nonconventional element is the test of ethical adequacy that helps to determine which principles belong to the soundest theory of the settled law. Whether some norm is part of the soundest theory, and so part of the law itself, depends in part on what is conventionally agreed to within the legal community, but it also depends on the substantive ethical soundness of the norm.

Let us assume for the moment that Dworkin is correct in arguing that the principles of the soundest theory are themselves part of the law: such principles carry legal authority and do so because they are part of the soundest theory. It does not follow from this assumption that Hart is wrong to believe that the legal authority of a norm is ultimately a matter of convention alone. Before concluding that Hart is wrong, we must ask a further question: In virtue of what are the principles belonging to the soundest theory part of the law? If the answer is "in virtue of a convention that gives the principles that status," we will have no grounds for rejecting Hart's contention that law is ultimately a matter of convention. For the key word here is *ultimately*. Hart recognizes the possibility of legal conventions that make the legal authority of a norm dependent in part on its ethical soundness. Hart's point is that to the extent that considerations of ethical soundness play such a role, it is some convention that explains why they play it.[24]

Dworkin tacitly concedes this point, thus defeating his own argument against Hart. When he addresses the question of why the principles of the soundest theory carry legal authority, he invokes his description of how judges characteristically reason about and decide hard cases in our legal culture.[25] He tells us that their reasoning characteristically aims to discover the soundest theory of the settled law and that their decisions rest on the principles which their reasoning points to as the most likely candidates for belonging to the soundest theory. But these claims about the practice of

[24] See Hart, *Concept of Law*, p. 199. Cf. Jules Coleman, "Legal Duty and Moral Argument," *Social Theory and Practice* 5 (1980): 377–407.

[25] Dworkin, *Taking Rights Seriously*, pp. 283–84.

judicial reasoning would not show that the principles of the soundest theory carry legal authority unless one assumed that the conventional practices of judges was what gave these principles their authority. In other words, Dworkin's argument rests on the premise that the principles of the soundest theory are part of the law because conventional judicial practice regards them as such.[26] But, if that is true, then Hart's claim that legal authority is ultimately conventional is confirmed rather than defeated.

An alternative would be to argue against Hart that the nature of law is what ultimately gives legal authority to the principles of the soundest theory. But Dworkin does not and cannot accept such an alternative because he concedes the possibility of a legal system that is exhausted by the settled law—by the noncontroversial norms, doctrines, and decisions. To be sure, he argues that a system of law that goes beyond the noncontroversial in the manner which he describes is, other things being equal, a better system than one that does not. But such an argument presupposes the possibility of a legal culture that restricts the legally authoritative norms and decisions to what all legal officials agree to, and that presupposition is inconsistent with the idea that the very nature of law is what gives legal authority to the principles of the soundest theory of the settled law.[27]

Indeterminacy and Legal Reasoning

Even if legal authority ultimately rests on convention alone, as Hart argues, it still may be true that there is no significant degree of indeterminacy in our legal system. Dworkin's argument is that the settled law and the principles of its soundest theory provide a determinate answer to virtually every case. That argument does not necessarily fall with the adoption of Hart's position that legal authority is, at its foundation, purely conventional. If there is a conventional practice of regarding the principles of the soundest theory as having legal authority and if the meaning and weight of

[26] The interpretation that I have given of Dworkin's argument for why the principles of the soundest theory carry legal authority is also given in Philip Soper, "Legal Theory and the Obligation of a Judge: The Hart/Dworkin Dispute," *Michigan Law Review* 75 (1977): 513. However, unlike Soper, I believe that there is good reason to reject the idea that Dworkin has provided a descriptively accurate account of the conventional practice of judicial reasoning in our legal culture. The basis for my belief is elaborated later in this section.

[27] A more detailed critique of Dworkin's view that legal authority is in part nonconventional can be found in Jules Coleman, "Negative and Positive Positivism," in *Ronald Dworkin and Contemporary Jurisprudence*, ed. Marshall Cohen (Totowa, N.J.: Rowman and Allanheld, 1984), pp. 28–48.

those principles are sufficiently precise to determine almost all outcomes that the settled law alone would leave open, then Dworkin would be right in his insistence that our legal system is almost wholly determinate. However, serious doubts can be raised about both of the preceding *ifs*.

One line of argument against Dworkin would run as follows: Even conceding that there are principles underlying the settled law that carry legal authority and that the appeal to those principles can help resolve some cases left open by the settled law, a significant degree of indeterminacy would still remain because the relevant underlying principles will often be insufficiently precise or will be in conflict with other equally authoritative underlying principles. Hart adopts this line of argument against the Dworkinite view on indeterminacy.[28]

I am going to press another line of criticism against Dworkin. His argument hinges on the dubious idea that the way judges typically think about and decide hard cases can be accurately described as searching for the implications of the soundest theory of the settled law. While Dworkin is correct in suggesting that judges do not leave their lawbooks behind when they think about and decide such cases, it does not follow that judges are basing their decisions on what they regard as the soundest theory of the settled law. In the next part of this section, I argue that there are good reasons to hold that there is no conventional practice in our legal system of deciding cases on grounds of (what is thought to be) the principles of the soundest theory and that Rolf Sartorius is closer to the truth when he suggests that considerations of *logical fit*, and such considerations alone, ultimately determine the identity and weight of the authoritative principles underlying the settled law. I then suggest that there is some room for Dworkinite reasoning in our legal culture, though it does not occupy the central position he attributes to it.

Sartorius and Logical Coherence

Sartorius explains his view thus:

> [T]he obligation of the judge is to reach that decision which coheres best with the total body of authoritative legal stan-

[28] Hart concedes that judges appeal to underlying principles when the settled law seems to leave a legal question open and appears to agree with Dworkin's view that such principles carry legal authority. But he then goes on to argue that this will still leave significant areas of legal indeterminacy. Hart, *Essays in Jurisprudence and Philosophy*, pp. 6–7, 136–40.

> dards which he is bound to apply. The correct decision in a given case is that which achieves "the best resolution" of existing standards in terms of systematic coherence as formally determined, not in terms of optimal desirability as determined either by some supreme substantive principle or by the judge's own personal scheme of values. . . . [I]t is the distinctive feature of the institutionalized role of the judiciary, in contrast to the legislative, that it may not directly base its decisions on substantive considerations of the value of competing social policies.[29]

Sartorius is claiming that the general rule in our legal culture is that the underlying principles relied upon to decide hard cases must have their identity and weight determined on grounds of logical fit with the settled law, considerations of moral adequacy playing no independent role.[30] In other words, he is contending that the reigning convention prescribes that legal decisions and the reasoning that supports them achieve maximum coherence with the body of settled norms, doctrines, and decisions.

Dworkin points out that the determination of which decision best coheres with the settled law is not a mechanical procedure.[31] It involves the rather sophisticated task of determining which potential principle of decision gives the settled law itself maximum systematic coherence. Dworkin's point here is fully consistent with Sartorius's view that considerations of ethical soundness play no role independent of the coherence test in the conventions that guide legal reasoning in our system. Dworkin's distinctive claim is that in addition to the sophisticated task of determining the degree of logical coherence with the settled law that potential principles of decision may have, legal reasoning conventionally incorporates independent considerations of the ethical soundness of such principles.

Although I will argue that Sartorius is essentially right in his

[29] Rolf Sartorius, *Individual Conduct and Social Norms* (Encino, Calif.: Dickenson, 1975), pp. 196–97. Notice Sartorius's insistence on the law-politics distinction in the last part of the passage and the implied contrast with Dworkin. C. L. Ten has also argued against Dworkin that the principles embedded in the settled law are determined ultimately by their logical fit with the settled rules and not by independent considerations of moral adequacy. See Ten, "The Soundest Theory of Law," *Mind* 88 (1979): 535.

[30] There could, of course, be a norm that is part of the settled law prescribing that considerations of ethical soundness be taken into account in certain sorts of cases. See note 32. Sartorius's claim is that the conventions of legal reasoning in our system exclude such ethical considerations unless the considerations are prescribed in that way.

[31] Dworkin, *Law's Empire*, p. 247.

description of the reigning convention, that convention does not tell the whole story about the operation of legal reasoning in our system. At the margins of the system, there is room for considerations of moral adequacy in the manner described by Dworkin. I do not think that it would be accurate to say that there is actually a Dworkinite counterconvention that operates at the margins of the system. This is because I do not believe that there is enough agreement among judges about when, or even if, the reliance on moral considerations in the manner described by Dworkin is a legitimate mode of legal reasoning. But I will argue that nonetheless, Dworkinite reasoning does play a significant role in the legal system, even if it is not the central role which his theory attributes to it.[32]

The considerations that lead me to conclude that there is no conventional Dworkinite judicial practice stem from a common argument made by judges who are disputing the soundness of some legal decision. This argument claims that the allegedly faulty decision rests on reasoning that has illegitimately included ethical considerations. A typical version of the argument claims that the decision rests on a principle that was embraced due to its ethical soundness, even though contrary principles have a better fit with the settled body of rules, doctrines, and decisions. This line of criticism contends that such reasoning is essentially illegitimate, that the principle of decision should be the one that best fits the settled law, not one that fits less well but is superior on ethical grounds. It is also typical for this line of criticism to suggest that the proper domain for ethical considerations is the legislative arena and that the (allegedly) faulty decision represents a usurpation of legislative authority.

Such criticism of a legal decision would be widely dismissed as wrongheaded in principle if the Dworkinite convention reigned. Yet the fact is that the criticism is not dismissed in that way, and the rejoinders to it by judges trying to justify their decisions typically concede that the criticism would be a powerful one if the decisions actually relied on ethical considerations as claimed by the critics. The rejoinders try to show that the principle of decision

[32] It can be argued that some authoritative norms in our legal system contain terms that more or less explicitly require judges to introduce ethical considerations into their grounds of decision—e.g., norms that are formulated in terms of fairness or due process. However, Dworkin's theory makes a general claim about reasoning in our legal culture, whatever the norms pertinent to a case. In order to test Dworkin's theory, then, we should largely restrict our attention to cases involving legal norms that do not explicitly license the judge to engage in ethical reasoning.

does fit better with the settled law than the alternatives, not that it is ethically more sound than they are. There is a great reluctance among judges to admit that ethical reasoning plays any role in their decisions. Even in cases where it seems obvious that ethical reasoning plays a significant role, judges will often refuse to concede that it is so and fashion their opinion solely in terms of how well the decision fits with the settled body of rules, doctrines, and decisions.

One of Dworkin's own model cases, *MacPherson v. Buick*, illustrates the points I am making.[33] In that case, a plaintiff who was injured when a wheel on his automobile broke sued the manufacturer of the vehicle. The plaintiff had bought the automobile not from the manufacturer but from a dealer. Cardozo rendered his decision on the basis of the principle that despite the absence of privity, a manufacturer has a duty of care to a third party if the product he manufactures poses a danger to life and limb when negligently constructed. Cardozo virtually conceded that this principle represented an expansion of the rule laid down in the key precedent, *Thomas v. Winchester*.[34] According to that rule, despite the absence of privity, a manufacturer has a duty of care to a third party if the product he manufactures is "inherently dangerous," in the sense that it is designed to be destructive of life or limb. In point of fact, Cardozo not only expanded the rule in *Thomas* but flipped the structure of doctrine inside out. The rule in *Thomas* had been treated as an exception to the general principle that the absence of privity entails the absence of any duty of care to a third party. Cardozo's expansion of the rule in *Thomas* had the crucial structural effect of making the privity requirement the exception rather than the rule; more accurately, this was the effect once Cardozo's principle became generally accepted by judges.

Over the dissent of the Court's chief judge, Cardozo argued for his expanded version of the *Thomas* rule on the grounds that the legal principle it embodied fit better with the settled law. He did not explicitly appeal to the greater moral or political adequacy of his expanded version of the rule in *Thomas*. The reasoning in his opinion tried to show that his decision and the principle on which it rested were more coherent with the relevant portion of the settled law than the alternatives.

I think that a persuasive case can be made that Cardozo's deci-

[33] *MacPherson v. Buick*, 111 N.E. 1050 (1916).

[34] *Thomas v. Winchester*, 6 N.Y. 397 (1852).

sion in *MacPherson* did rely on something very much like Dworkinite reasoning. The fact is, however, that both Cardozo's and the dissenting opinions presented their arguments as turning on the question of the best fit with the settled rules, doctrines, and decisions; neither appealed to the ethical adequacy of the principles that formed the grounds of decision. Moreover, in his dissenting opinion, Chief Judge Bartlett suggested that Cardozo had illegitimately relied on ethical considerations, claiming that if the rule in *Thomas* had been rendered socially undesirable by new technologies such as the automobile, then "the change should be effected by the legislature and not by the courts."[35] The implication is unmistakable: Cardozo had violated the distinction between the role of the legislature and that of the court by injecting ethical reasoning into his decision.

Dworkin's theory cannot account for the persistence or popularity of the line of argument found in the *MacPherson* dissent that criticizes a legal decision for injecting ethical considerations into the grounds of decision.[36] Nor can it explain why the rejoinders to these criticisms typically refuse to concede that independent ethical reasoning had any part in the decision. Nor can it explain why opinions such as Cardozo's are so resistant to conceding what appears obvious—that considerations of ethical soundness did play a role in the reasoning. If Dworkinite reasoning were conventionally practiced, one would expect that the line of criticism claiming that a legal conclusion rested (in part) on ethical reasoning would be widely dismissed by judges as wrongheaded and that the rejoinders to such criticism would concede happily that ethical reasoning played a role in the decision. One would expect that decisions such as Cardozo's would explicitly invoke considerations of ethical adequacy. In fact, however, these expectations are disappointed.

[35] *MacPherson v. Buick*, 111 N.E. 1050, 1057 (1916), Bartlett, C.J., dissenting.

[36] This line of criticism is by no means restricted to dissenting opinions. In the majority opinion of a case that raised the issue of the constitutionality of a Georgia statute that criminalized sodomy between consenting adults and that had been used to prosecute someone for homosexual sodomy, Justice White wrote, "This case does not require a judgment on whether laws against sodomy between consenting adults in general, or between homosexuals in particular, are wise or desirable." *Bowers v. Hardwick*, 478 U.S. 186, 190 (1986). White's statement was an implicit criticism of both the concurring opinion in the case by Chief Justice Burger and the dissenting opinion by Justice Blackmun. Both of the latter opinions quite explicitly introduced ethical judgments into the grounds of decision. Of course, Burger and Blackmun made opposing ethical judgments about the matters raised by the case.

The Role of Dworkinite Reasoning

Despite the problems with Dworkin's theory, it is difficult to deny that there are cases in which ethical reasoning does play a role in roughly the way Dworkin suggests, whether judges concede it or not. Cardozo may have crafted his opinion in terms of the decision's fit with settled law, but it is hard to deny the dissent's argument that if fit were the only ground of decision, then the majority handed down the wrong decision. Moreover, there are some cases in which the judge does explicitly concede a role for ethical reasoning.[37]

We need a theory that recognizes both the Dworkinite and the non-Dworkinite elements in our legal culture. My solution is to suggest that the reigning convention is the one Sartorius describes but that the convention breaks down in some cases. When it breaks down, some judges engage in Dworkinite reasoning but do not admit it; other judges engage in such reasoning and do admit it; still others reject the legitimacy of any Dworkinite reasoning and insist on the maximum-coherence criterion.[38]

Thus, Dworkinite reasoning is part of our legal culture, but wherever it appears, explicitly or implicitly, it is likely to raise controversy on account of the role that ethical considerations play. It is important to keep in mind that the controversy to which I refer is not fundamentally about the correctness of a decision but about the legitimacy of the mode of reasoning that led to it. Dworkinite reasoning is, in our legal culture, not conventional but inherently controversial.

It might be pointed out in defense of Dworkin that there is an important distinction between rendering a decision based upon the principles of the soundest theory of the settled law and rendering one based upon ethical reasoning that is unconstrained by existing legal conventions. In Dworkin's account, the settled law

[37] For example, in *Escola v. Coca-Cola Bottling Co.*, 24 Cal.2d 453 (1944), Judge Traynor explicitly introduces ethical considerations into the grounds of decision. When ethical reasoning is injected into legal argument in this way, it is usually under the rubric of "public policy."

[38] In some areas of law, the breakdown of the convention demanding maximum coherence with the settled law occurs with relatively higher frequency than in others. Such breakdowns occur most frequently, I believe, in constitutional law, perhaps in part because of the unusual gravity of the moral and political issues that are often at stake.

exerts a considerable constraint on the judge's moral and political convictions, even in a hard case.

This part of Dworkin's account can be conceded, but it still misses the central point that I am making against his theory. The reigning *convention* among judges in our legal culture prescribes that legal decisions achieve the best fit with the settled law, and to the extent that independent ethical considerations play a role in legal reasoning, the reasoning is likely to prove controversial rather than conventional. Dworkin argues, of course, that decisions in hard cases will be controversial. But again, the controversy to which I refer is not over the outcome but over the mode of reasoning.

Dworkin might also argue that legal interpretation is always value-laden. Indeed, his general theory of interpretation suggests that all efforts to interpret the products of human social action contain an essential and ineliminable value dimension. The theory claims that interpretation "is a matter of imposing purpose on an object or practice in order to make of it the best possible example of the form or genre to which it is taken to belong."[39]

Dworkin's claim about the value-laden character of interpretation can be conceded, however, without giving up the claim that the convention that reigns in our legal culture demands decisions having a maximum coherence with the settled law. Dworkin still respects the distinction between interpretation and invention.[40] Unlike the invention of meanings, interpretation is constrained by features of an object that are independent of the interpretation. My argument against Dworkin is that there are salient features of our legal culture that are incompatible with his account but fully compatible with the idea that the reigning convention demands decisions having maximum coherence with the settled law, irrespective of any independent judgment of the ethical soundness of the principles on which the decisions rest.

There may well be a value dimension to the task of determining which decisions have the best fit. For example, considerations of simplicity or "elegance" may play a role in the determination of which legal principle governs certain kinds of cases. It may even be true that more recent cases are conventionally accorded greater weight when coherence with the settled law is determined and that one could justify this practice on the grounds that the law is

[39] Dworkin, *Law's Empire*, p. 52.
[40] Ibid., pp. 67–68.

and should be an ever-evolving effort to grapple with the problems of social life. However, conceding the existence of such value dimensions in legal decision making is in no way incompatible with the claim that our conventional practice requires a judge to render the decision that has maximum coherence with the settled law, without regard to any independent judgment about the moral or political soundness of the principles on which the decision rests.[41]

Its controversial character does not prevent Dworkinite reasoning from having a significant influence on the shape of doctrine. What seems to happen is this: When the convention of maximum coherence breaks down, some judges make decisions that explicitly or tacitly appeal to the moral and political adequacy of principles that cohere with a substantial portion of the settled law. Other judges reject such reasoning and dissent, claiming that the decisions do not accord with the convention demanding maximum logical coherence with the settled law. But whenever a judge makes a decision relying on Dworkinite reasoning, it is easier for the next judge to render a similar decision in a similar case on grounds of maximum logical coherence. The earlier decision becomes a precedent, and the outcome, if not the reasoning, becomes part of the settled law. The doctrine of *precedent* thus creates a kind of bootstrap effect that can eventually lead to a situation in which even the most strict adherents to the convention of maximum coherence will acknowledge that the initially controversial principle fits the settled law better than its competitor. Legal principles and doctrines initially the product of controversial legal reasoning thus come to be an uncontested part of the law. Yet the

[41] Dworkin might be inclined to place the theory that I have proposed into the category that he calls *soft conventionalism.* Such a category encompasses theories which contend that the law consists not merely of the conventionally agreed upon norms and meanings but also of the principles that are implicit in those conventional materials. He claims that soft conventionalism is an inchoate version of his account of law. See *Law's Empire,* pp. 124–28.

Dworkin's claim about soft conventionalism rests on a peculiar reading that he gives to the term *implicit.* See *Law's Empire,* p. 123. On that reading, the principles that are implicit in the conventional materials are the principles that score highest on some combination of both logical coherence with those materials and inherent ethical soundness. If that is what *implicit* means, then soft conventionalism is a version of Dworkin's account, and my theory is not a form of soft conventionalism. On the other hand, if a principle can be implicit by virtue of being maximally coherent with the conventional materials, irrespective of its ethical soundness, then my theory is a form of soft conventionalism, but there are types of soft conventionalism that are not versions of Dworkin's account.

general mode of reasoning that initially invoked the principle remains controversial.

Sources of Indeterminacy

If the account of legal reasoning that I have been defending is sound, it defeats Dworkin's argument for the thesis that virtually all legal cases have a single correct answer in our legal system. It also shows that there are a number of potential sources of legal indeterminacy in the system and that indeterminacy is a significant phenomenon in our legal culture.

The major source of indeterminacy is the breakdown of the convention prescribing decisions and reasoning having a maximum coherence with the settled law.[42] There are several kinds of cases in which this breakdown is likely to occur. Consider, for example, those cases where a conscientious inspection of the legal materials leads many judges to conclude that conflicting principles of decision fit the law more or less equally well, with no single principle the decisive winner. Perhaps the judges would concede that a certain principle might really fit a millimeter better than another; the point is that they see the difference in fit as governed by the principle *de minimis non curat lex* (the law does not notice trifles). In such a situation, judges would go beyond the convention demanding maximum fit with the settled law in rendering their decisions. A convention would still be operative prohibiting a judge from choosing as the ground of decision some principle that fits the settled law to a much lower degree than the principles that score highest on the coherence criterion. However, such a convention by itself would clearly be insufficient to dictate a unique legal outcome, and different judges would invoke incompatible criteria

[42] Some theorists have argued that even when the law fails to dictate a single determinate outcome, it still establishes a frame within which the outcome and the reasoning for it must be located. I think that such a view is correct. See Hans Kelsen, *Pure Theory of Law* (Los Angeles: University of California Press, 1967), pp. 351–52, and Kent Greenawalt, "Discretion and Judicial Decision: The Elusive Quest for the Fetters that Bind Judges," *Columbia Law Review* 75 (1975): 382.

Even when the convention that prescribes a (principle of) decision having maximum coherence with the settled law completely breaks down, there is still a convention operating that demands that the (principle of) decision fit with a substantial portion of the settled law. The breakdown of the convention demanding maximum coherence does not mean the breakdown of all conventions of reasoning within the legal culture. This point will become important when we examine the CLS attack on the law-politics distinction.

in order to take up the slack and choose from among the best-fitting principles.

Some judges would appeal in Dworkinite fashion to the principles of critical morality in order to settle on a norm of decision—with many disagreements among them, of course, about what those principles were. Other judges would appeal to the principles of positive morality—with similar disagreements as well. Others would appeal to the intentions of the legislature, again with disputes about what those intentions were. Still others would insist on sticking with the criterion of maximum coherence in order to detect that millimeter of difference, rejecting the idea that the *de minimis* principle applied here. Yet, the maximum-coherence criterion would be reduced, in such cases, to just another controversial basis for a decision; its conventional status would be suspended relative to such cases. The conventions of legal reasoning that did remain in force (e.g., the convention that demands of any principle of decision substantial coherence with the settled law) would be insufficient to dictate unique legal outcomes. The law would thus be indeterminate.

The convention of maximum coherence sometimes breaks down even when one possible principle of decision clearly fits the settled law better than its competitors. For example, sometimes a norm that loses on grounds of coherence is far and away the morally better principle and will become the basis of decision for that reason. Since judges are somewhat loath to acknowledge departure from the maximum-coherence convention, they will sometimes refuse to concede that their reasoning takes this form or invoke in some vague way the demands of "public policy." But I believe that it is quite plausible to see a number of cases as fitting this model, including Cardozo's opinion in *MacPherson*.

It is important to note that none of my arguments for the existence of legal indeterminacy hinges on the premise that disagreement between legal officials about the outcomes of cases entails indeterminacy. Dworkin contends that sincere disagreement between legal professionals about the correct outcome of a case does not entail the conclusion that there is no correct legal outcome. I do not dispute that contention. In fact, the account of legal reasoning that I have given is perfectly consistent with it.

Some judges are likely to be much better than others at grasping the logical connections among the elements of a large body of propositions and seeing which (principle of) decision coheres best with the settled law. These variations in cognitive ability could lead judges to disagree about a case, even if there is one decision that coheres with the settled law better than the alternatives. In such a situation, there will be disagreement about the correct outcome, even though there will be a single correct legal answer to the case. Given the reigning convention of maximum coherence and our very complicated body of law, it is perfectly possible that disagreement is a sign not of a gap in the law but of the differential cognitive abilities of judges.

Reasoning in our legal culture, then, is governed by a convention that makes it possible for judges and lawyers to be divided on the correct outcome in a case without that division entailing that there is no single, correct decision for the case. To the extent that Hart's argument for indeterminacy rests on the premise that disagreement about outcomes entails legal indeterminacy, the argument overlooks the possibility of such a convention and so is not sound. However, there is a persuasive case for the existence of a significant degree of legal indeterminacy that does not hinge on that premise. I have argued that legal reasoning usually proceeds in accordance with a convention that demands a decision having maximum fit with the settled law. This convention sometimes breaks down, though, and it is mainly in the spaces created by that breakdown that indeterminacy arises.

Law and Politics

It might be concluded that my account of legal reasoning effectively concedes the CLS contention that the law-politics distinction and the rule of law are illusions. When the maximum-coherence convention breaks down, it seems, ethical and political judgments infiltrate into legal reasoning in a way that subverts the liberal commitment to the rule of law. But to draw such a conclusion at this point would be to rely on the patently false premise that anything short of an absolute distinction is no distinction at all.

We have examined several liberal models of the rule of law, each allowing a different degree of infiltration of ethical or political judgment into legal reasoning. A Dworkinite model of law would surely involve such infiltration to a far more significant degree than a system that relies on the convention of maximum coherence with the settled law, even when the convention sometimes breaks down in the manner I have described. And the model of legal reasoning that I have defended as capturing the character of reasoning in our legal culture surely allows a greater infiltration than alternatives such as the generic model. But one cannot validly conclude from these points that my model, or even Dworkin's, effectively destroys the law-politics distinction and with it, the rule of law. Such a conclusion would rest on the indefensible notion that if two domains share some important similarities, there is no genuine distinction between them. On the other hand, the concession that there is a significant infiltration of ethical or political judgment into legal reasoning certainly raises the question of whether the CLS position is sound. Thus, we need to examine in detail the CLS arguments against the law-politics distinction and the liberal rule of law. That examination begins in the next chapter. The final section of this chapter is devoted to the claims of Hayek and other liberals that the rule of law has broken down in the contemporary liberal state because of the growth of its administrative-regulatory apparatus.

The Destruction of the Rule of Law?

The most powerful arguments from the liberal tradition that the rule of law has broken down in contemporary liberal democratic states stem from a consideration of the implications of the existence of administrative-regulatory regimes in those societies. The emergence of the administrative-regulatory state has cast serious doubt on the idea that the rule of law effectively constrains and regulates the power of state organs in contemporary liberal society. Administrative and regulatory agencies exercise extensive discretionary powers, guided by the vaguest of standards. Review of the actions of these agencies by the judiciary is, at best, relaxed. Even when an issue is deemed reviewable by the courts—and it is not always so deemed—substantial deference is accorded to the judgments of regulatory agencies, on grounds of their alleged expertise in the relevant area of social life. In addition, people can be deprived of their property or liberty by regulatory agencies without a full and fair hearing by an independent judicial body. These developments appear to make nonsense of the idea that the organs of the state are legally accountable for their actions in a way that truly regulates and confines their power. Pointing to such developments, liberals hostile to the administrative-regulatory apparatus of the contemporary liberal state have argued forcefully that the rule of law has been virtually destroyed.[43]

[43] It is important to recognize the fundamental differences between the claim of

It is clear that certain formulations of the rule of law have been rendered completely obsolete by the development of the administrative-regulatory state. As J. Roland Pennock points out, Dicey's influential formulation is blatantly inconsistent with the institutions of the administrative-regulatory regime. Dicey argued that the rule of law required "that no man is punishable or can be lawfully made to suffer in body or goods except for a distinct breach of law established in the ordinary legal manner before ordinary Courts of the land."[44] Pennock points out that under the regulatory regime of the twentieth-century liberal democratic state, "there are countless instances in which men can be 'made to suffer in goods' for breaches of law established in other ways than 'in the ordinary legal manner.' "[45] And Pennock may just as well have added that such losses are often suffered at the hands of agencies quite different from ordinary courts.

However, it would be premature to conclude from the foregoing that the principle of the rule of law has been destroyed. Dicey's version of the rule of law was excessively tied to institutional details. All liberal accounts contend that courts, or their functional equivalents, are required in practice to establish the rule of law. But it is going too far to suggest, as Dicey did, that the rule of law requires that no state organ other than an ordinary court impose a loss on anyone. Courts there must be, but precisely how they fit into the overall scheme of government is a matter that will vary from situation to situation and should not be incorporated into the very idea of the rule of law. The idea of the rule of law should be formulated at a level of abstraction that leaves considerable room for institutional variation, as is done in the theories of Dworkin and Hart. Only in this way can we keep our eye on the guiding moral purpose of the rule of law and distinguish the achievement

---

liberals such as Hayek that the rule of law has broken down and the claims associated with the CLS charge that the liberal rule of law is a myth. For those liberals, the liberal rule of law did once exist and presumably could be resurrected. A main line of CLS argument, examined in the next chapter, is that the liberal rule of law never did exist and never could exist. In addition, liberals who mourn the death of the rule of law do not attribute its demise so much to a pervasive legal indeterminacy as to the extensive discretionary powers of administrative and regulatory agencies. The problem is not that the law is indeterminate but that the law clearly confers on such agencies the power to do very much as they please. For CLS, on the other hand, it is the pervasiveness of legal indeterminacy that constitutes one of the main reasons for concluding that the rule of law is a myth.

[44] A. V. Dicey, *An Introduction to the Study of the Law of the Constitution*, 6th ed. (New York: Macmillan, 1902), pp. 183–84.

[45] J. Roland Pennock, *Administration and the Rule of Law* (New York: Farrar and Rinehart, 1941), p. 10.

of that purpose from the establishment of particular institutional arrangements that may serve that purpose best only in a certain limited social or historical context.

It should not be surprising, then, that the liberals who first alleged the destruction of the rule of law essentially accepted Dicey's version of it.[46] If Dicey's version *is* the rule of law, then it has been destroyed by the administrative-regulatory regime of the twentieth-century state. However, once one moves to an understanding of the rule of law that is less tied to institutional detail, it is far less obvious that it has been destroyed by the developments which have been briefly summarized. The issue becomes much less clear-cut.

Dworkin provides us with a useful hint for dealing with the issue. The rule of law, he tells us, demands that a normative principle must have at least some substantial degree of logical coherence with the settled law if it is to carry any legal authority. Yet this raises the question of how much coherence is "substantial." Dworkin points out that the answer to that question depends in part on the answers to questions of normative political philosophy; in particular it depends on the answers to questions about the ethical and political purposes that are served by the rule of law and the importance of those purposes in the overall scheme of worthy human aims.[47] I believe that the same is true of the question whether the rule of law has been destroyed. The answer hinges in part on questions of normative political philosophy. I do not propose to answer those questions here. Instead, I propose the more modest approach of showing how the dispute between liberals who affirm and liberals who deny the destruction of the rule of law rests largely on a normative conflict within the liberal tradition of political philosophy.

It is possible to imagine a total collapse of the rule of law in which no reasonable person, whatever his or her political philosophy, could affirm that it existed. Neither side in the liberal debate holds that we are in such a situation. If legal norms can constrain and regulate public and private power at all—and all liberals agree that they can—then there is at least a fair degree of such constraint and regulation in contemporary liberal states.

First, substantial areas of legal doctrine remain in which precision in the formulation of the rules is insisted upon—notably, the

[46] See, e.g., Lord Hewart of Bury, *The New Despotism.*
[47] Dworkin, *Law's Empire*, p. 257.

criminal law. Second, much of the state's activity in denying people liberty or property remains subject to due-process guarantees. Third, the vague standards that guide administrative and regulatory agencies when they issue their authoritative rules and edicts still operate within a broader framework of rules that constrain the power of these agencies. No agency of government is given the unrestricted mandate to "maximize social utility" or "do as justice requires." The Consumer Product Safety Commission has a mandate to enact safety rules for consumer goods and even to ban goods judged to be unreasonably unsafe. But the commission may not enact rules for an industry that pertain to matters other than product safety (e.g., conditions in the workplace); nor may it nationalize industries, even if there were good reasons to think that it would promote product safety to do so. Fourth, there is a difference between uncontrolled state power and state power controlled by vague laws and relaxed judicial oversight; vague laws may not constrain state power with the same force as that of precise ones. But if one believes that laws can constrain power at all, then there is no good reason to deny that vague laws exercise some constraining force. Judicial oversight that exhibits much deference to the judgment of the executive agency may not constrain state power with the same force as that of strict judicial oversight. But if one believes that judicial oversight can constitute some independent check on the actions of other government organs, there is no good reason to deny that relaxed judicial oversight can exercise some constraining force.

The contemporary liberal state may have more power and more kinds of power than earlier versions of the liberal state. However, it does not follow that any organ of the state has the power to do whatever it pleases or even whatever it judges to be for the good of the political community.

The foregoing points are not meant to dispose of the question whether the rule of law has broken down. Rather, they are meant to help us locate the issue that lies at the bottom of the debate about the alleged breakdown. If all sides agree that the law exercises some constraint on the exercise of power, then the source of the dispute must be whether there is enough constraint. How much is enough?

Liberals of all stripes hold that the principal purpose of the rule of law is to secure individual freedom by constraining the illegitimate use of power. The proper degree of constraint will be a function of the degree needed to secure a sufficiently wide zone of individual freedom. This is not to say that establishing the required degree of constraint will by itself be sufficient to secure such a zone of freedom. Recall that I argued at the beginning of the chapter against the view that the rule of law was by itself sufficient to establish an ample zone of liberal freedom. "Enough" constraint is the minimal level below which a sufficiently wide zone of individual freedom either cannot exist or can do so only in an unacceptably precarious condition.

What is a sufficiently wide zone of individual freedom? It is here, I think, that we come to the issue that lies at the bottom of the intramural liberal debate. Liberals like Hayek would claim that the legal constraints on the organs of the administrative-regulatory state are too weak for the state to secure a sufficiently wide zone of individual freedom. Hayek subscribes to a political philosophy according to which the freedoms infringed upon by the administrative-regulatory apparatus are of such vital importance, and their infringement so severe, that it has become impossible for the state to do its job of securing individual freedoms. From Hayek's point of view, essential liberal freedoms have been lost, and they have been lost because certain organs of the contemporary state have been licensed to operate in ways that are substantially unconfined by the rule of law. Thus, Hayek's claim about the breakdown of the rule of law rests largely on his moral assessment of the state's new powers of regulation and administration. To the extent that like Hayek, one is critical of such powers and condemns them for encroaching grievously on vital freedoms, one does indeed have reason to say that the rule of law has broken down. The moral purpose of the rule of law has, in such a view, been subverted.

On the other hand, many liberals make the opposing moral judgment about the liberal state's powers of regulation and administration.[48] They deny that vital liberal freedoms have been destroyed by such powers and argue that although individual freedoms have been circumscribed for some, the result has been a society that comes closer to the liberal ideal of the greatest equal

[48] In his critique of Hayek, Raz clearly downplays the importance for individual dignity and autonomy of the economic liberties that Hayek holds dear. However, Raz's basic strategy is to argue that there are crucial values other than those served by the rule of law and that we should not rigidly insist on meeting the requirements of the rule of law when we can serve those other values by departing from those requirements. See Raz, *Authority of Law*, pp. 226–29. My argument is different from Raz's and focuses instead on the fact that competing political philosophies will lead to conflicting judgments about how the administrative-regulatory state has affected those values that the rule of law should be serving.

freedom for all. Such liberals need not deny the obvious—that in many cases, the legal accountability of the organs of the administrative-regulatory state is relatively relaxed. But they can argue that the relaxation has not undermined the essential moral purpose of the rule of law. Thus, they can argue that there are no good grounds for concluding that the rule of law has been destroyed. The degree to which law confines and regulates power is enough to make essential liberal freedoms secure.

The intramural liberal debate thus hinges in large measure on a more fundamental split in the liberal camp. The more fundamental split concerns the legitimate role of the state in economic and social affairs and the importance of the individual freedoms affected by contemporary government administration and regulation. Critics of the administrative-regulatory regime have reason to conclude that the rule of law once reigned but has broken down. Defenders of the regime have reason to conclude that it still reigns. Both groups agree in regarding the rule of law as a feasible set of institutional arrangements that serves as an indispensable condition for securing a morally acceptable zone of individual freedom. They disagree in their judgments about the conditions under which that set of arrangements can be said to operate because they disagree about the kind and degree of individual freedoms that the rule of law is to secure.

It is now time to turn to a challenge to the rule of law that comes from outside the liberal camp, a challenge far more radical than that mounted by Hayek and company against the administrative-regulatory state. The aim of the challenge is to show that the liberal rule of law is simply not possible, given the kind of moral, religious, and political pluralism that prevails in any liberal society. This is the challenge of Critical Legal Studies.

THREE

THE POSSIBILITY OF THE LIBERAL RULE OF LAW

The literature of Critical Legal Studies (CLS) is filled with contentions that liberal legal and political theory are "incoherent," "internally inconsistent," "self-contradictory," and the like. At the center of these contentions is the charge that it is impossible for a state to satisfy both the requirements of the rule of law and the demands of liberal political morality. The key thesis around which the charge revolves is this: In any society characterized by moral, religious, and political pluralism, the rule of law will be impossible to maintain without violating the key liberal principle that the state must remain neutral on questions regarding what gives meaning and value to human life. Let us use the term *liberal rule of law* to refer to the rule of law that obtains under conditions where pluralism prevails and the state abides by the rule of law and the liberal principle of neutrality. The CLS thesis in question, then, entails that the liberal rule of law is an impossibility. This is indeed a serious charge: an incoherence at the very core of liberal thought.

There are three main arguments in the CLS literature for the thesis that the liberal rule of law is an impossibility. The first contends that there can be no neutral process for the enactment of legal rules in the context of moral, religious, and political pluralism. Since the liberal rule of law requires such a process, it must be impossible. The seminal CLS statement of this line of argument is in Roberto Unger's *Knowledge and Politics*.[1]

The second argument claims that there can be no neutral pro-

[1] Roberto Unger, *Knowledge and Politics* (New York: Free Press, 1975), pp. 83–88. Also see Unger, *Law in Modern Society* (New York: Free Press, 1976), p. 180. Unger has changed his views over the years and no longer argues that the idea of the liberal rule of law is incoherent. Indeed, as we see in the final chapter, Unger's latest position is in many important respects quite close to liberalism's. The rationale for examining in detail his earlier positions and arguments is that they have had and continue to have an enormous influence in the CLS movement.

cess for the interpretation of legal rules in the context of moral, religious, and political pluralism. This argument has two variants. The more radical contends that legal rules are inherently devoid of any meaning and can be filled with semantic content only through a process that is nonneutral. This view can be found in the work of Gary Peller, Clare Dalton, Girardeau Spann, and, with some qualification, James Boyle.[2] The less radical variant denies that legal rules are inherently devoid of meaning but claims that their full interpretation necessarily involves a process that is not neutral. The seminal CLS statement of this variant is again in Unger's *Knowledge and Politics*.[3] In either variant, the liberal rule of law breaks down because it requires something that cannot be delivered—a neutral process of legal interpretation.

The third argument focuses on a distinction whose institutionalization liberalism takes to be vital for maintaining the neutrality of the legal process, the distinction between law and politics. The argument claims that, paradoxically, to institutionalize this very distinction is to undercut neutrality because it exhibits a bias against certain conceptions of the good and the right in a pluralist setting. Protecting the neutrality of the legal process, a task crucial to the maintenance of the rule of law, turns out to be normatively biased and thus violates the liberal neutrality principle. This argument can be found in a number of CLS authors, including Peller, Boyle, and Mark Kelman.[4]

In this chapter, I examine these three lines of attack on the conceptual coherence of the liberal rule of law. In the course of the examination, it is necessary to provide a precise account of the liberal commitment to neutrality. It is also necessary to sketch an account of legal meaning and interpretation. In light of the accounts which I defend, my conclusion is that the three lines of CLS argument fail to establish the incoherence of liberal theory. This conclusion leaves open the question of whether the legal doctrine of any particular liberal state, such as that of the United States or England, is in some sense incoherent or self-contradictory. In the next chap-

[2] See Gary Peller, "The Metaphysics of American Law," *California Law Review* 73 (1985): 1167–75; Girardeau Spann, "Deconstructing the Legislative Veto," *Minnesota Law Review* 68 (1984): 534; Clare Dalton, "An Essay in the Deconstruction of Contract Doctrine," *Yale Law Journal* 94 (1985): 1102; and James Boyle, "The Politics of Reason," *University of Pennsylvania Law Review* 133 (1985): 712 n. 90.

[3] Unger, *Knowledge and Politics*, pp. 88–100.

[4] Peller, "Metaphysics of American Law," pp. 1153–55; Boyle, "Politics of Reason," p. 696; and Mark Kelman, *A Guide to Critical Legal Studies* (Cambridge: Harvard University Press, 1987), chap. 9.

ter, I take up the CLS claim that existing legal doctrine, particularly in the United States, is to be characterized in that manner.

Unger: The Contradictions of Liberalism

In *Knowledge and Politics* and *Law in Modern Society*, Unger contends that there are two fatal contradictions at the heart of liberal political and legal theory. Both contradictions stem from the same basic deficiency, in Unger's view, and both destroy the possibility of the liberal rule of law. The deficiency is liberalism's "inability to arrive at a coherent understanding of the relations between rules and values in social life."[5] Many of the theoretical arguments to be found in the CLS literature in favor of the thesis that the liberal rule of law is impossible derive directly from Unger's contention that liberal legal and political theory are incapable of providing a coherent account of rules and values.

The first of the two contradictions attributed to liberalism concerns the process by which legal rules are enacted. Unger argues that there is no process which can satisfy the demand of liberal political morality for a neutral procedure of legislation. The second contradiction concerns the process by which legal rules are interpreted. Unger argues that there is no process which can satisfy the demand of liberal political morality for a neutral process of interpretation. The second contradiction is the "antinomy of rules and values."[6] He does not give a name to the first, but we can call it the antinomy of legislation.

According to Unger's account, both antinomies are rooted in the fact that in liberal theory and in liberal society, values are regarded as subjective. Unger uses the term *values* to cover both the ends or goals that people pursue and the conceptions that people hold of what is good and bad in human life. For purposes of clarity, it will help to focus on values as conceptions rather than ends, although the two senses are clearly related.

The subjectivity of values means that no conception of what is good or bad in human life has any warrant or basis beyond the choice of a given individual to embrace it. No such conception can be "correct" in the sense of being sound, regardless of what anyone may think or choose, nor can any such conception license an

[5] Unger, *Knowledge and Politics*, p. 63.
[6] Ibid., pp. 88ff.

individual who embraces it to coerce those who do not to conform to its dictates.

Conceptions of good and bad ways to live may be shared by a number of individuals in the context of the liberal state, but such sharing is regarded by liberal theory as having no significance as far as any claim regarding their objective correctness or their authority to license coercion is concerned. Sharing is an accidental feature of the social situation and may not be construed as evidence that the shared conception has any foundation that transcends individual choice or that warrants the coercion of those who decline to choose the way of life recommended by the conception. Such are the implications, at any rate, of the doctrine of the subjectivity of values which Unger attributes to liberalism.

Moreover, liberal theory attempts to solve two crucial problems that quickly emerge once reflective awareness is attained regarding this subjectivity of values. The first is the problem of order: How can social order be established and maintained if there are no objective values around which it can be built and stabilized and if every sharing of values must be regarded as an accidental and transitory feature of social life? The second is the problem of freedom: How can the establishment and maintenance of a social order avoid the unjustifiable subjugation of some people to the subjective choices of others?

The liberal answer to these problems, Unger tells us, is "that the eternal hostility of men to one another requires that order and freedom be maintained by government under law."[7] This is understood as rule by prescriptive positive norms to which all can agree. "The need for rules arises . . . [b]ecause there are no conceptions of the good that stand above the conflict and impose limits on it. . . . Peace must therefore be established by rules."[8]

According to Unger's reconstruction of liberalism, a key liberal idea is that even if people choose to embrace and pursue competing conceptions of what is good and bad in human life, they can still agree to a set of ground rules to abide by in pursuit of the ends that they regard as worthy of their efforts. The establishment and enforcement of such ground rules is the rule of law. Just as opponents in an athletic contest can agree to the rules, despite their pursuit of directly incompatible goals, people who inhabit the same territory but disagree about which ways of life are better and which are worse can agree to a set of rules to regulate their inter-

[7] Ibid., p. 67.

[8] Ibid., p. 68.

action, association, and competition. Whereas reliance on common conceptions of what is good in human life is unstable or impossible in the context of liberal society where there are many such conceptions and none is regarded as having an authority independent of individual choice on which to rest, the liberal believes that reliance on a set of rules to regulate social life can be stable. If the rules are neutral between the competing conceptions of the good life, then all can accept the rules, and the consequence will be a stable social and political order in which no one is subjected to illegitimate political domination by another.

The rule of authoritative and positive rules, that is, the rule of law, is thus a crucial component in the liberal solution to the problem of creating a stable social order in a pluralist setting and preventing illegitimate domination. The antinomies of legislation and of rules and values mean that this solution cannot possibly work, given the framework of liberal thought. Unger believes that the doctrine of subjective value undercuts the rule of law as a solution to the problems of order and freedom. The doctrine entails two insurmountable difficulties for liberalism. First, it makes impossible any neutral process for the enactment of the authoritative rules. A nonneutral legislative process will be biased against those who have embraced certain conceptions of what is good and bad in human life. Second, the doctrine of subjective value makes impossible any neutral process for the interpretation of the authoritative rules. A nonneutral interpretive process will be similarly biased. Since liberal political morality demands that both processes be neutral—or else, not everyone could voluntarily agree to the rules as authoritatively interpreted, and the consequence would be illegitimate domination—the liberal rule of law turns out to be a theoretically incoherent concept. Such is Unger's argument.

A neutral legislative process is impossible, according to Unger, for two main reasons:

> First, procedure is inseparable from outcome: every method makes certain legislative choices more likely than others. . . . Second, each lawmaking system itself embodies certain values; it incorporates a view of how power ought to be distributed in the society and of how conflicts should be resolved.[9]

Yet even if a neutral process of legislation were possible, the liberal rule of law would be defeated by the fact that there can be no neutral process for interpreting the rules generated by the legisla-

[9] Unger, *Law in Modern Society*, p. 180.

tive process. The principal reason that neutral interpretation is impossible, according to Unger, is that the interpretation of rules requires a reliance on values. He argues that conceptions of what is good and bad inevitably play a role in construing the meaning of legal rules. The choice of different conceptions of good and bad in the light of which to interpret legal rules will generate conflicting interpretations of their meaning. Yet, by liberalism's own principles, there is no conception of the good that is objectively correct or that licenses those who embrace it to coerce those who dissent from it. Different people can and will construe legal rules in the light of competing conceptions of the good. Since there is no privileged conception of the good, there can be no privileged interpretation of the rules.

If social stability requires rules whose meaning all can agree to, stability is undercut, for the instability of relying on controversial conceptions of the good will reemerge in the reliance on rules whose meanings fall into dispute. If freedom from illegitimate political domination prohibits anyone from imposing a particular conception of good and bad on one who dissents, freedom is undercut, for the authoritative interpretation of the legal rules will be a reflection of the values in the light of which a given judge or other public official has chosen to read the law. Thus, Unger claims that, given liberal premises, "laws or rules (legal justice) can neither dispense with a consideration of values in the process of adjudication, nor be made consistent with such a consideration."[10]

The reliance on values in the interpretation of rules is claimed to be inevitable, given the context of liberal ideas, because of certain conceptions of meaning and reality which have been embraced by liberalism. These conceptions decisively reject the older view that words, including those that constitute legal rules, have "plain meaning." The idea of plain meaning rests on the metaphysical premise that there is some natural categorization of facts and things, some privileged way of parsing reality that follows the contours and folds which are in reality itself and are cognizable by humans. Linguistic meaning is taken to map these independent cognizable contours. To understand meaning is to cognize the contours to which a given linguistic formulation refers. Meaning is presumed to be "plain" because the contours of reality to which it corresponds are taken to be readily cognizable.

[10] Unger, *Knowledge and Politics*, p. 91.

Unger calls the metaphysics which he attributes to the plain-meaning view the doctrine of *intelligible essences*,[11] and he tells us that liberal theory repudiates the doctrine and adopts in its stead the view that all categories constituted and defined by human languages are inescapably responsive to human ends and purposes. Languages are not the mirrors of nature but the mirrors of the particular plans and purposes pursued by those who speak them. Once the metaphysics of intelligible essences is dropped in favor of the liberal approach to meaning, legal rules must be interpreted in light of the ends they are meant to serve. But Unger claims that such a mode of interpretation reintroduces the very problems that liberal theory invoked the rule of law to solve, because interpreting legal rules in the light of their purposes invariably relies on the values that the interpreter has chosen to embrace.

This is true for two reasons, according to Unger. First, a single legal rule will serve multiple purposes, and there will be any number of cases in which different purposes come into conflict. The judge who is interpreting the law must then make a judgment about which purpose is most worthy. Such a judgment, Unger tells us, necessarily relies upon certain conceptions of what is good and bad in human life. And the need for reliance on such conceptions undercuts the rule of law as the stabilizing, freedom-protecting institution that liberalism takes it to be. Disagreement over the meaning of legal rules is authoritatively resolved only through the state's imposition of a particular conception of the human good, an imposition that must be condemned by the very principles of liberal political morality.

For Unger, there is a second reason that the interpretation of legal rules in the liberal state invariably relies on the values of the interpreter. Purposive legal interpretation cannot confine itself to the purposes of a single rule. There will always be a number of rules that are potentially applicable to a given case, and there will be any number of cases in which the purposes of these different rules pull in different directions. Again, the interpreter must determine which purpose is most worthwhile, inescapably relying on his or her conceptions of which ways of human life are best. Again, the liberal rule of law is undercut; there will be insufficient agreement in a pluralistic population on the meaning of the legal rules for such rules to stabilize social life without some coercive power to render an authoritative interpretation. And the authori-

[11] Ibid., p. 92.

tative interpretation and execution of the rules by public officials and their agents will amount to what liberal principles must regard as the illegitimate exercise of political domination.

Unger's claims regarding legal interpretation may be illustrated by reference to *Boys Markets v. Retail Clerk's Union*.[12] The case revolves around the question of whether a federal court has the authority to issue an injunction ordering union employees back to work in a situation where the union contract has a no-strike provision and requires binding arbitration for the settlement of disputes. The Norris-LaGuardia Act (1932) denies federal courts the jurisdiction to issue injunctions in any case involving a labor dispute. The Taft-Hartley Act (Labor Management Relations Act, 1947) gives federal courts jurisdiction to enforce collective-bargaining contracts. In an earlier case, *Sinclair Refining v. Atkinson*, the Supreme Court had held that the jurisdiction granted in Taft-Hartley did not extend to the issuance of a back-to-work injunction; Norris-LaGuardia's virtual blanket prohibition of such injunctions remained in force.[13] In *Boys Markets*, the Court reconsidered the issue and decided to overrule *Sinclair*.

On Unger's analysis of legal interpretation, the decisions in *Sinclair* and *Boys Markets* hinge on the formulation and assessment of the policies and purposes meant to be served by the two statutes and related law. Writing for the majority in *Boys Markets*, Justice Brennan gives an admirably clear description and illustration of the kind of purposive interpretation that Unger regards as vital to liberal legal reasoning:

> The literal terms of section 4 of the Norris-LaGuardia Act must be accommodated to the subsequently enacted provisions of section 301(a) of the Labor Management Relations Act and the purposes of arbitration. Statutory interpretation requires more than concentration upon isolated words; rather, consideration must be given to the total corpus of pertinent law and the policies that inspired ostensibly inconsistent provisions.[14]

Brennan proceeds to cite what he regards as the overriding purpose of federal labor law: "the encouragement of collective bargaining and . . . [of] administrative techniques for the peaceful resolution of industrial disputes."[15] In addition, he claims that the

[12] *Boys Markets, Inc. v. Retail Clerk's Union*, 398 U.S. 235 (1970).
[13] *Sinclair Refining Co. v. Atkinson*, 370 U.S. 195 (1962).
[14] *Boys Markets*, 398 U.S. at 250.
[15] *Boys Markets*, 398 U.S. at 251.

main purpose of Norris-LaGuardia was "to foster the growth and viability of labor organizations. . . ."[16] In light of this conception of the relevant purposes, Brennan argues that the correct decision becomes clear: Allowing the issuance of an injunction is the correct decision because it will serve the overriding purpose of federal labor law and will not defeat the main purpose of Norris-LaGuardia.

While Brennan provides a model case of liberal legal interpretation, he neglects what Unger's account takes to be the central problem of such a mode of interpretation: There are conflicting but equally plausible ways of reading the purposes behind Norris-LaGuardia, Taft-Hartley, and federal labor law in general. From Unger's point of view, Brennan merely hides this crucial point by reasoning as though there were a single privileged reading of those purposes and their relative importance that could be derived from a knowledge of the intent of Congress. Invoking congressional intent will not solve the problem of conflicting accounts of the purposes of federal labor law because it is equally easy to come up with conflicting accounts of congressional intent. Indeed, this is precisely what was done in *Sinclair* and in Justice Black's dissent in *Boys Markets*.[17] It was argued that the Congress which passed Taft-Hartley had no intention of curtailing the essential purpose of Norris-LaGuardia—to establish a general proscription of federally issued labor injunctions.

From Unger's point of view, the invocation of congressional intent to give authoritative status to a particular account of the purposes of labor law merely hides the fact that such accounts are reflections of the judge's assessment that certain purposes and policies are better than others. For Brennan, securing industrial tranquility and channeling labor-management struggles into administrative modes of conflict resolution were the controlling purposes, rather than protecting employee self-help and letting labor and management resolve their conflicts without management's being able to wield the weapon of the federal back-to-work injunction. But there was nothing in the law that made such an assessment of the competing purposes and policies the privileged one. Although liberal legal reasoning may obscure the nonneutral value choices that lie behind the interpretation of the law, it cannot eliminate such choices.

To sum up Unger's attack on the coherence of liberal theory, he

[16] *Boys Markets*, 398 U.S. at 252.

[17] *Boys Markets*, 398 U.S. at 255, J. Black dissenting.

is suggesting that the pluralism of the liberal state makes the rule of law both necessary and impossible, given liberal premises. The existence of liberal pluralism means that the order of social life cannot stabilize around common conceptions of good and bad. Social conflicts cannot be resolved and contained by an appeal to such conceptions since the conflicts are bound to be in large degree a reflection of conflicting conceptions of what is good and bad in human life. Rules that can be agreed to by persons who share no such conceptions must be the stabilizing force—or so the liberal argues in Unger's account. But for rules to stabilize social life in a manner consistent with liberal political morality, we must—despite our differences over the good—be able to agree on both the procedures by which the authoritative rules are enacted and the processes by which they are interpreted. Unger's claim is that the very pluralism that on liberal premises, makes rules to govern social life necessary makes it impossible for us to agree on any process for enacting those rules and interpreting their meaning. If there is insufficient consensus on conceptions of good and bad in human life for such conceptions to stabilize the terms of social life, then there will be an insufficient consensus on either the procedures for enacting rules or the processes by which their meaning is construed for rules to stabilize the terms of social life in a manner consistent with the liberal commitment to neutrality. That problem is the crux of the contradictions that afflict liberal legal and political philosophy in Unger's account.

The Right-Good Distinction

One of the crucial flaws in Unger's argument for the antinomies of legislation and of rules and values is his failure to take explicit account of the vital liberal distinction between the *right* and the *good*. The distinction is papered over by Unger's use of the term *values*. Indeed, in my reconstruction of Unger's arguments, I have papered over the distinction by the loose use of the terms *good* and *bad*, terms which are broad enough to cover virtually any form of assessment.

For the liberal tradition, though, there are two very different kinds of *values* to be considered. One set of normative directives, or *values*, concerns the demands of justice and moral obligation. This is the realm of the *right*. Another set of normative directives concerns the ends we should strive for, once we have insured that we are living above the moral threshold set by the requirements of justice and moral obligation. This is the realm of the *good*.

While there is a sense in which liberal theories have held that the good is subjective, the dominant position in the liberal tradition makes no such claim about the right. The good has been held to be subjective in the sense that no conception of the good licenses those who embrace it to coerce those who dissent. Sometimes this has been conjoined to the further claim that there is no such license because no conception of the good is correct or true in the sense of being sound whether anyone accepts it or not. But there are many liberal theorists who refrain from that further claim. The key point here, though, is that liberalism does not deny the legitimacy of coercion or the applicability of the concept of objective truth when it comes to matters of the right. If it did, it would be subject to the very contradictions of which Unger complains, and the concept of the liberal rule of law would be incoherent.

But it seems that Unger's arguments hinge on the mistaken premise that liberalism embraces the subjectivity of all normative directives, of both the good and the right. Thus, consider his response to the claim of utilitarian liberals that the principle of utility provides the standard for aggregating preferences and generating legislative outcomes. Unger claims that if the principle of utility is so regarded, that is tantamount to treating the maximization of utility as "precisely the objective good whose nonexistence drove us into the attempt to devise a liberal doctrine of legislation."[18] In other words, his claim is that to use the principle of utility as the standard for legislation would introduce an objective value inconsistent with the liberal commitment to the subjectivity of values.

Yet such a claim is based on a confusion: The utilitarian principle belongs to the realm of the right, at least according to utilitarian theory, not to the realm of the good. Whether a convincing argument for the binding character of the principle can or need be produced is another question. Unger's claim here is not that utilitarian liberals cannot adduce sufficient reasons for the acceptance of their principle but that they incoherently endorse both the principle of utility and the subjectivity of values. The claim is just wrong. The utilitarian view may be mistaken, but it is not incoherent in the manner that Unger suggests.

Similar problems afflict Unger's argument about the need to in-

[18] Unger, *Knowledge and Politics*, p. 86.

troduce values into the process of legal interpretation. Given the standard liberal understanding of the right-good distinction, the neutrality principle certainly cannot be taken as demanding neutrality with respect to conceptions of justice and right. It is neutrality with respect to conceptions of the good that standard liberal theories demand. This means that legal rules should be restricted to enforcing the requirements of justice and moral obligation. Yet when so restricted, it is not at all clear why it would be necessary to introduce considerations of the good into their interpretation. And if considerations of the good are not needed for the authoritative interpretation of legal rules, then the subjectivity of the good poses no problem for the liberal state.

In regarding the right as a domain where normative conceptions can be objectively true and can license the coercion of those who dissent, the liberal is tacitly committed to what Unger might describe as a doctrine of *intelligible moral essences*. But all this doctrine amounts to is the idea that some things really are wrong or unjust (religious persecution, for example) and that others really are right and just (religious toleration, for example). Of course, a few thinkers have tried to throw overboard entirely all notions of objective correctness, truth, reality, and so forth, and to succeed in doing so would be to sweep away the presumed objectivity of the right as well as the good. Unger presumably has in mind such a total rejection of objectivity and truth when he speaks of the liberal rejection of metaphysical essences. But it is difficult to see why such a view should be characterized as liberal. It was embraced by Nietzsche but not by any of the great nineteenth-century defenders of the liberal creed—not by Mill, not by Constant, not by Humboldt. It is suggested in the work of contemporary deconstructionists but not by any of the central figures in contemporary liberal thought—Rawls, Dworkin, or Feinberg.

It is not truth but teleology that liberal theorists have sought to jettison. The doctrine of metaphysical essences which they repudiated was the Aristotelian version which held that all things, including human beings, had inherent natures constituted by their tendency to pursue certain goals. Liberalism was indeed born in the intellectual revolution that overthrew Aristotelian metaphysical teleology. The revolution helped to liberate political thought from the classical idea that there was a single relatively restrictive mode of living that was best for human beings and that the function of the state was to inculcate in its citizens the qualities that would enable them to lead it. It helped to establish the liberal distinction between the right and the good. But the rejection of Aristotelian teleology cannot be equated with the wholesale repudiation of truth and objectivity.

Unfortunately, Unger does not grapple directly with the problems raised for his arguments by the liberal right-good distinction. Let us see if we can construct a response for him; without one, his antinomies collapse with barely a push.

One response from Unger would go as follows: In the context of liberal pluralism, the very issue of where to draw the boundary that separates the right from the good will be in dispute. Proponents of laissez-faire and defenders of the welfare state hardly agree on what the principles of justice and right require. Those who denounce abortion as murder and those who defend it as a morally permissible choice for a woman hardly agree on where the line that defines our obligations to others is to be drawn. Liberal pluralism is characterized by deep disagreement about the right and the just, not merely about the good, the better, and the best. Now, given a form of pluralism where the very line between the right and the good is a matter of dispute, it would be impossible to stabilize social life around any particular conception of the right in a manner consistent with the liberal principle that the state remain neutral regarding all conceptions of the good. For the state to enforce any conception of the right would be to override conceptions of the good which draw the line between the good and the right at a different place and thus to violate the neutrality requirement.

This Ungerian argument makes the sound point that in a context where the very line between the right and the good is at issue, the question whether public power is being exercised in a neutral way will have no noncontroversial answer. From the moral perspective of those who contend that women ought to be free to choose an abortion, the state is neutral among competing conceptions of the good when it lets each woman decide for herself whether to have an abortion or not. From the moral perspective of the antiabortion forces, the state is not neutral, for the choice to have an abortion does not belong to the domain of the good; the choice fails to satisfy the principles of right and justice. Agreement breaks down, then, on the question of neutrality if the state permits the choice of abortion. Of course, the breakdown would also occur, but from the opposite direction, were the state to outlaw abortion. And thus it seems that, given disagreement over where to draw the line between the right and the good, the state invariably violates the liberal requirement of political neutrality with respect to conceptions of the good.

A liberal counterargument to this Ungerian response may begin by pointing out that there is a crucial equivocation in the response's construction of the liberal commitment to neutrality. In one interpretation, the state must be neutral among all (and only) those normative conceptions that endorse ways of life actually above the threshold of right and justice. In the second interpretation, the state must be neutral among all conceptions of the good, no matter what way of life they endorse or where they draw the line between the right and the good. Liberalism, the counterargument contends, is committed to the former interpretation, not the latter. Yet the argument that the state necessarily violates the neutrality principle whenever it overrides some conception of the good depends on construing liberalism as committed to the latter interpretation.

One way to respond to this defense would be to argue that liberalism is in fact committed to the second interpretation of the neutrality principle. If this interpretation were the correct one, the distinction between the good and the right would collapse, subjectivity would swallow up both domains, and the state would violate neutrality no matter what it did or refrained from doing. For any given way of life, there is some conceivable moral position that would regard it as above the threshold of justice and obligation and another such position that would regard it as below that threshold. Anything regarded as a matter of the right from one moral perspective could be regarded as a matter of the good from another, and so the state could not, consistent with neutrality, enforce any rules, no matter which set of principles of justice and right they embodied.

Unger can be understood as suggesting that liberalism ought to be interpreted in this way: Its commitment to neutrality ultimately results in the collapse of the distinction between the good and the right and drowns both domains in the sea of subjectivity. Such an interpretation could explain why Unger appears rather careless with respect to the right-good distinction, virtually ignoring it with his rather imprecise notion of "values." But it would be an interpretation of liberalism that has little foundation in the history of modern Western legal and political philosophy. This is explicitly recognized, even within the CLS literature, by Mark Kelman, who criticizes Unger for failing to acknowledge that liberalism is not committed to total moral subjectivism.[19] A doctrine of total moral subjectivity, covering both the right and the good, has had some role to play in the liberal tradition, but it has been a minor one. The dominant position is that there are objective standards of right and justice that carry an authority independent of actual human choices and indeed place normative constraints on such choices.

There is, however, something disquieting about the suggestion that the liberal can escape Unger's antinomies by claiming that there is some objectively true conception of the just and right and that political neutrality means merely the absence of state bias with respect to any normative view above the threshold set by that objective conception. There are, I think, two sources of this disquiet. First, the strategy has the effect of robbing the neutrality principle of any distinctively liberal character. All the real work of distinguishing liberalism from, for example, an antiliberal opposition which argues against religious toleration would be done by the principles of right. Antitolerationists could just as well accept the principle demanding neutrality with respect to what is not a matter of the right. They would simply be drawing the line that distinguishes the right from the good in a different location because of their different conception of the content of the principles of right. There would be nothing distinctively liberal about acceptance of the neutrality principle; its endorsement would tell us virtually nothing about the degree of liberty, plurality, or toleration which a theory was prepared to embrace.

The second source of disquiet stems from the idea that the notions of compromise and accommodation must play a vital role in any full account of liberalism. Liberal compromise and accommodation must extend not only to the realm of the good but also to the realm of the right. Liberalism at its best takes seriously the existence of disagreement about principles of justice and obligation and not merely disagreement about what we should strive for once the demands of justice and obligation have been met. Taking such disagreement seriously means being prepared to endorse an institutional structure that requires groups holding conflicting conceptions of the right to work out compromises and accommodations they can live with. The outcomes of such arrangements will not track the principles of justice and obligation embraced by any one group. And the liberal should not defend the outcomes as em-

[19] Kelman, *A Guide to Critical Legal Studies*, pp. 83–84.

bodying the complete truth about the right but defend them as embodying a workable and defensible compromise.

If this view of liberalism is accepted, it may appear that liberalism must banish considerations of moral truth from the arena of politics. Consensus, not truth, would seem to be the foundation upon which liberalism would be prepared to embrace a set of institutional arrangements. But this appearance is deceptive in some important ways. The appeal to moral truth cannot be banished from the liberal tradition, even in the name of consensus, compromise, and accommodation. The liberal who endorses institutional arrangements that require compromise and adjustment is implicitly appealing to moral truth. Such arrangements are not optional for the liberal; they are not on a par with arrangements that allow one of the contending groups to exercise a monopoly over the deployment of state power and violence. Rather, such arrangements are, in a pluralist society, required by justice. This is a proposition that liberal theory must be prepared to defend as a *moral* truth. Moreover, we will see that there are certain moral claims regarding individual rights on which the liberal must refuse to compromise. These claims do not exhaust the domain of right and justice, but the liberal must be prepared to defend them as moral truths.

Nonetheless, the foregoing considerations suggest that it is a mistake for liberals to interpret neutrality simply as an indifference to those normative conceptions above the moral threshold set by the true principles of justice and right. In a robustly pluralist society, where there was vigorous dispute about the right as well as the good, it would be unlikely that the compromises and deals worked out would faithfully track the complete moral truth about justice and right. If one takes seriously the liberal commitment to compromise and accommodation in a pluralist context, a different conception of liberal neutrality is required.

Liberal Neutrality: Four Forms

There are at least four forms of neutrality that are defended within the liberal tradition. The first concerns the legitimate bounds of politics and is premised on the idea that there are certain domains of human experience and activity that are beyond the legitimate reach of the state. To say that the state must be neutral with respect to such aspects of human life is to imply that they are not to be subject to the processes of deliberation, compromise, and negotiation that constitute the normal political life of the liberal state.

Those domains involve matters that are not legitimate subjects for the concern and regulation of the political community. Rather, they are to be regarded as areas of individual autonomy into which politics may not properly intrude. The neutrality of the state, in this first form, places certain matters beyond the bounds of legitimate politics.

Liberal theory conceptualizes the boundaries which thus confine legitimate political activity in terms of individual rights. Such rights represent constraints on what political activity may legitimately aim for or accomplish. We may thus label this form of neutrality as *rights neutrality*. The right of conscience is paradigmatic. The right to property has also played a central role in liberal thought, although the exact contours of that right, as well as those of all other liberal rights, have been the subject of much controversy within the tradition. The general point to be made here, though, is that despite their intramural controversies, liberals all agree on placing rather substantial restrictions on the permissible reach of politics in the name of individual autonomy.[20]

The second form of neutrality concerns the epistemological basis for claiming that there are individual rights that seriously confine the legitimate role of politics. More specifically, it concerns requirements on acceptable arguments for the principles that are alleged to demarcate the boundaries of permissible politics. Let us call it *epistemological neutrality*.

One version of this form of neutrality contends that the principles for demarcating the acceptable bounds of politics (i.e., for specifying individual rights) must be derived from premises that are noncommittal on questions of the human good. However, as the formulation of a requirement for acceptable arguments, it is questionable whether this version of epistemological neutrality makes sense. It clearly would make sense if one could define the realm of the good independently of the principles of right, but such an independent definition seems impossible. Questions

[20] Utilitarians have serious problems with the idea of moral rights, and this makes it difficult to give a concise description of liberal theory in a way that clearly allows utilitarians to be liberals. However, we should not get hung up on the term *rights*. The crucial question to ask in determining whether a theory is committed to what I have called rights neutrality is this: Does the theory endorse substantial and enduring limitations on the legitimate bounds of politics in order to free the individual from the regulation of the political community? A utilitarian liberal would answer affirmatively and then add that freeing the individual from the regulation of the political community is the right thing to do because it promotes utility. A deontological liberal would answer affirmatively and then add that it is the right thing because individuals have moral rights against the community.

about the good are questions about how to live and organize society once one is above the moral threshold set by the principles of right. Because of this, a theory's noncommittal orientation with regard to questions of the good is logically guaranteed once its principles of right are formulated, if the principles are the true ones. But prior to the formulation of the principles of right, it seems that there is no way to specify the domain of the good; therefore, there is no way, in advance of a cogent argument for specific principles of right, to determine whether a given theory is in fact neutral on questions of the good.

It may be possible to overcome such difficulties by using the method of *reflective equilibrium.* We start out with intuitive judgments about what belongs to the domain of the good and adjust our intuitions as we attempt to formulate and defend the principles that embody normative constraints on politics. However, there are difficulties with the method of reflective equilibrium. For example, the conclusions one reaches are deeply influenced by the intuitions one starts with, and yet the method places no restrictions—or only very weak ones—on the initial intuitions.[21]

Some liberals have tried another approach. In their conception of what epistemological neutrality requires, a theory of right satisfies the demands of neutrality when its principles can be derived from premises that all parties to any moral controversy would accept. The idea is to derive substantive moral conclusions from relatively noncontroversial premises—for example, from the premise that humans are capable of intentional action. This theoretical project makes sense, but there are serious philosophical obstacles to carrying it off. Deriving a substantive principle of justice or obligation would require a number of premises, and it seems that anyone who dissented from any derived principle would be able to reject one of the premises rather than accept the principle. This problem could be circumvented if it could somehow be shown that the premises had greater inherent plausibility than the normative principle derived from them or that rejecting the premises would logically entail unacceptable revisions elsewhere in anyone's sys-

[21] Criticisms of reflective equilibrium as a general method of moral reasoning can be found in R. M. Hare, "Rawls' Theory of Justice," in *Reading Rawls*, ed. Norman Daniels (New York: Basic Books, n.d.), pp. 82ff; Richard Brandt, *A Theory of the Good and the Right* (New York: Oxford University Press, 1979), chap. 1; and Peter Singer, "Sidgwick and Reflective Equilibrium," *Monist* 58 (1974): 494. An effort to reconstruct and defend reflective equilibrium can be found in Norman Daniels, "Wide Reflective Equilibrium and Theory Acceptance in Ethics," *Journal of Philosophy* 76 (1976): 256–82.

tem of belief. But success in these strategies has thus far remained beyond the grasp of our most persistent and sophisticated thinkers.

Some liberals have adopted a pragmatic conception of epistemological neutrality. Their idea is that the derivation of principles of right should rest on premises that can be widely shared in a given society, culture, or epoch. This is somewhat more relaxed than the requirement that the premises be acceptable to all those on any side of any moral question and to that extent, has somewhat greater chances of being successfully carried out. One problem, of course, is that a society or culture may have such a distorted sense of morality that working from premises that can be widely shared within it may be traveling in exactly the wrong direction. Another problem is that the pluralist character of liberal society may make it impossible to find widely accepted premises sufficiently strong to generate any interesting results.

Which conception of epistemological neutrality should liberalism adopt? I think that the soundest form of liberalism would formulate and adopt an epistemological neutrality requirement that operates at a higher level of abstraction than those which I have discussed. It would not require any specific form of argumentation or reasoning. The epistemological neutrality of liberalism, in other words, ought to consist of an indifference toward the specific moral epistemology that accompanies the commitment to individual rights as substantial constraints on politics. Of course, any liberal should retain the minimal requirement that an epistemology must be conceptually coherent, but aside from such minimal demands, the idea of epistemological neutrality is to let a thousand epistemologies bloom. What counts for liberalism is the commitment to substantial constraints on politics in the name of individual autonomy and not the particular epistemology that lies behind that commitment.[22] This idea is, I believe, a key element in the position which Rawls is defending when he claims that liberalism should be construed as extending the principle of toleration to philosophy.[23] As Rawls and Larmore have recently argued, liberalism

[22] This approach to neutrality is thus consistent with recent work in liberal theory that attempts to base liberal political principles on some conception of the human good. See, e.g., William Galston, "Defending Liberalism," *American Political Science Review* 76 (1982): 621–29, and Joseph Raz, *The Morality of Freedom* (New York: Oxford University Press, 1986).

[23] Rawls, "The Idea of an Overlapping Consensus," *Oxford Journal of Legal Studies* 7 (1987): 15. See also Bruce Ackerman, *Social Justice in the Liberal State* (New Haven: Yale University Press, 1980), p. 361.

is best conceived as a stripped-down political philosophy that does without its own comprehensive epistemology, metaphysics, and personal morality.[24] It is a political philosophy deliberately constructed to abstract, as its ancient and medieval predecessors did not, from many issues concerning the nature of knowledge, reality, and the good life.

The third form of liberal neutrality concerns the process of legislation; institutional arrangements should guarantee that political power in a liberal pluralist society is sufficiently widespread and equalized so that each group, with its own conceptions of the good and the right, must engage in processes of normative compromise and accommodation with the other groups in order to exercise significant influence over the deployment of state power. Moreover, the arrangements should be calculated to insure that no single group or fixed coalition can gain lasting control of the power of government. Let us call this *political neutrality*. Its classic formulation is by Madison in *The Federalist*, Nos. 10 and 51.[25] It must be remembered, though, that political neutrality is strictly subordinate to rights neutrality in this sense: The compromise and negotiation that the former kind of neutrality involves must operate within the borders set by substantial constraints on politics that are imposed in order to protect and promote individual autonomy.

The fourth form of liberal neutrality concerns the process of adjudication. Neutrality in adjudication means that once the appropriate political processes have settled some normative clash and have declared authoritative (or have enacted) some particular rule, then the rule is interpreted and applied by public officials in a way that is insulated from the influence of any fresh assessment of the contending normative views. The political arena is the one in which the contending views are to be assessed and weighed, and some settlement among them reached. The legal arena is the one in which the settlement is interpreted and applied without any new assessment or weighing of the contending normative views. In this sense, the process of legal interpretation should bracket out the normative controversies of the political arena and so not be

[24] John Rawls, "Justice as Fairness: Political Not Metaphysical," *Philosophy and Public Affairs* 14 (1985): 223–51, and Charles Larmore, *Patterns of Moral Complexity* (New York: Cambridge University Press, 1987), chap. 4.

[25] In his most recent work, Unger has given a good account of this form of neutrality in terms of the idea of preventing the state from becoming hostage to a faction. See Roberto Unger, *False Necessity* (New York: Cambridge University Press, 1987), p. 369. This is not, however, to endorse Unger's belief that liberal democracy is incapable of preventing the state from becoming hostage to a faction.

responsive to differing assessments of the soundness of the normative views expressed there. Let us call this *legal neutrality*. It is the form of neutrality that is embraced by liberals who insist upon a separation of law and politics.

In chapter 2, we examined several liberal approaches, each having a distinct conception of the law-politics distinction. All the approaches recognized that in practice at least, it was impossible to insulate the legal process completely from assessments of the normative views that competed in the political arena. The approaches differed in the degree of infiltration of such assessments they allowed. The generic model insisted upon as little infiltration as possible. The models proposed by Hart and Dworkin, as well as the modified version of Sartorius's model that I employed, allowed a significant degree of reliance on political judgment in the process of legal interpretation.

Yet in all the liberal models, legal reasoning should proceed, for the most part, without reliance on political judgments about the views that compete in the legislative arena. For Hart and Dworkin, it is only the hard cases that require political judgment; the easy cases, which constitute in their view the bulk of the material on which the system operates, can and should be decided without recourse to an assessment of the normative views that compete with one another in the political arena. On the model which I develop, most cases (including many that are not easy cases) are governed by a convention that excludes any independent political judgments by judges. Thus, the idea of legal neutrality is a central part of the liberal conception of law, even if no liberal theory insists that in practice, all cases must be decided without recourse to political judgments.

Reopening the CLS *Attack*

At this point, Unger and his CLS colleagues may reenter the argument, for it seems that the account which I have offered of the nature of liberal neutrality reintroduces the very antinomies that Unger describes. Political neutrality appears afflicted by the antinomy of legislation, since it seems that there will always be a bias against conceptions of the good and right held by certain groups in any robustly pluralist society, no matter which procedures for the enactment of legal rules are adopted. Legal neutrality appears afflicted by the antinomy of rules and values, since that antinomy seems to show that legal interpretation will never succeed in sufficiently bracketing the normative controversies that battle in the political arena of a pluralist society.

In addition, the other two forms of liberal neutrality have been targets of CLS attack. With regard to epistemological neutrality, CLS thinkers have challenged the tenability of deriving normative principles from premises that are noncontroversial (e.g., the premise that humans can act intentionally) or are noncommittal on questions of the good.[26] Some nineteenth- and early-twentieth-century legal thinkers attempted to derive logically determinate rules of property and contract from noncontroversial facts about humans. Following in the footsteps of their legal realist predecessors, CLS thinkers have vigorously rejected the logical soundness of such derivations.[27] The key CLS-realist point is that these allegedly noncontroversial derivations are guilty of smuggling in controversial moral or political premises. We will not examine the CLS-realist arguments on this score, although I do take them to be persuasive. However, as we examine the CLS arguments against legal and political neutrality, it is helpful to keep in mind the following point: The CLS-realist arguments against the allegedly noncontroversial derivations of legal rules do nothing to discredit the conceptual coherence of the other three forms of liberal neutrality—rights, legal, and political. Moreover, such arguments discredit, at best, only one version of epistemological neutrality and leave entirely untouched the higher-order epistemological neutrality which consists of the principle of epistemological toleration.

Finally, there is a very important element in the CLS critique of liberalism that does directly attack rights neutrality. CLS thinkers have argued vehemently that the limits placed on politics by liberal theory are far in excess of what is justified. The liberal commitment to individual rights is attacked on the grounds that such a commitment unduly confines the scope and power of political activity. This crucial line of CLS argument is examined in detail in the final chapter. The remainder of the present chapter focuses on political and legal neutrality and on CLS arguments holding that

[26] Unger, *False Necessity*, p. 571.

[27] For a relatively detached CLS analysis, see Duncan Kennedy, "Toward an Historical Understanding of Legal Consciousness: The Case of Classical Legal Thought in America, 1850–1940," *Research in Law and Sociology* 3 (1980): 19–21. For more polemical ones, see Elizabeth Mensch, "The History of Mainstream Legal Thought," in *The Politics of Law*, ed. David Kairys (New York: Pantheon Books, 1982), pp. 23–29, and Morton Horwitz, "The Doctrine of Objective Causation," in *Politics of Law*, pp. 201–11.

neither of these forms of neutrality can be satisfied within the framework of a liberal pluralist society.

Legal Neutrality and the Law-Politics Distinction

In his manifesto, *The Critical Legal Studies Movement*, Unger construes the position known as *legal formalism* in terms somewhat broader than those traditional in the jurisprudential literature. Traditionally, formalism has been thought of as the doctrine that legal rules form a consistent and complete whole from which the answer to any legal question can be logically deduced simply by discovering the applicable rule and applying it to the facts of the case.

Unger sees such formalism as merely the extreme case of a view much more widely held among liberal legal theorists. In its less extreme forms, the view is that the authoritative interpretation of legal rules can and should be insulated from the normative controversies that contend in the political arena of a liberal pluralist society. Of course, the particular legal rules that are in force will be a product of the competition and compromise of the contending normative views. But the formalist view is that the interpretation of those rules should not depend on any fresh assessment of the soundness of the conceptions of the right and the good that compete in the political arena. In other words, the interpretation of laws can and should proceed upon the basis of the distinction between law and politics. Unger thus broadly defines formalism as involving "a commitment to, and therefore also a belief in the possibility of, a method of legal justification that contrasts with open-ended disputes about the basic terms of social life, disputes that people call ideological, philosophical, or visionary."[28]

Legal formalism, as Unger describes it, is the jurisprudential position that vouches for the possibility of what I have called legal neutrality, the neutrality that liberal legal theory has traditionally demanded of the process by which legal rules are authoritatively interpreted. Unger's attack on legal formalism is an attack on this form of neutrality. The rejection of the law-politics distinction, repeated throughout the CLS literature, is a rejection of both liberal legal formalism and legal neutrality. James Boyle has put the CLS position straightforwardly: "Much critical legal scholarship consists of a series of complicated and erudite explanations of the idea

[28] Roberto Unger, *The Critical Legal Studies Movement* (Cambridge: Harvard University Press, 1986), p. 1.

that law cannot be interpreted neutrally and thus that the law/politics distinction and the legitimating story on which the liberal state depends must inevitably collapse."[29]

The antinomy of rules and values is the central CLS explanation of why legal neutrality is not possible. As an attack on liberal legal formalism, the pivotal aspect of the antinomy is the idea that the full interpretation of legal rules will require reliance on some assessment of the contending conceptions of the good and the right whose competition in the political arena helped to generate the rules. This reliance is necessary (according to the argument which we examined earlier in the chapter) in order to rank the multiple purposes of a single rule or the conflicting purposes of different rules implicated in a given case. Because of the reliance, the normative controversies of the political arena cannot be bracketed from the process of legal interpretation. Such interpretations will invariably be responsive to differences in assessing competing conceptions of the good and the right. According to CLS, such responsiveness makes legal neutrality an impossibility; it destroys the law-politics distinction and with it the possibility of the liberal rule of law.

This reconstructed version of Unger's antinomy can be clarified and criticized by raising a liberal objection that employs a distinction made in Hart's analysis of the concept of law.[30] It may be claimed that the reconstructed argument (and the original) ignores the crucial distinction which Hart draws between primary and secondary rules, a distinction which can help us to see how the rule of law can be maintained in the context of liberal pluralism without violating the liberal principle of legal neutrality. Let us set the stage for the argument by briefly recounting Hart's distinction.

Primary rules are rules of obligation that specify the social duties which people are bound to discharge. Hart argues that all societies will have primary rules of some kind to regulate social interaction. But only a relatively simple, small, and homogeneous society can get by with primary rules alone; as societies become larger and more heterogeneous (i.e., as they become increasingly pluralistic), more and more disputes will break out over just what the truly binding primary rules are. These disputes will threaten social sta-

[29] Boyle, "Politics of Reason," 697. The "legitimating story" to which Boyle refers involves the liberal claim that the liberal state is morally legitimate because it is neutral among conflicting conceptions of the good.

[30] H.L.A. Hart, *The Concept of Law* (New York: Oxford University Press, 1961), pp. 84–96.

bility unless some way can be found to forestall and/or resolve them. Secondary rules serve, among other purposes, the vital function of establishing procedures for identifying the primary rules that bind people. The "rule of recognition" is the master rule for such a purpose, and the rule of law, Hart suggests, is the rule of a system of primary and secondary rules.

Hart makes passing reference to the possibility of secondary rules that would serve to pin down the authoritative interpretations of the binding primary rules identified by the rule of recognition.[31] Such secondary rules might be needed when the terms of the primary rules are vague, subject to dispute, or require a special legal meaning. For current purposes, we are especially interested in cases where there would be a dispute about the meaning of a primary rule that arises from conflicting normative conceptions. In those cases, secondary rules that pin down the meaning could serve the very same purpose that Hart's rule of recognition serves: forestalling and/or resolving disputes that would break out regarding social duties if social stability were to rely solely on primary rules. Let us call such rules *secondary rules of meaning*. Thus, while it may be true that the value dissensus of a liberal pluralist society would invariably lead to widespread dissensus over the meaning of rules were primary rules the only ones in force, the same result does not invariably follow when there are secondary rules of meaning to pin down meanings for the primary rules. And since the rule of law is, as Hart suggests, the rule of a system that combines primary rules with secondary ones, value dissensus does not invariably entail widespread dissensus over the meaning of legal rules.[32]

[31] H.L.A. Hart, *Essays in Jurisprudence and Philosophy* (New York: Oxford University Press, 1983), p. 106.

[32] Stanley Fish has made an argument denying that secondary rules of meaning can help to pin down the meanings of primary rules. Although Fish is by no means a proponent of CLS, his conclusion on this score converges with what critical scholars would claim. Fish's argument is directed at Owen Fiss, who claims that "disciplining rules" constrain legal professionals in their activity of interpreting legal texts. Fiss's disciplining rules are, in essence, secondary rules of meaning. Fish argues that such rules cannot constrain interpretation because they too are texts standing as much in need of interpretation as the primary legal texts. What constrains all interpretive activity, including the interpretation of disciplining rules, is the framework of conventional practices within which interpretation proceeds. See Fish, "Fish v. Fiss," *Stanford Law Review* 36 (1984): 1326–34. However, Fiss has cogently responded that Fish's argument rests on a non sequitur. He agrees with Fish that interpretation always proceeds within the framework of conventional practices, "but that does not reduce (in either a logical or practical sense) the content or meaning of a rule to its various interpretations, nor does it mean that one text

Unger appears to have three responses to this liberal objection. First, "if individuals can know the meanings of laws but are unable to accept the values that inform the rules, the problems of order and freedom will not have been solved."[33] He is suggesting here that it is one thing to have secondary rules of meaning which enable everyone to know with sufficient precision the meanings of the primary legal rules but that it is another for everyone to find the primary rules acceptable under those interpretations. For any set of secondary rules of meaning, a society of liberal pluralism will contain some conception of the good and right from whose perspective the rules under the meanings assigned to them by the secondary rules are unacceptable. Even granting that people embracing such a normative conception could know the authoritative meaning of any given rule, the enforcement of that interpretation by the state would still amount to what liberalism must regard as the illegitimate violation of the neutrality requirement. For rather than being neutral among the controversial conceptions of the good and the right, the state would be taking sides by forcing a particular conception on those who find it unacceptable.

Unger's response here rests on a confusion of legal and political neutrality and on a faulty conception of the latter form of neutrality. The liberal principle of legal neutrality has nothing to do directly with the acceptability of a legal rule to the population. As long as the rule is interpreted in a manner that does not rely on any fresh assessment of the normative views implicated in the political deliberations over the rule, legal neutrality is satisfied, even if there are people who cannot accept the rule so interpreted.

Political neutrality, on the other hand, has some connection to the acceptability of legal rules to the population, but it is not the connection Unger assumes. He assumes that political neutrality requires that the rules, both primary and secondary, by which the liberal state governs society must be found acceptable by all in the society, whatever their conceptions of the good and the right. But

(disciplining rules) cannot constrain the interpretation of another text." See Fiss, "Conventionalism," *Southern California Law Review* 58 (1985): 186. It should also be pointed out that Fish's argument rests on a narrow understanding of what a rule is; he thinks of rules as abstract linguistic formulas and sharply distinguishes them from behavioral regularities. Hart's concept of a rule, however, clearly regards rules as types of behavioral regularities. Hart does not draw Fish's sharp contrast between rules and practices, and given this broader conception of rule, it seems that Fish could agree that secondary rules of meaning can help to pin down the meanings of primary rules. Cf. Steven Burton, "Legal Reasoning and the Left," *Journal of Legal Education* 36 (1986): 365 n. 28.

[33] Unger, *Knowledge and Politics*, p. 101.

this is sheer confusion. Certainly, the early liberal theorists did not labor under the illusion that the system of political arrangements for which they fought had to be found acceptable by their anti-liberal opponents who, for example, were uncompromising enemies of the principle of religious toleration. Moreover, the rules of the liberal state will prove unacceptable to any group whose conceptions of the good and right are so inflexible that there are no significant political issues on which it would be willing to seek accommodations and compromises with other groups.

This does not mean that the liberal state will be open to compromise on all important issues of political morality: rights neutrality forbids that. But in the liberal state, there will be a significant range of normative issues that are open to such negotiation and compromise. Unger is correct in suggesting that invariably there will be groups who refuse to recognize the legitimacy of a system that allows, indeed demands, negotiation and compromise on a significant range of political issues. But that is simply to say that such groups do not accept the sort of neutrality that liberalism demands in the political arena, and liberal theory need not pretend that such neutrality would be acceptable to all. The same points apply to groups that reject the liberal premise that there must be substantial limits placed on politics in the name of individual autonomy. One might, of course, say that this means that the liberal principle of political neutrality is not neutral. But to take such a statement as a sign of the incoherence of liberalism is to conflate quite different senses of the idea of neutrality.

Unger's second response to the argument invoking secondary rules of meaning is that differences in conceptions of the good and the right can be so wide that agreement will break down, even on the meanings the secondary rules assign to the primary ones. Unger may be perfectly willing to grant that such differences must be greater than those that would lead to disagreements over the meanings of primary rules in a system that incorporated no secondary rules. There is no suggestion in Unger's work that secondary rules are wholly incapable of pinning down in any degree the meanings of primary ones. But he does claim that as conceptions of the human good diverge, the prospects decrease for pinning down meanings in such a way that all can agree on the correct meanings, until such prospects are reduced to zero.

Unger's claim rests in part on an idea that I have already accepted—that major differences in substantive normative views can set off semantic reverberations that generate conflicting interpretations of legal rules. Terms such as *human life* or *due care* may be construed quite differently, depending upon whether they are being interpreted by an antiabortionist or prochoice advocate, by a defender of laissez-faire, or by a proponent of socialism. Even granting this idea, however, there are two serious problems in parlaying it into an argument that secondary rules of meaning cannot solve the problem of competing interpretations of primary rules.

First, Unger never provides an argument that it is possible for differences in conceptions of the good and the right to be so vast that all efforts must fail to pin down (through secondary rules) determinate meanings for primary rules that all can agree to as the legally authoritative meanings. Antiabortionists and prochoice advocates may disagree about whether the human fetus should count as a human life for the purpose of construing the laws against homicide. Without any secondary rules of meaning, there would no doubt be endless controversy over the legally correct interpretation of the primary rule. Once such secondary rules are introduced, however, there is no problem in specifying, in a way that all sides can understand, which interpretation is to have authoritative status.

To take another example, the ambiguity that the Supreme Court faced in *Sinclair* and *Boys Markets* was resolved, in effect, by the pronouncement of a secondary rule of meaning explicitly dictating the scope of the prohibition of labor injunctions laid down in Norris-LaGuardia and specifying the range of remedies which federal courts have at their disposal in enforcing collective bargaining agreements under Taft-Hartley. It would have been perfectly possible for the Congress that enacted Taft-Hartley to have incorporated such a secondary rule in the legislation (or in a preamble or some text that would have been regarded as authoritative), thereby avoiding the need for the courts to resolve the disputed cases by settling on a definitive interpretation of the laws in question. The fact that a court had to settle the meaning does not establish the view that secondary rules of meaning cannot help to pin down meanings. Nor does the fact that the Supreme Court reversed its initial decision on the issue raised in *Sinclair* and *Boys Markets* establish such a view. Quite the opposite: These facts show that secondary rules can do the job of pinning down meanings. Everyone understands that *Sinclair* settled the issue in one way, *Boys Markets* in another. Even CLS authors who are critical of the holding in *Boys Markets* demonstrate through their criticism that they know the specific meaning that the decision gave to the labor statutes in question.[34]

The second problem with Unger's argument against the use of secondary rules to settle meanings is this: Even granting that sufficiently vast differences in conceptions of the good and right can set off semantic reverberations that defeat any effort to specify a commonly agreed upon conventional meaning for legal rules, it does not follow that the liberal rule of law is impossible. All that follows is that there are limits to the pluralism that liberalism can accommodate under the rule of law. These limits would not be the ones discussed earlier—those limits derived from the demand for flexible and compromising conceptions of the right and from the requirement that individual autonomy place substantial limits on politics. Rather, they would be the limits beyond which it is impossible, even with secondary rules of meaning, for some people to understand the way public officials interpreted the meanings of primary legal rules. If there were people whose differences with the public officials who authoritatively interpreted the legal rules were of the magnitude Unger suggests, such people would be in the Kafkaesque situation of being wholly incapable of comprehending the meanings that the state attributed to the rules that governed the duties of social life. The primary rules which the state coercively applied to these people would be in a code undecipherable by them. It is difficult to imagine a more stunning breakdown of the rule of law.

The liberal rule of law surely could not accommodate the presence of such radically different conceptions of the good and the right. Yet there is no good argument that liberal states invariably incorporate such radically opposing normative conceptions. Indeed, it would be difficult to argue that they ever do so. Surely, actual liberal societies contain groups that oppose the authoritative interpretations given of the primary rules that govern them, but I have yet to see Unger or anyone else cite a case where there were those who, because of a radically different moral vision of the world, literally could not comprehend those interpretations. And even if such a case could be cited, it would only establish that the rule of law had broken down in a certain highly unusual pluralist setting. It would be far from establishing the CLS claim that the liberal rule of law is an impossibility.

[34] For a CLS criticism of *Boys Markets*, see Karl Klare, "Critical Theory and Labor Relations Law," in Kairys, *Politics of Law*, pp. 67–82.

Unger's third response to the possibility of using secondary rules of meaning to bracket the normative controversies of the political arena is a direct assault on what he regards as liberal legal formalism. The argument proceeds on the basis of the claim that, were moral and political assessments fully bracketed from the process of legal interpretation, the law would be so riddled with indeterminacy as to violate the rule of law. The core of Unger's argument is this:

> [E]very branch of doctrine must rely tacitly if not explicitly upon some picture of the forms of human association that are right and realistic in the areas of social life with which it deals. . . . Without such a guiding vision, legal reasoning seems condemned to a game of easy analogies. It will always be possible to find, retrospectively, more or less convincing ways to make a set of distinctions, or failures to distinguish, look credible. A common experience testifies to this possibility; every thoughtful law student or lawyer has had the disquieting sense of being able to argue too well or too easily for too many conflicting solutions. Because everything can be defended, nothing can; the analogy-mongering must be brought to a halt.[35]

Unger proceeds to claim that it is the appeal to some background normative theory that brings the "analogy-mongering" to a halt. It is in the light of the ideas and principles of such a background theory that certain analogies appear convincing and others unpersuasive.

Consider the following example. In *Hurley v. Eddingfield*, it was claimed that a physician refused, without good reason, to accept the offer of his usual fee in return for attending to someone who was ill.[36] The person died of the illness, and the physician was sued for wrongful death. To the extent that the facts of the case could be analogized to a standard contract case, there could be no good cause of action against the physician. There is no duty to accept an offer in contract doctrine. However, to the extent that the physician could be analogized to an innkeeper or common carrier, there might be a good cause of action, because traditional common law rules place affirmative duties on innkeepers and common carriers. Unger's point is that it is only in the light of

[35] Unger, *Critical Legal Studies*, p. 8.
[36] *Hurley v. Eddingfield*, 59 N.E. 1058 (1901).

some background conception of the good and the right that a defensible conclusion can be drawn about which analogy is more convincing and that such a background conception will include controversial ideas about the scope and strength of our affirmative moral obligations to others. Thus, it is the appeal, explicit or tacit, to some controversial background conception of the good or the right that overcomes what would otherwise be a pervasive and incorrigible indeterminacy in the system of legal rules. Liberal legal formalism thus breaks down and, with it, the neutrality of legal interpretation.

Unger's argument serves to pose the following apparent dilemma for those who believe that secondary rules of meaning can save the neutrality of legal interpretation: Either the rules will license the appeal to controversial conceptions of the right and good in the interpretation of the extant primary rules, in which case neutrality will be violated, or they will prohibit the appeal to such conceptions, in which case the system of rules will be riddled with indeterminacy.

There are three fatal problems with Unger's argument. The first is that, again, Unger is confused about what legal neutrality requires. Legal neutrality does not demand that the judge (i.e., the interpreter of the law) avoid any reliance on norms that embody controversial moral or political conceptions. It simply is not relevant that some secondary rule that a judge may be called on to follow in the course of interpreting a primary rule embodies some controversial moral or political position. All the judge need do to conform to the dictates of legal neutrality is to apply the secondary rule in question without making any fresh assessment of the normative views that it implicates.

On the other hand, there is some connection between the liberal principle of political neutrality and the controversiality of normative views, but it is not the connection that Unger's argument supposes. This is the second problem with the argument: It supposes that political neutrality demands that there be no legal rules, primary or secondary, that embody controversial moral or political views. But the liberal conception of political neutrality requires no such thing. It requires that institutions embody some fair set of procedures that compel different groups, each having its own controversial moral and political views, to compromise and negotiate with one another. But it does not follow that controversial moral and political views are thereby excluded from being written into the legal rules of society. All that follows is that to the extent that they are so written, it will be as a result of fair processes that involve compromise, negotiation, and accommodation.

Yet one may still argue that when judges inscribe their own controversial political and moral positions into the secondary rules of meaning—as Brennan did in *Boys Markets*, for example—both legal and political neutrality are violated. Legal neutrality is violated because the judge is making a fresh assessment of the normative views whose clash in the political arena led to the laws that needed to be interpreted. The judge cannot rely on the assessment generated by the political process because it is precisely one of those cases where the political process arrived at a settlement that was studiously silent on the relative worth of the various aims that could be attributed to the laws, and cases such as *Boys Markets* hinge on these judgments of relative worth.

However, this elaboration of Unger's argument fails to destroy the law-politics distinction and to demonstrate the impossibility of the liberal rule of law, unless one adds an additional premise—that cases requiring judges to make fresh assessments of controversial political and moral positions are *necessarily* so pervasive in any liberal state as to be inconsistent with any liberal model of the rule of law. Unger never provides any reason for accepting the additional premise. That is the third flaw in his argument. Let us examine it in greater detail.

As a purely conceptual matter, there is no reason why a liberal legal system must contain cases such as *Boys Markets* in which the judiciary is compelled to rely on moral or political judgments in order to render a decision. To see why this is so, begin by considering an actual liberal legal system, which is likely to contain a significant number of cases requiring moral or political judgments. The applicable legal rules in these cases are ambiguous or vague so that they render a decision impossible without some reliance on such judgments. Every one of those cases will be resolved when a court, in effect, settles on some secondary rule of meaning that resolves the ambiguity or vagueness sufficiently for a determinate decision to be rendered. Imagine now a legal system that is just like the actual one, with one key difference: The secondary rules that the courts appeal to in order to decide these cases have all been authoritatively enacted by the legislature in advance of the cases in question. For example, instead of letting the courts decide how to handle the reconciliation of Norris-LaGuardia and Taft-Hartley in back-to-work cases, the legislature laid down the rule in advance of any such case. There is no conceptual impossibility in imagining this sort of situation for every case that in some actual legal system requires judicial resolution. This means that there is no conceptual incoherence in the ideal of the generic liberal model of a legal system in which every case has a predetermined legal answer. To the extent that Unger's argument aims to establish such an incoherence, it fails.

Perhaps Unger intends only to argue that in any actual liberal system, the extent of cases requiring judicial reliance on moral or political judgments is too great for any liberal to accept. While not as philosophically striking as the conceptual incoherence claim, such an argument would still be devastating to the liberal view if it could be made persuasive. Nonetheless, Unger does not make a persuasive case. He merely assumes that *some* infiltration of moral and political judgment into the process of legal interpretation is sufficient to defeat the liberal view. Yet every liberal model of the rule of law allows for some infiltration of that sort. The generic model has the strictest requirements for the exclusion of such assessments and thus the least room for their infiltration. It demands the strongest possible distinction between law and politics, but Unger even fails to show why no actual liberal system could be a reasonable approximation of the generic model.

Moreover, even if he could show that no such approximation were possible, it would provide no grounds for rejecting the other liberal models of the rule of law examined in the previous chapter. The models of Dworkin and Hart, as well as the modified version of Sartorius's model that I defended, portray legal reasoning as involving some reliance on moral and political judgments. For example, in the model that I defended, there is a dominant convention that prescribes decisions whose grounds have the best fit with the settled law, and when that convention breaks down, there is a convention that prescribes decisions whose grounds fit with some substantial portion of the settled law. In the latter case, there are likely to be competing grounds of decision, all of which fit the settled law well enough, so judges will often appeal, implicitly or explicitly, to their own moral or political convictions in selecting among those potential grounds of decision.

Whether or not I am wrong to suggest that our legal system operates in accordance with such conventions, there is no reason to think that it is impossible for there to be an actual liberal system of law that does operate in that way. Yet such a system would be governed by the rule of law. Although there would be no airtight law-politics distinction, legal reasoning would, for the most part, operate without any reliance on moral or political assessments of the normative views that compete in the political arena, and when such reliance did come into play, it would do so within the confines of a legal convention that required the grounds of decision to cohere with a substantial portion of the conventionally accepted decisions, doctrines, and norms. While this system would not correspond to the generic liberal model, it would reflect a recognizable model of the rule of law in which there was indeed a contrast between legal argument and open-ended ideological or philosophical dispute about the basic terms of social and political life.

In summary, Unger's arguments against liberal legal neutrality and the law-politics distinction fail. In making these arguments, Unger's main aim was to show that the liberal understanding of the rule of law was conceptually incoherent. His strategy hinged on the idea that the liberal understanding placed an impossible demand on the rule of law, viz., the demand that legal interpretation and reasoning remain neutral on the moral and political controversies that fragment liberal pluralist society. However, we have seen that Unger's strategy rests on confusions about the meaning of the liberal commitment to neutrality in law and in politics. He conflates the sort of neutrality required in the legal sphere with that required in the political, in addition to misinterpreting the demands of liberal political neutrality. A careful examination of the different forms of liberal neutrality reveals that once such confusions are remedied, Unger's arguments fail to establish that liberal legal and political philosophy are incoherent or even unrealistic. Moreover, Unger's argumentative strategy fails to take account of the significant differences among various liberal models of the rule of law. For all Unger has shown, there is a perfectly coherent and defensible liberal understanding of the rule of law.

Radical Indeterminacy

Unger's arguments against the coherence of the liberal rule of law are widely endorsed in the CLS literature, but they are not the only arguments in the literature that seek to establish the impossibility of the liberal rule of law. There is in addition a much more radical line of CLS argument. This more radical strain rests on the view that legal rules are "empty vessels" into which individuals can pour virtually any content they please. To put the same point in a different way, legal rules have no determinate meaning and therefore no semantic content that could help to dictate the decision in any case. It is not just that the rules are, by themselves, semantically incomplete and must be interpreted by officials in the light of background moral and political principles in order to draw out their implications for many legal cases; it is that the decisions officials make about the meanings of rules amount to creating meanings for the rules when there is none there to begin with.

This more radical view of meaning lies behind Mark Tushnet's claim that "radical indeterminacy of meaning is, within a liberal community, inevitable."[37] It is also reflected in CLS assertions to the effect that the bases of judicial decision making are value choices unconstrained by what the existing rules and doctrines happen to say. David Kairys's assertion is characteristic: "The ultimate basis for a decision is a social and political judgment. . . . The decision is not based on, or determined by, legal reasoning."[38] And Clare Dalton gives graphic expression to the radical view by describing the central categories of legal discourse as "empty vessels."[39]

This radical view of legal meaning must be distinguished from Unger's.[40] For Unger, judicial decision making operates on the basis of legal rules as interpreted in the light of judicial value choices. One cannot dispense with the value choices, but neither can one dispense with the rules, because the process of legal interpretation is one of filling out their partial or incomplete meanings when regarded in isolation from any value choices. Such a view of meaning is inconsistent with the idea that legal rules are semantic empty vessels that the judge can fill with whatever meaning content he or she chooses.

The radical view is that legal rules are just such vessels, implying that it is misguided to talk of "interpreting" the meaning of legal rules at all. One is engaged in the unconstrained creation of meaning, and this entails that any moral or political conception can be the basis for a judicial decision. These implications are regarded as flowing from the character of meaning and so cannot be safeguarded against to any degree by secondary rules of meaning.

[37] Mark Tushnet, *Red, White, and Blue: A Critical Analysis of Constitutional Law* (Cambridge: Harvard University Press, 1988), p. 63.

[38] David Kairys, "Law and Politics," *George Washington Law Review* 52 (1984): 247.

[39] Dalton, "Essay in Deconstruction," p. 1002.

[40] Unger is not the only CLS thinker who rejects the idea that judges can read their moral and political values into the law unconstrained by existing rules and doctrines. See, e.g., Paul Brest, "Who Decides?" *Southern California Law Review* 58 (1985): 663–64, and Joseph Singer, "The Player and the Cards: Nihilism and Legal Theory," *Yale Law Journal* 94 (1984): 23–24.

The meaning of any such rule would itself have to be created in the act of "interpretation" and could be created in a way that permits the introduction of any moral or political conception. If the conception of meaning on which the radical indeterminacy view rests is persuasive, then the liberal rule of law will indeed be impossible. Liberal models of the rule of law can and do allow a significant degree of moral and political assessment into the process of legal interpretation. But even the more permissive liberal models are utterly incompatible with the position that what passes as legal interpretation can be nothing more than the unconstrained creation of meaning, based on whatever moral or political conceptions the official happens to embrace.

The radical indeterminacy view within CLS is a reflection and elaboration of a position articulated forcefully by Foucault:

> Humanity does not gradually progress from combat to combat until it arrives at universal reciprocity, where the rule of law finally replaces warfare; humanity installs each of its violences in a system of rules and thus proceeds from domination to domination. . . . Rules are empty in themselves, violent and unfinalized; they are impersonal and can be bent to any purpose. . . . [I]nterpretation is the violent or surreptitious appropriation of a system of rules, which in itself has no essential meaning, in order to impose a direction, to bend it to a new will, to force its participation in a different game.[41]

This fecund passage contains two principal themes, both of which have been picked up by the radical indeterminists in CLS: (1) the inherent semantic emptiness of legal rules and (2) the notion of interpretation as an act of power that forces meaning into otherwise semantically empty rules. Let us begin by examining the first theme.

Gary Peller gives one of the more sustained CLS arguments in favor of the radical view. He contends that words and sentences are not self-contained units of meaning; rather, meaning is relational, the meaning of one term being wholly a function of the meaning of others. But this raises a serious problem for Peller. He argues that "the attempt to fix the meaning of an expression leads to an infinite regress. One must follow traces pointing away from expressions to other terms, which themselves contain traces lead-

[41] Michel Foucault, "Nietzsche, Genealogy, History," in *Language, Counter-memory, Practice*, ed. D. F. Bouchard (Ithaca, N.Y.: Cornell University Press, 1977), pp. 151–52.

ing to still other terms, and so on."[42] The consequence of this infinite regress, he tells us, is that "meaning is ultimately indeterminate."[43]

Peller's argument revolves around the deconstructionist idea that when we try to pin down the meaning of a term or sentence, we are simply "deferring" the meaning from one set of terms to another. We have not succeeded in pinning down the meaning but have merely transferred the problem of meaning from one location to another, in a process roughly analogous to that of borrowing from Peter to pay Paul. There may be an illusion of advance, but there is no real advance.

That there is something seriously awry in Peller's argument may be gleaned from the fact that like all forms of radical relativism, this one is self-refuting.[44] The implications of the argument extend not merely to the domain of legal discourse but to all language. If all words are indeterminate in meaning, then so are the words of Peller's argument, and if that is so, then the argument means nothing and establishes nothing. Clearly, Peller regards the argument as establishing something—moreover, something that is inconsistent with a standard view of meaning. But that is impossible where meaning is wholly indeterminate: there can be no inconsistency where there is no determinate meaning.

It also follows from Peller's argument that the charge that the liberal rule of law is a theoretical impossibility makes no sense. For theoretical impossibilities can exist only when words have determinate meaning. In fact, Peller's argument does not even allow for

[42] Peller, "Metaphysics of American Law," pp. 1167–68.

[43] Ibid., p. 1169.

[44] Seyla Benhabib has recently written: "The deconstructionist knows that s/he will be accused of self-referential absurdities . . . by those who still take seriously the claim of reason to justify itself. . . . In what ways is the charge of self-referential absurdities damaging for a mode of thinking that only too willingly acknowledges this to be its virtue?" See Benhabib, "Review of Jürgen Habermas, *The Philosophical Discourse of Modernity*," *Journal of Philosophy* 84 (1987): 755. The response to Benhabib's puzzled query does not seem to me to be especially difficult to provide. Taking seriously "the claim of reason to justify itself" simply amounts to taking logical coherence seriously. If one is trying to do what philosophical theorizing tries to do, viz., to make sense of (some aspect of) human experience, then I fail to see how that can be done without taking logical coherence seriously. On the other hand, if one is playing games, then one can dispense with coherence. But if one is playing games, then no issue is joined with those who are doing philosophical theorizing. If CLS is simply playing games (and I do not intend to denigrate playing games as such), then there is no issue between it and liberal legal theory; they are simply up to totally different things. I think that there are issues between the two, and if I am right about that, then one must take seriously whether CLS claims are logically coherent.

the creation of meaning, vital to the radical attack on the liberal rule of law. Even if it is conceded that words do not come with determinate meaning already "attached," the creation of meaning still presupposes the possibility of infusing words with determinate meaning. Yet such infusion seems impossible on Peller's argument: Creating meaning would be liable to the same problem of deferral as would the process of trying to determine a meaning that is thought to be already there.[45] We will see shortly that in a subsequent argument, Peller himself effectively gives up the argument that meaning is ultimately indeterminate due to the problem of deferral and tries instead to save the notion, borrowed from Foucault, that meaning is created through acts of power.

At this stage, though, it is not enough for us to point out the problems with the sort of argument given by Peller. We should attempt to determine where the argument goes wrong and what grains of truth it may contain. My suggestion is that this can best be accomplished by looking at legal interpretation in the light of Quine's celebrated article "Two Dogmas of Empiricism."[46]

Among the claims Quine makes is that the empirical meaning of our terms and sentences is a function of the role they play in the total body of sentences to which we subscribe. Languages are seen as having internal structures. Some sentences are at the periphery—closer to direct contact with sense experience and more likely to be revised in the face of recalcitrant experience. Other sentences are nearer the core—further from sense experience and less likely to be revised. In addition, there are inferential connections between the sentences at the core and those at the periphery. To use Dummett's suggestive phrase, Quine gives us an "image of language as an articulated network."[47]

Quine is driven to this network image of language by reflection on Duhem's thesis that it is impossible to conduct an experimental test of an isolated physical hypothesis. Testing requires that predictive conclusions be drawn from the hypothesis, but that requires auxiliary premises. These premises must draw on principles and laws from the parts of physical theory that are not regarded, for the purposes of the test, as hypotheses. Moreover, additional

[45] Don Herzog raises some of the other paradoxes of the radical indeterminacy position in "As Many as Six Impossible Things before Breakfast," *California Law Review* 75 (1987): 629.

[46] W.V.O. Quine, "Two Dogmas of Empiricism," in *From a Logical Point of View* (New York: Harper Torchbooks, 1963), pp. 20–46.

[47] Michael Dummett, *Frege: Philosophy of Language* (Cambridge: Harvard University Press, 1981), p. 608.

premises are required regarding the accuracy of the instruments employed for the test, and these premises implicate further laws and principles of physical theory.

If we think of the empirical meaning of a hypothesis in physical theory as represented by the conditions that would serve to confirm its truth, it becomes clear that isolated hypotheses do not carry fully determinate empirical meaning. Only as part of a system of sentences would a given hypothesis have a fully determinate meaning, since only as part of such a system would a hypothesis have confirmable consequences. Quine generalizes Duhem's point by arguing that every one of our beliefs about the physical world is semantically tied in a similar way to the total body of beliefs to which we subscribe and that the total body confronts sense experience as a systematic corporate whole.

My suggestion is that, with an important proviso, a similar kind of analysis be applied to the meaning of legal rules and terms. This is not to endorse a verificationist theory of meaning. It is the Quinean picture of language as a structured network, not his verificationism, that is relevant here.

The proviso is that we should not accept Quine's holistic view that single sentences have no meaning at all in isolation and that it is only a body of discourse (or a theory) as a whole that has any meaning. Quine's holism makes it impossible to explain how we can understand what anyone else is saying. As Dummett has pointed out, it would be necessary to know the total body of sentences to which a person subscribes to comprehend what he says.[48] This is because only the total body of sentences would have any significance, no subset of that total body would have any meaning. Given that communication in fact takes place with less than the utterance of the total body of sentences to which one subscribes—and anyone who disagrees with that premise refutes himself by that very disagreement—the holistic thesis must be rejected. Indeed, Peller's account of meaning can be construed as committed to precisely this offending holism.

The Quinean picture of language as an articulated network of terms and sentences suggests that interpretation is not a process of "deferring" meaning, as the deconstructionist view would have it, but a process of filling out the meaning of a sentence by tracing its implications as part of a wider body of terms and sentences. The problem of specifying meaning is not merely shifted from one

[48] Ibid., pp. 598–99.

set of terms to another; rather, meaning is made fuller as more and more inferential connections within the body of sentences are traced and the implications of those connections are drawn. Peller is correct insofar as he believes that terms and sentences are not fully self-contained units of meaning. This is just as true for physical theory as it is for law. Sentences, including legal rules, will lack fully determinate meaning to the extent that they are read in isolation from the body of sentences that helps to give them semantic content. However, the conclusion to draw is not that legal rules, even when considered in isolation, are wholly indeterminate but that the determinate meaning of a legal rule will be to a large degree a function of its role in the wider body of legal discourse.

Why accept this semantic theory for legal terms and rules? In any reasonably sophisticated legal system, the issue of whether a certain action is legally permitted or prohibited, authorized or *ultra vires*, cannot be answered by looking at any legal rule in isolation. One must examine the given rule in the context of the wider body of legal rules in order to arrive at a judgment regarding its implications for any particular case. This is not to say that a legal decision can be deduced from the body of legal rules in the same way that a prediction can be deduced from the laws of physical theory. But it is to say that (a) the meaning of a legal rule is constituted (at least in part) by the implications it has for particular cases and (b) the implications of any given rule are in significant part a function of its place in the wider body of rules.

The relational character of legal meaning can be illustrated by an example from tort law. Consider the *negligence* standard. The terms which form the heart of this standard—*due care, reasonable care*, and the like—are highly indeterminate when regarded in isolation from the other rules and doctrines of the legal system. However, in combination with the other rules and doctrines, the negligence standard takes on much more determinate content. For example, safety rules from other areas of the law help to define negligence. In *Martin v. Herzog*,[49] Cardozo ruled that the violation of a traffic safety rule by a buggy which was traveling without a light along a road after dark constituted negligence. In a similar fashion, criminal statutes are used to fill in the semantic content of the negligence rule.

It might be suggested that the radical indeterminacy position can easily be resurrected on the network model of meaning. One

[49] *Martin v. Herzog*, 126 N.E. 814 (1920).

could pour virtually whatever semantic content one wished into any legal rule simply by adopting the appropriate set of background organizing principles for structuring the mass of legal norms. Boyle suggests this line of argument when he contends that contemporary philosophies of language hold that language "is, or can be, used in an infinite number of ways."[50] The idea here is that once intelligible essences have been rejected as providing the natural referents of linguistic terms, the world becomes a kind of undifferentiated mass that can be carved up and structured by language in limitless ways. No sets of categories or systems of classification are metaphysically privileged over any other. It appears to Boyle and other CLS proponents that the mass of legal rules and doctrines is likewise subject to a limitless variety of organizational and classificatory schemes, different schemes infusing the rules and doctrines with different meanings.

There are two key problems with this line of argument. First, it incorrectly supposes that legal rules have no meaning at all when regarded in isolation from the body of legal rules and doctrines. This supposition runs into the same problems as Quine's thesis that only whole theories have meaning: It cannot explain how a language (or a theory or a discourse) is learned or how communication occurs. Second, the argument incorrectly presupposes that the principles of organization which give structure to the mass of legal rules have no objective status whatsoever and are merely relative to the choices or perceptions of any given individual. This presupposition that the structure of law is merely in the eyes of the beholder is mistaken.[51]

Each legal system incorporates principles that give structure to the mass of legal norms, and this structure is independent of the choice or perception of any particular individual. For example, the division of the mass of rules into various departments such as the law of torts, the law of crimes, and so forth, reflects those objective organizing principles.[52] Clearly, such divisions change, and certain traditional distinctions may all but collapse with the passage of time. But the division of the mass of rules into certain departments is not something that depends on the choice or perception of any individual. Someone who decided to redraw such divisions would not thereby change the law but would become unintelligible or unconvincing to everyone else. Over the long term, enough people

[50] Boyle, "Politics of Reason," pp. 708–9.

[51] Cf. Dummett's criticism of Quine, in *Frege*, p. 600.

[52] See Dworkin, *Law's Empire*, pp. 250–54.

can decide to redraw a traditional division so that it will change, but it takes time and more than one person precisely because there is a structure to the law that is independent of the choice or perception of any particular individual.

Skeptics may still demand to know how it is that the law in any particular legal system gets its structure. This is an important question and raises crucial issues regarding the ontology of law and of social reality generally. We must delay the answer to the question until the final chapter, when we have the opportunity to explore those issues in some detail.

If the meaning of legal rules were radically indeterminate, there would be a quick and easy argument that the rule of law could not be maintained in a pluralist society without violating the liberal commitment to neutrality. One would only have to argue that the officials called on to "interpret" the rules would be compelled to rely on controversial conceptions of the good and the right in what would amount to a process of creating the meaning of the rules. In this section, I have tried to throw serious doubt on whether such a victory over the liberal rule of law is available, although we must wait until the final chapter's examination of social ontology to complete the argument against the radical indeterminacy position. In concluding this chapter, I consider another popular CLS argument against the conceptual coherence of the liberal rule of law. The argument revolves around the idea that the establishment of any system of law automatically violates the liberal commitment to neutrality. Again, Peller provides one of the more extended versions of the argument.

Power, Neutrality, and Legalism

Peller contends that semantic determinacy is achieved in any legal system by the repression of competing ways of ordering and structuring the mass of rules and doctrines. These competing ways are tied to moral and political conceptions that radically challenge the prevailing system of power and privilege. Their repression is itself an act of power, says Peller, and exposes the legal system's absence of neutrality. Echoing Foucault, Peller claims that meaning is thus a "produced effect of social power institutionalized in social representational conventions."[53] Moreover, the law-politics distinction is seen by Peller as a "myth about the social world" be-

[53] Peller, "Metaphysics of American Law," p. 1170.

cause it pretends to a political neutrality that it necessarily lacks and represents the product of "an act of power through which other ways of understanding and experiencing the world are marginalized."[54] To set up a system of law in which legal interpretation represses radical normative visions is itself a political act. Furthermore, to set up a system of law at all is a political act that involves the rejection of certain moral and political visions. Even if there is a relatively impermeable membrane constructed around the law that screens out much moral and political controversy, thus creating a law-politics distinction, the commitment to law itself is far from politically neutral.

Peller's argument is an extension of one made by Unger against the possibility of any system of law meeting the liberal requirement of political neutrality. Unger argued that "each system of lawmaking itself embodies certain values; it incorporates a view of how power ought to be distributed in the society and of how conflicts should be resolved."[55] Peller extends this argument in two ways. First, he claims (following Foucault) that it is the exercise of power (i.e., repression, force, threats, violence) which gives legal rules and doctrines sufficient semantic determinacy to embody certain values rather than others. Second, he argues that to establish a legal system in the first place is to opt for a way of handling social conflict and difference that reflects certain ideas of the good and the right rather than others. It is not simply that some legal systems embody certain values and others embody conflicting values, but that law as such is just one means of dealing with difference and conflict in social life, a means which embodies certain values rather than others.

The crucial claim of these CLS arguments is that the rule of law automatically violates the liberal commitment to political neutrality. Peller's contention that the rule of law is a creature of power is really beside the point. Liberals can concede that it is social power that gives life to the rule of law; what they insist upon is that such power be exercised in ways that are consistent with the principles of liberal political morality. Liberals need not be allergic to exercises of power. The issue is *how* power is exercised, on what principles and to what ends, not the simple fact of its exercise.[56]

[54] Ibid., pp. 1289, 1275.

[55] Unger, *Law in Modern Society*, p. 180.

[56] Thus, I disagree with Alan Hunt's claim that one of the accomplishments of the CLS project is to have "identified the fact that the concept and reality of 'power' is invisible to liberal jurisprudence." There is no such fact. See Alan Hunt, "The

In response to Peller's argument, it must be conceded from the beginning that any system of primary and secondary rules will be more consonant with some moral and political views than others. A system of law which does not tilt in favor of or against any conception of the good or the right is simply not possible. We have already seen how the liberal rule of law demands moral and political views that are capable of accommodation and compromise and impose substantial limits on politics in the name of individual autonomy. Political neutrality does not treat uncompromising conceptions of the right on a par with those open to compromise. That represents no small tilt in favor of certain conceptions of the right and against others. Similarly, rights neutrality is biased against views that place weak constraints on politics and in favor of those that place relatively strong constraints on the power and reach of political activity. However, it would be a simple failure to distinguish different senses of the idea of neutrality to claim that it is a self-contradictory idea because it is not neutral with respect to uncompromising normative views or views that do not endorse strong constraints on politics.

It must also be conceded that there are conceptions of the right and the good that are not intolerant or uncompromising but reject law as a means for dealing with difference and conflict in social life. Such conceptions reject the use of the formal procedures of law as a way to deal with social conflict and instead embrace nonlegalistic methods, such as mediation, designed to restore what is regarded as the torn fabric of a community united by common values. The establishment and maintenance of any system of law will be an act of political power that lacks neutrality in the straightforward sense that it will represent the repudiation of such antinomian conceptions.

Peller is thus correct in seeing the liberal commitment to the law-politics distinction as charged with controversial political values. It is charged with the values of legalism: the embrace of rules and formal procedures as ways of dealing with difference and conflict in social life.[57] Liberal theory embraces the values of legalism to

---

Critique of Law: What Is 'Critical' about Critical Legal Theory," in *Critical Legal Studies*, ed. P. Fitzpatrick and A. Hunt (New York: Blackwell, 1987), p. 15. I think that Hunt is led astray by misinterpreting claims such as Locke's that where law ends, force begins. Such claims do not mean that law has nothing to do with power but that political power exercised beyond the limits of the law is illegitimate. See John Locke, *A Letter Concerning Toleration* (Indianapolis: Hackett, 1983), p. 49.

[57] This does not mean that liberal theory must place overriding importance on formal procedures and rules in all contexts within liberal society. It is only to say

the extent that it regards the modern nation-state as forming a social context that is too pluralistic to rely exclusively, or even primarily, on nonlegalist modes of regulation. Formal dispute-resolving mechanisms are needed to deal with conflict in a fair and effective manner. Those who are committed to a thoroughgoing antinomian normative view will reject any form of political society in which values are insufficiently shared for exclusively nonlegalist methods of social regulation to work effectively and fairly. Insofar as the liberal rule of law represents an alternative to such a normative vision, it is by no means politically neutral. But then must we not conclude that the CLS attack on the coherence of the liberal rule of law is correct after all?

The answer is negative because liberal theory is not committed to neutrality in the sense that rejecting the antinomian vision of a society without law represents a departure from normative neutrality. First, recall that for liberal theory, rights neutrality takes precedence over political neutrality. Insuring that politics does not invade the zone of individual autonomy to an intolerable extent is the first order of liberal business. Liberals embrace the rule of law and the values of legalism because they believe that in the context of the modern nation-state, the rule of law is an essential element for constraining politics to prevent such an invasion. They believe that the nation-state is too pluralistic to rely solely on nonlegalistic modes of social regulation for dealing with social difference and conflict in a fair and effective manner. The liberal embrace of the rule of law and the values of legalism is thus not inconsistent with the liberal demands for neutrality. Rather, it is fully consistent with the overriding importance placed by liberalism on rights neutrality, given the liberal view of the modern nation-state.

In addition, it would be a distortion of liberal theory to suggest that it has no place for nonlegal modes of social regulation, such as mediation. Liberals can and do acknowledge the value of such nonlegal mechanisms in certain social contexts and can consis-

---

that the liberal view requires us to recognize that such procedures and rules have a central role to play in resolving fairly and effectively the conflicts that arise in a society characterized by moral, religious, and political pluralism. Thus, the liberal endorsement of legalism does not necessarily involve a commitment to *legalism* in the sense that Judith Shklar defines the term: "the ethical attitude that holds moral conduct to be a matter of rule following, and moral relationships to consist of duties and rights determined by rules." Shklar, *Legalism* (Cambridge: Harvard University Press, 1986), p. 1. Shklar understands full well that a commitment to the liberal rule of law does not entail an acceptance of legalism in her sense of the term. See *Legalism*, pp. xi–xii.

tently allow a place for them in liberal society. And those who reject the rule of law can argue in the political arena for extending the role of such informal mechanisms. Of course, a liberal state could not allow the antinomians to eradicate legal institutions; in that sense, one might say that the liberal rule of law is not neutral. But the kind of political neutrality which the liberal defends does not aim to guarantee that any normative view has an opportunity to remake society wholly in its vision. It does guarantee an opportunity to negotiate and compromise within a framework of individual rights, and there is no reason why those who defend nonlegal modes of social regulation cannot seize the opportunity under a liberal regime to carve out a significant role for nonlegal modes of social regulation within the liberal state. The liberal version of political neutrality demands that antinomians have such an opportunity, but there is nothing remotely inconsistent in liberal thought in making that demand or prohibiting antilegalism from going so far as to destroy all legal institutions.

Perhaps the liberal belief that law is essential and effective in protecting individuals from oppression is false. Perhaps informal institutions would protect people better than legal ones in the context of the modern nation-state. I argue against these possibilities in the final chapter. But even if the liberal beliefs that underlie the commitment to the rule of law are false, the CLS attack on the coherence of the liberal rule of law fails. The liberal embrace of the rule of law is a perfectly coherent response to the liberal assessment of the possibilities and dangers of social and political life within the framework of the modern nation-state.[58]

Summary

This chapter has examined three important lines of argument in the CLS literature. All three attempt to establish that liberal theory is internally inconsistent, and all three claim that the inconsistency

[58] In the final chapter of *A Guide to Critical Legal Studies*, Kelman sets out to argue that legal thinking as such is nonneutral in the sense that it blocks or subverts the kind of thinking that radically challenges the existing institutional structures of society. Such an argument would fit comfortably into the general line of CLS argument that I examine in the final section of this chapter. However, in the course of his chapter, Kelman gets diverted from the line of argument that he starts out with and ends up defending a quite different claim, viz., that legal thinking that employs the currently authoritative concepts and doctrines blocks radical social thinking. The coherence of the liberal rule of law, however, does not depend in any way on the denial of such a claim about current legal categories.

arises from the liberal embrace of pluralism, neutrality, and the rule of law. The central contention of these arguments is that it is impossible to satisfy both the demands of legality and those of neutrality in a context of moral, religious, and political pluralism. I found that the three main lines of argument deployed to support such a contention are all wanting. The arguments rest to a large degree on a confused understanding of the liberal commitment to neutrality. In addition, the more radical CLS arguments rest on a seriously inadequate understanding of linguistic meaning. Once those confusions and inadequacies are remedied, it becomes clear that the requirements of legality and neutrality can be met in a pluralist context.

FOUR

THE CONTRADICTIONS OF LAW

In the previous chapter, we examined the CLS claim that the liberal conception of the rule of law is incoherent. The claim rests on the charge that there is an inconsistency between the liberal theory of law and the liberal theory of politics. The legal side is committed to the rule of law. The political side is committed to neutrality and to moral, religious, and political pluralism. The claim that the liberal rule of law is conceptually incoherent is the charge that the rule of law cannot exist without violating liberal neutrality, given a pluralist context. I argued that the charge could not be sustained.

In this chapter, I turn to CLS charges of incoherence and contradiction at another level of liberalism. The claim is typically made in the CLS literature that liberal legal doctrine is riddled with contradiction. This is not a claim about the liberal theory of law but one about the set of rules and doctrines that constitute the law of a liberal state. Liberal *law*—and not merely liberal theorizing about law—is said to be riddled with contradiction.

In the CLS literature, this claim is defended almost exclusively by reference to Anglo-American legal doctrine and indeed mainly by reference to the law of the various jurisdictions in the United States. This is potentially a serious methodological weakness, since one can reasonably question whether Anglo-American law is representative of the law of all possible liberal states. However, I will not challenge CLS on its relatively narrow focus. I believe that its main points about Anglo-American law can be made with equal cogency about the law of other liberal states. This is not to say that the points are all convincing ones but only that they would be neither more nor less persuasive if applied to other liberal states.

Moreover, even if one could not assume that the main CLS points about Anglo-American law applied to other liberal states, it would still be theoretically important to examine the claims of contradiction within our legal doctrine. This is because CLS holds that such contradictions are inconsistent with fundamental elements of liberal legal theory. It would be no small matter if the CLS literature could establish a basic incompatibility between liberal legal theory and Anglo-American legal doctrine, for liberal theorists would then be unable to hold consistently that the doctrine met the requirements of their theory. One can regard this chapter, then, as an examination of whether the CLS literature does indeed establish such an incompatibility.

The charge of contradiction within legal doctrine is a kind of shorthand for a number of very specific theses about the character of the law. In this chapter, I examine in detail three such theses. They are, I believe, the most fundamental of the CLS theses about contradictions within doctrine.

The first is the thesis that our legal doctrine is an unprincipled patchwork of norms deriving from starkly incompatible ethical viewpoints. This is the *patchwork thesis*. The second is that the structure of legal doctrine can be organized in radically different ways, depending upon which of two incompatible ethical viewpoints one adopts. This is the *duck-rabbit thesis*, so named for reasons which are considered in due course. The third is that the principles that underlie legal rules are not consistently applied to all of the cases over which they claim moral authority but are truncated well short of the full range of cases over which they claim authority. This is the *truncation thesis*.

The charge that liberal legal doctrine is riddled with contradiction is typically viewed in the CLS literature as a serious criticism of the liberal conception of law. Behind this view, lie two premises: first, liberal legal theory demands that the legal doctrine of the liberal state be free of contradictions; second, the liberal view of law regards the United States, Britain, Canada, and so forth as leading examples of liberal states. These charges of contradiction are then thought to confront the liberal view with the difficult choice of rejecting its leading examples or rejecting the requirements of its legal theory.

The first premise seems noncontroversial, even trivially true. After all, how can any system of thought, liberalism included, countenance contradictions? The apparent triviality of the premise diminishes, however, when one focuses on the three specific theses for which the charges of contradiction stand. I argue that the truncation thesis is sound but that there is nothing in liberal theory incompatible with the thesis. In fact, the truth of the thesis is virtually guaranteed, given certain fundamental liberal principles.

Thus, the truncation thesis cannot force the liberal to choose between his leading examples and his legal theory.

The duck-rabbit thesis is less innocuous for liberal theory. In one common interpretation, it is incompatible with liberal legal theory. But I suggest that under such an interpretation, the thesis relies on a highly questionable social ontology, and in the next chapter I offer detailed criticisms of that ontology. In another interpretation, the duck-rabbit thesis is true but not incompatible with liberal theory. Finally, I argue that the patchwork thesis is not, by itself, inconsistent with liberal legal theory and that although it might tend to establish a conclusion inconsistent with any liberal model of the rule of law, the thesis has not been convincingly established by the CLS literature.

The three CLS theses are embedded in relatively complex arguments about particular aspects and elements of doctrine. I have tried to avoid extricating these arguments from their contexts. This means that the chapter focuses on a few specific CLS pieces and that a good deal of time is spent setting up the context. The two pieces that receive the lion's share of attention—Duncan Kennedy's "Form and Substance in Private Law Adjudication" and Roberto Unger's *The Critical Legal Studies Movement*—are widely regarded in the CLS movement as among the best and most influential of the critical accounts of legal doctrine. I will begin with Kennedy's piece, which formulates and develops some of the central concepts that are used within the CLS movement for the analysis of doctrine.

Form and Substance: Kennedy on Private Law

Duncan Kennedy's "Form and Substance in Private Law Adjudication" is one of the seminal pieces of the CLS literature.[1] Kennedy's style of legal analysis has been widely regarded in the CLS movement as paradigmatic, providing many of the conceptual resources relied upon in the literature to support the contention that legal doctrine is riddled with contradiction. It is helpful to have a close look at some of the key concepts and themes of "Form and Substance" before proceeding to a direct analysis of the relation of the article to the theses covered by the claim of contradiction.

Kennedy's article revolves around what I call *the problem of form*.

[1] Duncan Kennedy, "Form and Substance in Private Law Adjudication," *Harvard Law Review* 89 (1976): 1685–1778.

The most concise way to formulate the problem is with the question, What degree of formal realizability should legal norms have? Formal realizability is a quality that can be represented in terms of a continuum between two opposing poles. At one extreme are norms that legal thinkers characterize as *rules;* at the other are those characterized as *standards.* Kennedy explains it thus:

> The extreme of formal realizability is a directive to an official that requires him to respond to the presence together of each of a list of easily distinguishable factual aspects of a situation by intervening in a determinate way. Ihering used the determination of legal capacity by sole reference to age as a prime example of a formally realizable definition of liability. . . . At the opposite pole from a formally realizable rule is a standard. . . . A standard refers directly to one of the substantive objectives of the legal order. Some examples are good faith, due care, fairness, unconscionability, unjust enrichment, and reasonableness.[2]

The problem of form stems from the fact that there are good reasons for thinking that it is better for legal norms to have a higher degree of formal realizability, that is, better for them to be cast as rules; but there are also good counterreasons for thinking that they are better cast as standards. The problem of form is the problem of how legal norms ought to be cast along the dimension of formal realizability.

Kennedy points out that the rule form is traditionally regarded as having two principal virtues. First, it confines the discretion of officials: They are authorized to act only in well-defined situations and in well-defined ways. This is a virtue because it hampers the arbitrary exercise of public power. Second, the rule form provides citizens with a clear advance warning of the conditions under which public power will be deployed and how it will be deployed. This is a virtue because citizens can then choose their activities secure in the belief that they will not be bringing down the coercive hand of state power upon themselves.

But, the rule form also has two vices. In giving any rule authoritative status, the political community is acting for some substantive purpose. For example, a rule that a person's contract with another party is legally enforceable against that party only if she is at least eighteen years of age is meant to protect minors from con-

[2] Ibid., pp. 1687–88.

tracts that they enter into as a result of their immaturity or lack of experience. Should the minor have second thoughts and seek to back out, the law will allow her to do so. One of the vices of rules, though, is that they will invariably be overinclusive. Thus, consider rules intended to protect a certain class of people. Such rules almost invariably serve to protect some people who fall outside the favored class. For example, the eighteen-year minimum-age rule will allow minors who are as mature as most adults to cancel a contract.

Of course, rules also have the opposite flaw: They are underinclusive—they fail to protect some people who do fall within the class favored by the underlying purpose of the rule. Thus, the minimum-age rule for contracts allows me to enforce a contract against a nineteen-year-old who is two or three years behind normal emotional development. Moreover, it is clear that under- and overinclusiveness afflict rules having purposes other than the protection of some class. Whatever the substantive purpose behind a rule—protection, punishment, or something else—legal norms cast as rules virtually always fail to provide an airtight fit between the criteria for the application of the rule and the purpose underlying it.

The virtues and vices of standards are a mirror image of the virtues and vices of rules. Standards allow an official to tailor his decision to the specifics of an individual case and so better to promote the specific purpose of the political community. They thus seem less subject to the vices of over- and underinclusiveness than rules. Yet standards seem more liable to abuse by officials and also appear to provide a less clear-cut warning to citizens of when and how public power will be deployed against them.

Because rules and standards have both virtues and vices, the legal literature concerning form is filled with pro-rule arguments, invoking the virtues of rules and the vices of standards, and pro-standard counterarguments, invoking the virtues of standards and the vices of rules. The problem of form may appear to be, in the final analysis, a straightforward (albeit difficult) empirical issue: Which form more effectively serves the specific purposes for which the political community has given authoritative status to certain norms? For any given purpose, the problem of form would come down to the question of which degree of formal realizability would more effectively serve it. Kennedy suggests that the traditional approach to the problem of form regards it in precisely this way.

Kennedy rejects such an interpretation of the problem. He regards the problem as implicating fundamental normative conceptions about human life. He claims that "the pro-rules and pro-standards positions are more than an invitation to a positivist investigation of reality. They are also an invitation to choose between sets of values and visions of the universe."[3] Kennedy elaborates the point by contending that a jurisprudential position that favors rules is tied to a substantive ethical view that he characterizes as *individualism*, while a jurisprudential position that favors standards is tied to a substantive ethical view that he characterizes as *altruism*. These two ethical views represent fundamentally incompatible conceptions of the nature of the self, the scope of a person's basic moral duties to others, the principal virtues of human life, the proper role of law, the epistemological status of our ethical beliefs, and the nature of human freedom.[4]

Kennedy considers his principal contribution to the discussion of the problem of form to stem from his thesis that the problem is connected to the opposition of these two substantive views. To be sure, thinkers operating in the tradition of legal realism have long denied that there is a purely empirical, value-neutral way of answering the problem. Kennedy points this out explicitly.

But legal realism did not provide an account of the substantive normative visions to which the different *policy* arguments about rules and standards were tied. Realism taught that pro-rule arguments and their pro-standard counterarguments could not be resolved by value-neutral, empirical means, but it did not systematically relate the arguments to fundamental views about morality and politics. Kennedy's aim is to make those arguments more intelligible by exhibiting their connection to such substantive ethical visions:

> The ultimate goal is to break down the sense that legal argument is autonomous from moral, economic, and political discourse in general. There is nothing innovative about this. Indeed, it has been a premise of legal scholars for several generations that it is impossible to construct an autonomous logic of legal rules. What is new in this piece is the attempt to

[3] Ibid., p. 1712.

[4] For the purposes of this chapter, it will not be necessary to examine Kennedy's account of the epistemologies of individualism and altruism or their conceptions of freedom.

> show an orderliness to the debates about "policy" with which we are left after the abandonment of the claim of neutrality.[5]

The "orderliness" to which Kennedy refers is, of course, an order of opposites. Thus, Kennedy goes beyond the realist analysis both in postulating the connection of the problem of form to the most basic normative issues in personal and political life and in contending that there are fundamentally incompatible ethical conceptions implicated in the law's response to the problem.

Kennedy describes individualism as a view that rests on a sharp conceptual contrast between the interests of the self and the interests of others. It proceeds from this sharp separation of self and others to make three key claims. First, it is legitimate for a person to prefer his own well-being to that of others, as long as he abides by norms that make it possible for similarly self-interested and separate selves to coexist peacefully. Second, the central virtue of human life is self-reliance in the pursuit of one's goals. Third, the proper purpose of law is to give authority to the kinds of norms that make peaceful coexistence among separate, self-interested, self-reliant selves possible.

It is important to understand the connection between self-reliance and self-interest in the individualist model. Kennedy does not make this connection explicit, but I believe that doing so helps to fill out his model of individualism. Self-reliant individualists do not necessarily accomplish their goals without the assistance of others. Rather, the assistance of others is asked for and received on the basis of the others' self-interest. When the self-reliant person asks for help, he does not do so by appealing to the sympathy or benevolence of others. He appeals to their self-interest by offering something in return. Adam Smith articulates this individualist view with characteristic clarity:

> It is not from the benevolence of the butcher, the brewer, or the baker that we expect our dinner, but from their regard to their own interest. We address ourselves, not to their humanity, but to their self-love. . . . Nobody but a beggar chooses to depend chiefly upon the benevolence of his fellow-citizens.[6]

Thus, the individualist is not reduced to the status of a supplicant when he requests the assistance of others. He can retain his

[5] Kennedy, "Form and Substance," p. 1724.

[6] Adam Smith, *Wealth of Nations: Books I–III* (Harmondsworth: Penguin, 1970), p. 119.

dignity because he has something to offer to those who help him; he helps them as much as they help him.[7]

Altruism proceeds from a rejection of this sharp individualist contrast between the interests of the self and the interests of others. People are sometimes obligated to act on behalf of another's well-being, even if such action is not required by the norms of peaceful coexistence of separate, self-reliant and self-interested selves. Moreover, the central virtues of human life are sharing and sacrifice, the kind of actions that discharge one's obligations to look after the well-being of others. And the proper function of law includes the enforcement of such obligations.

One of the central contentions of "Form and Substance" is that individualism is tied to the idea that legal norms ought to be cast in the form of rules, while altruism is tied to the idea that legal norms ought to be cast in the form of standards. The key question to be addressed in the interpretation of Kennedy's piece concerns the nature of the connection postulated between individualism and rules on one side, and altruism and standards on the other.

In discussing "Form and Substance," CLS scholar Mark Kelman has suggested that the connection has been widely misinterpreted.[8] He says that many commentators have taken Kennedy to assert that there is a connection of the following sort: People whose ethical thinking is dominated by individualism, if they are logically consistent, will inevitably favor the rule form for any legal norm; people whose ethical thinking is dominated by altruism will, if they are logically consistent, inevitably favor the standard form. Kelman rejects this interpretation, and he is surely right to do so. First, Kennedy is clearly skeptical of virtually any nontrivial claim about human social life that asserts something to be "inevitable." Second, the article mentions several examples of rulelike norms that have been consistently promoted by those holding altruist principles—for example, progressive income-tax laws. It would be difficult to maintain that Kennedy was oblivious to the significance of such examples for the connection between form and substance.

Kelman suggests that we interpret Kennedy as postulating an "aesthetic" connection between form and substance. He characterizes such a postulate as the "invaluable" insight of "Form and

[7] Cf. Don Herzog, "As Many as Six Impossible Things before Breakfast," *California Law Review* 75 (1987): 617.

[8] Mark Kelman, *A Guide to Critical Legal Studies* (Cambridge: Harvard University Press, 1987), p. 17.

Substance."[9] Kelman claims that the "rule *form* may always tend to appeal to the *substantive* individualist because its formal virtues match up aesthetically with the virtues he is inclined to admire."[10]

The principal formal virtue of the rule form, as Kelman seems to see it, is that it provides people with a clear and unequivocal specification of what the state requires of them. The rule form thus provides a clear notice of the requirements that the state is laying down. In the jargon of legal theory, rules provide "fair notice."

Kelman's suggestion is that the virtue of fair notice matches aesthetically the individualist virtue of self-reliance. But such a suggestion seems to me to be hopelessly confused. What can it mean to assert that self-reliance matches fair notice aesthetically? Kelman is of no help here. Not only does he fail to give an account of what this aesthetic connection amounts to but his discussion of it implies that the kind of connection which he has in mind ultimately has nothing to do with aesthetic considerations. Consider his statement "The self-reliant person wants to know just what is expected of him: even if a lot is expected, he can do it, as long as there are no surprises, as long as he can plan his life anticipating and controlling all obligations that he will ultimately be asked to meet."[11] What these remarks help to show is nothing about the aesthetics of self-reliance or rules but rather that the individual who regards self-reliance as a central moral virtue has reason to prefer the rule form: It will do a better job of letting him know what to expect, so that he may plan his life accordingly and thereby avoid being put in the position of having to rely on the benevolence of others in order to achieve his ends. The individualist has a good reason to choose the rule form because it helps him to realize the virtue which he regards as central to human life: self-reliance. This is a logical connection (one might say, practico-logical) between form and substance insofar as it concerns reasons for choice. It is not an aesthetic connection.

Kelman is perfectly correct to claim that rules and standards do not necessarily correspond to the substantive values of individualism and altruism, respectively. He cites convincing examples of rules that promote altruist values, such as the progressive income tax, and standards that can promote individualist values, such as the negligence standard.

An additional argument for Kelman's point comes from anthro-

[9] Ibid.

[10] Ibid., p. 59.

[11] Ibid., p. 60.

pological evidence. A number of cultures have highly individualist values but do not govern themselves in conformity to norms that take a rule form. Robert Edgerton has described three such cultures: "The Siriono, Paliyans, and Chenchus, for example, paid little apparent heed to rules most of the time. They ignored many, permitted all manner of exceptions to others, and often considered what was right or wrong to be dependent on the situation."[12] Neither Kennedy nor anyone else gives us reason to think that these cultures are somehow guilty of logical or practical inconsistency for their simultaneous acceptance of individualism and standard-like norms. It is simply unfounded, then, to claim that the logically consistent embrace of individualism entails that one must always choose the rule over the standard, and it is equally unfounded to claim that the logically consistent embrace of altruism entails that one must always choose the standard over the rule.

Yet Kelman goes astray when he infers from the unfounded character of these claims that there can be no logical connection of any kind between form and substance. There may still be some sort of logical tie between form and substance, though a weaker one than that postulated in the unfounded claims that we just rejected. For example, it may be—as Kelman's own remarks about self-reliance suggest—that individualism provides reasons for choosing rules over standards, though the reasons are defeasible ones. Similarly, it may be that altruism provides reasons for choosing standards over rules, although the reasons are again defeasible. These postulated connections between form and substance are logical, albeit modest ones.

Kelman's description of the connection between form and substance as aesthetic suggests that the individualist's preference for the rule form is not logically grounded in any of his substantive ethical commitments: The preference represents a judgment of what is pleasing to his aesthetic sensibilities, having no logical tie to his ethical conceptions. In addition to rendering the exact nature of the connection obscure, such a suggestion is difficult to square with important parts of Kennedy's piece. For instance, Kennedy contends that the problem of form is an aspect of the issue of which substantive ethical view is superior and that the same normative arguments are used in addressing both problems.[13] This appears to imply that there is some kind of logical tie

[12] Robert Edgerton, *Rules, Exceptions, and Social Order* (Berkeley: University of California Press, 1985), p. 197.

[13] Kennedy, "Form and Substance," pp. 1710, 1712, pp. 1776.

between substantive ethical commitments and the problem of legal form, not some elusive aesthetic connection.

I believe the best interpretation of "Form and Substance" construes Kennedy as postulating the relatively modest logical connections between form and substance I mentioned earlier. Individualism provides general but defeasible reasons for choosing rules over standards, while altruism provides general but defeasible reasons for choosing the opposite. If these connections hold, then the cogency of competing answers to the problem of form will depend to a significant degree on the relative merits of individualist and altruist tenets, and this seems to be just what Kennedy has in mind. This interpretation is further supported by the fact that Kennedy does provide arguments attempting to establish these modest logical links between form and substance. Let us begin with the argument for the connection between individualism and rules.[14]

Individualism aims to foster self-reliance. Yet when the norms of private law are vaguely formulated, individuals will likely find themselves in situations where they are faced with unexpected losses: The contracts they thought valid turn out unenforceable; the conduct they thought innocent turns out tortious. Under such conditions, the individualist may well be put in the position of having to depend on the benevolence of others. Self-reliance is undercut. Individualism thus provides reason for choosing rules over standards. (Once we dispense with his talk of aesthetics, the foregoing is also, in essence, Kelman's argument for the connection between self-reliance and rules.)

Note that it is perfectly consistent with the foregoing argument to say that there are situations in which standards could do as well, or better, in providing the conditions that encourage self-reliance. For example, the term *unconscionable* may be quite vague generally and liable to widely conflicting interpretations, but to businesspersons who are operating in a certain commercial context, the term may have a relatively clear and definite meaning, and may provide a much more economical way of specifying forbidden commercial practices than a compendium of rules. Given the tenets of individualism, the presumption may be in favor of the rule form, but the presumption will remain rebuttable.

Also, note that this argument for a connection between individ-

[14] The following is my reconstruction of one of the strands of argument found in "Form and Substance," pp. 1738–40.

ualism and rules will be stronger in the context of a pluralist culture where basic moral notions are likely to receive widely conflicting interpretations. In the context of such pluralism, standards will typically fail to have unequivocal meanings, since they are typically formulated in terms of such moral notions. On the other hand, in a relatively homogeneous cultural setting, such notions are likely to receive a uniform interpretation, so that the meanings of standards will tend to be less equivocal. The example of how *unconscionability* is construed within the context of commercial transactions illustrates this in the setting of a particular subculture. And it could well be argued that the individualist societies described by Edgerton illustrate this at the level of the general culture.

The other side of Kennedy's argument linking form and substance concerns the logical link between altruism and standards. If self-reliance is not regarded as a central virtue, then the individualist reason for choosing rules over standards is removed, and we would not be primarily concerned with casting legal norms in a form that would encourage self-reliance. If we adopted altruism, we would be primarily concerned to cast legal norms in ways that would assist in the enforcement of the principles of sharing and sacrifice. I construe Kennedy as suggesting that standards are generally superior for such a task because they give the state more flexibility in deciding when it is appropriate to spread the burdens (or advantages) of social life more widely across the population and determining who should be required to share those burdens.

Again, the link posited here consists of defeasible reasons. In certain cases, there may be rules that do a better job of implementing the altruist principles of sharing and sacrifice than the standards that could replace them. Recall the oftmentioned progressive income tax laws. But conceding the existence and altruistic efficacy of such rules is not inconsistent with what I take to be Kennedy's claim: The tenets of altruism provide general (but not indefeasible) reasons for choosing standards over rules.

Kennedy's position that there are these modest logical links between rules and individualism, standards and altruism, is a persuasive one. If our primary aim is to encourage self-reliance, we have good reason for choosing a system of law that will avoid imposing losses that are difficult or impossible to anticipate. We need legal norms that make it clear to everyone what the legal consequences will be under a given set of facts. In that way, individuals will be able to plan their lives to avoid appealing to the benevolence of others.

It is true that vague or ambiguous legal norms may lead to unexpected gains as well as unexpected losses. But unexpected gains will not assist the self-reliant individual in his efforts to avoid appealing to benevolence because he will already have planned his life to avoid such an appeal.[15] On the other hand, unexpected losses can materially undercut such plans and make it difficult or impossible to avoid the appeal to benevolence. The rule form makes it possible for the individual to anticipate the losses that the law may impose on him, because rules are, by definition, couched in terms relatively simple to apply in a given situation. The facts that form the basis of applying the rule can usually be determined in a noncontroversial manner, and the directive that the rule issues to the relevant official is a clear-cut specification of what is to be done.

The modest link postulated by Kennedy between altruism and standards is equally persuasive. From an altruist standpoint, burden-spreading rules will be less desirable than burden-spreading standards because of the problems of over- and underinclusiveness. Easily applicable rules are likely to be relatively clumsy, often spreading the burden to those who should not shoulder it (overinclusiveness) and failing to spread it to those who should be shouldering it (underinclusiveness). Rules can be effective in spreading burdens, but their effectiveness is offset by the invariably loose fit between their simple criteria and the class of people that would be targeted by the burden-sharing principles of an altruist political order. Standards allow for more fine-tuning in the spreading of burdens, and thus, given a commitment to altruism, there are good (though defeasible) reasons for casting legal norms as standards rather than rules.[16]

[15] The individualist position presupposes that individuals will have sufficient resources, at least at some appropriate initial moment, so that dire need does not undercut efforts to avoid the appeal to benevolence. Thus, individuals will have enough resources to plan a life of self-reliance before any unexpected windfalls come their way.

[16] Individualism is not entirely free of the problem of the over- and underinclusiveness of rules. For example, legal norms must specify who is to count as an individual of whom self-reliance is expected. Any specification of this by rules (such as a minimum-age rule) is likely to suffer from the problem. But the over- and underinclusiveness of rules would be a far more pervasive problem in an altruist legal order that saw the main function of legal norms as shifting the benefits and burdens of social life in accordance with substantive principles of sharing and sacrifice than in an individualist legal order that saw the main function of legal norms

We have been examining in some detail Kennedy's seminal piece, "Form and Substance in Private Law Adjudication," because it develops some of the central concepts and claims that CLS authors have come to rely upon in arguing that liberal legal doctrine is a logically incoherent patchwork of norms deriving from starkly incompatible ethical viewpoints. We have called this CLS contention the patchwork thesis, and we are now prepared to examine the principal CLS arguments for it. We have seen that Kennedy's piece makes some cogent claims about the connections between the form of legal doctrine and the opposing ethical viewpoints of individualism and altruism. However, the following sections will show that the patchwork thesis goes well beyond those claims and that no CLS author has been able to provide convincing arguments for the thesis.

The Patchwork Thesis

The patchwork thesis is best construed as a conjunction of two connected but distinct claims: first, that it is impossible to provide a rational reconstruction of the body of legal doctrine by deriving its norms from a consistent set of underlying principles; second, that the reason for this impossibility is that the reconstruction of certain important elements of doctrine will require principles from a particular ethical viewpoint, while the reconstruction of other important elements of doctrine will require contradictory principles from an incompatible ethical viewpoint. In most CLS literature, Kennedy's models of individualism and altruism are the incompatible ethical viewpoints in question.

The central importance of the patchwork thesis for CLS resides in the belief of critical theorists that the thesis is inconsistent with the requirements of liberal legal theory. Liberal theory, it is held, demands that our legal doctrine be amenable to rational reconstruction in terms of some consistent set of normative principles. The patchwork character of doctrine defeats the possibility of any such rational reconstruction, according to the CLS position, and so

as encouraging self-reliance. Moreover, for the individualist order, rules have the great virtue of providing clear warning of when the state may act to impose a loss on the individual. For altruism, there is no such counterbalance to the problem of the over- and underinclusiveness of rules but there is the reason that we have just specified for preferring standards, so altruism but not individualism is logically tilted toward a preference for standards.

confronts liberals with the choice of rejecting our system of law or rejecting the requirements laid down by the liberal theory of law.

Indeterminacy and the Patchwork Thesis

What is the CLS argument for the incompatibility of the patchwork thesis with the requirements of liberal legal theory? It revolves around the contention that the law would contain what liberal theory would have to regard as an intolerably high level of indeterminacy if it were not amenable to rational reconstruction. This argument is an offshoot of Unger's in *The Critical Legal Studies Movement*, where he contends that doctrinal rules contain so many gaps, conflicts, and ambiguities that they must be supplemented by an appeal to underlying principles in order to attain a degree of determinacy acceptable to liberalism and consistent with its commitment to the rule of law.[17]

The problem that the patchwork thesis is thought to pose for liberalism is that when one goes to the level of principles, one simply finds the doctrinal conflicts replicated in a more abstract form. According to the argument, the problem of indeterminacy is not resolved but merely pushed to another level, given the truth of the patchwork thesis. In deciding a case, the judge tries to find guidance on how to resolve an apparent conflict between different elements of the settled law by moving to the level of underlying principles, but at that level, one does not leave the conflicts behind. Rather, one finds that there are incompatible ethical and political principles underlying the different elements of the settled law. According to the CLS argument, the result is that the judge must choose which of the incompatible principles to rely on in deciding the case, and this is a choice that the law cannot dictate.

If there were a single consistent set of principles in terms of which doctrine could be rationally reconstructed, then the judge could appeal to it in resolving some apparent conflict within the settled law. But because there is no such set of principles, judges can only choose one or another of the incompatible principles that underlie the settled doctrine. Different judges can and will choose different principles, but none can provide a convincing legal argument that her choice is the legally correct one. Each judge can

[17] See chapter 3 for a critique of Unger's use of the argument to show that the rule of law necessarily violates liberal neutrality. In this context, the issue is not the neutrality of the rule of law but the extent of indeterminacy in existing systems of liberal law.

only cite the doctrinal materials that support her favored principle and attempt to downplay the ones that support the opposing principle. Clare Dalton neatly summarizes the CLS view of the significance of the patchwork thesis: "[D]octrinal inconsistency necessarily undermines the force of any conventional legal argument, and . . . opposing arguments can be made with equal force."[18]

There are serious problems with this CLS view of the implications of the patchwork thesis. Even if there are incompatible principles that underlie different segments of doctrine, it does not follow that the judge is free to choose which principle to rely on in deciding a case. Recall from the discussion in chapter 2 that our legal culture incorporates a convention that requires that cases be decided in a way that provides the greatest degree of logical coherence with the settled rules and decisions. Suppose that in most cases a decision relying on a particular principle fits better with the settled materials than one relying on a competing principle. The supposition is not inconsistent with the patchwork thesis, but if it is true, then it would be wrong to claim, as Dalton does, that equally forceful legal arguments could be given for both sides in almost any case. The better legal argument would be the one that displays the better fit with the settled decisions and norms, and the law itself would be highly determinate, even if the patchwork thesis were true.

Given that our legal culture contains the convention demanding decisions whose grounds have maximum coherence with the settled law, in order for CLS to parlay the patchwork thesis into an argument for excessive legal indeterminacy, the following premise would have to be added: There is an unacceptably high percentage of cases in which (a) there are several different principles that underlie the relevant doctrinal materials, (b) the principles would lead to contrary decisions, and (c) a decision resting on one of the principles would fit the doctrinal materials as well as a contrary decision resting on another principle.

The premise goes well beyond the patchwork thesis. Part (c) could well be false, even if the patchwork thesis were true, and it is impossible to find in the CLS literature much more than assertions of the truth of (c), usually slipped in on the heels of the more plausible patchwork thesis. It should be conceded that if the patchwork thesis could be established, that would advance CLS

[18] Clare Dalton, "An Essay in the Deconstruction of Contract Doctrine," *Yale Law Journal* 94 (1985): 1007.

some distance toward its conclusion that our law is riddled with indeterminacy. However, I do not believe that the CLS literature has even given a convincing argument for the patchwork thesis. Let us examine its arguments on this matter in some detail.

Kennedy and Kelman: Rules v. Standards

Many CLS authors have tried to show that the conflict between individualism and altruism, as Kennedy defines them, is one of the principal ethical clashes that make legal doctrine an unprincipled patchwork. Kennedy is ambiguous on this. At times in "Form and Substance," he suggests that certain legal norms can be characterized as individualist and others as altruist, and that overall doctrine is an unprincipled patchwork quilt of the two sorts of norms. Thus, he suggests that those contract doctrines that allow judges to police the substantive fairness of an exchange are altruist, while those that restrain a judge from doing so are individualist.[19]

But in other places, Kennedy paints a quite different picture of the law. He suggests that virtually any of our legal doctrines is compatible with either individualism or altruism.[20] The point he stresses about the relation of these conflicting ethical viewpoints to legal doctrine is, rather, that the doctrines that individualism regards as central to the law are ones that altruism regards as peripheral exceptions, and vice versa. In this picture, the law can be organized according to two radically incompatible ethical positions. The incompatibility between the positions does not manifest itself in the inconsistency of certain doctrines with one or another of the incompatible ethical positions. Rather, it manifests itself in conflicting modes of conceptually organizing the mass of legal rules and standards.

If this picture of the law is accurate, it would be more appropriate to speak of doctrine as a kind of Wittgensteinian duck-rabbit than as a patchwork quilt.[21] In any event, the patchwork thesis is not consistent with the claim that the mass of legal rules and standards can be organized according to individualist or altruist principles, simply because the latter claim presupposes that both in-

[19] Kennedy, "Form and Substance," pp. 1732–33.

[20] Ibid., pp. 1737, 1762.

[21] Ludwig Wittgenstein, *Philosophical Investigations*, 3d ed., trans. G.E.M. Anscombe (New York: Macmillan, 1958), p. 194. Kennedy employs another metaphor with the same import: The law is like a glass of water that can be seen as half full or half empty. See "Form and Substance," p. 1762.

dividualism and altruism are compatible with virtually all of the doctrinal norms.

It can be reasonably argued that the duck-rabbit interpretation of "Form and Substance" is the better one, but I will delay an examination of the duck-rabbit thesis until later in this chapter. In this section I focus on the patchwork thesis and its implication that legal doctrine is unprincipled. "Form and Substance" has often been interpreted within the CLS literature as defending the patchwork thesis, and in later writings, Kennedy appears to embrace the thesis explicitly (though in still other places he appears committed to its denial).[22] On the basis of such an interpretation, some critical theorists have extended Kennedy's argument by trying to show that there is a patchwork of individualist and altruist norms in tort doctrine and in other areas of private law left largely unexplored in "Form and Substance." (I examine one such effort, by Allan Hutchinson, shortly.) Moreover, the patchwork thesis has been defended by critical theorists who have seen clashes other than that between altruism and individualism at work in making the law an unprincipled patchwork. For example, Kelman postulates a clash between a hard determinist and a libertarian conception of human agency in the criminal law that renders its doctrine an unprincipled patchwork in just the way Kennedy can be interpreted as portraying private law doctrine.[23]

Kennedy does not provide any explicit and sustained argument for the patchwork thesis in "Form and Substance." Yet some may think that the following argument can easily be spun out of what Kennedy does explicitly claim. Legal doctrine is a mix of rules and standards. What is the best explanation for this? The presence of rules is due to the influence of individualism in our culture; the presence of standards is due to the influence of altruism. Thus, the character of doctrine is the outcome of the clash of incompatible ethical viewpoints, and so doctrine itself must be a patchwork of norms unamenable to rational reconstruction in terms of a consistent set of principles.

This argument is easily defeated. It conflates the patchwork the-

[22] Kennedy speaks explicitly of contract doctrine as a patchwork in "The Political Significance of the Structure of the Law School Curriculum," *Seton Hall Law Review* 14 (1983): 15. But in other works, he writes of the principles that underlie doctrine as being so abstract as to be consistent with virtually any of the doctrinal norms. See "Distributive and Paternalist Motives in Contract and Tort Law, with Special Reference to Compulsory Terms and Unequal Bargaining Power," *Maryland Law Review* 41 (1982): 577, 580–82.

[23] Kelman, *A Guide to Critical Legal Studies*, chap. 3.

sis with the empirical thesis that the character (or content) of doctrine is the result of a sociocultural clash of incompatible ethical views.

The patchwork thesis is, rather, a logical one about the possibility of rationally reconstructing doctrine to exhibit it as conceptually derivable from a single coherent ethical view. The thesis is that such a reconstruction is not possible because any reconstruction of private law will inevitably encounter the problem that one ethical view is needed to derive certain important aspects of doctrine, but an incompatible view is required to derive other important aspects. Even if the empirical thesis that the character and contents of doctrine are the product of a clash of incompatible ethical views is true, the patchwork thesis does not follow. (Later, I explore in more detail the non sequitur involved when one infers the truth of the patchwork thesis from the empirical claim that our doctrine has been influenced by incompatible ethical viewpoints.)

Our examination in the previous section of the connection between form and substance also defeats any effort to infer the truth of the patchwork thesis from the presence of both rules and standards in our legal doctrine. If the embrace of altruism, and only such an embrace, necessarily entailed a commitment to standards and the embrace of individualism, and only such an embrace, likewise entailed a commitment to rules, then one could argue that our system's mix of rules and standards makes rational reconstruction of doctrine impossible for exactly the reasons invoked by the patchwork thesis. But we saw that individualism provides only defeasible reasons to prefer rules and that the link between altruism and standards is equally modest. Given these relatively modest logical links between form and substance, the argument for the patchwork thesis based on the fact that doctrine contains both rules and standards collapses. A pure individualist could well include many standards in his legal doctrine, just as a pure altruist could include many rules in hers.

Kelman insists upon describing the relation of rules and standards as one of "contradiction," even though he explicitly denies any logical connection between legal form and the ethical substance of individualism and altruism. What does this description amount to? I take it that its intent is to convey the point that there is too much variation in form from legal norm to legal norm for any consistent set of background principles to account for legal form in our system of law. The principle of fair notice, for example, might account for the more rulelike norms but cannot account for the many vague and open-ended standards found in our law.

Let us grant that any adequate rational reconstruction of the doctrinal division of labor between rules and standards would have to introduce more than one normative principle. No single principle, such as that of fair notice, could consistently account for the range of variation in legal form found in our system of law. However, it would be a mistake to describe the situation as one of contradiction, unless one could also argue cogently for the premise that the different principles needed to provide a rational reconstruction are logically incompatible with one another. Kelman must establish the premise that the acceptance of one such principle logically requires the rejection of the others, but he has no argument at all for this crucial premise. In fact, he has no sustained discussion of the different principles that might be needed to provide a rational reconstruction of how our legal system deals with the problem of form. There is nothing in Kelman's work, or in that of other CLS authors, that provides any good reason for thinking that the patchwork thesis can be vindicated by examining legal form.

Hutchinson v. Dworkin: Tort Doctrine

Some CLS theorists have sought to vindicate the patchwork thesis by looking to legal content rather than legal form. The idea has been to see the content of different legal norms in terms of the clash between individualism and altruism. Allan Hutchinson has taken this line.[24] Let us examine his argument.

One of the issues addressed by the law of torts concerns the extent of the harm for which a person is liable when he has acted negligently. Hutchinson tells us that the dominant principle in current tort law is that people are liable only for the reasonably foreseeable harm that they cause when acting without due care. But he points out that there is also a counterprinciple that holds people liable for the direct consequences of their negligent conduct, whether or not such consequences were reasonably foreseeable. (Hutchinson is presumably referring to Canadian law; in the United States, the situation is the reverse: the direct-consequences principle is the rule, and reasonable foreseeability is the excep-

[24] Allan Hutchinson, "Of Kings and Dirty Rascals: The Struggle for Democracy," *Queens Law Journal* (1985): 273–92.

tion.) The counterprinciple stems from the fact that strict adherence to the principle of reasonable foreseeability "might deprive entirely innocent and worthy victims of compensation."[25] Hutchinson proceeds:

> Each principle derives from and is empowered by two entirely different visions of a just democratic order. One rests on an individualism which represents a world consisting of independent and self-sufficient individuals, confidently drawing up and robustly pursuing their own life plans. . . . The legal regime is committed to protecting private property, enforcing bargains and creating autonomous spheres of activity. The other vision flows from a collectivism that views the world as made up of interdependent and cooperating persons. Recognizing the vulnerability of individuals, it encourages greater solidarity and altruism.[26]

The evocation of Kennedy's models of individualism and altruism is deliberate: Hutchinson explicitly cites "Form and Substance" in a footnote to this section of his paper. Hutchinson appears to suggest that the principle and counterprinciple are logically incompatible: If one is accepted, logical consistency demands that the other be rejected. The principle of reasonable foreseeability is embodied in one patch of the settled law, albeit a relatively large one; the counterprinciple of direct consequences is embodied in another, clashing patch of the settled law, albeit a somewhat smaller one. Overall, legal doctrine is contradictory.

In defending liberal legal philosophy, Ronald Dworkin has responded to Hutchinson's claims by making two basic points.[27] First, any morally decent legal system will contain both doctrines for limiting the scope of liability of negligent people—otherwise, people could be held liable for huge damages as a result of a freak causal chain that magnifies a minor instance of negligence into extensive losses for the plaintiff—and doctrines for enabling innocent people in certain cases to recover for damages when the harm negligently done to them could not be foreseen—otherwise, such innocents would always be unfairly required to bear the costs of the unforeseeable consequences of another's negligence. Second, Hutchinson has not established that the principle and counterprin-

[25] Ibid., p. 281.

[26] Ibid., p. 282.

[27] Ronald Dworkin, *Law's Empire* (Cambridge: Harvard University Press, 1986), pp. 441–44.

ciple he cites are in fact logically incompatible. If the two principles were applied to all of the same cases, then one would surely have inconsistent results. Because of that, Dworkin suggests that the principles might be said to be in "competition" with each other. But he argues that Hutchinson has failed to show that they are contradictory or incompatible—that if one is accepted, consistency demands that the other be rejected.

Dworkin's first point does not get to the heart of the issue. Hutchinson, Kennedy, and everyone else associated with CLS would be more than willing to grant the point that any morally decent legal system will have to do just what Dworkin says. The lesson they draw from the point is exactly the opposite of Dworkin's—that any decent legal system will invariably embody contradictory principles from incompatible moral visions. Indeed, one of the prominent themes of "Form and Substance" is that few if any of us would regard it as morally decent to be either a pure individualist or a pure altruist. As Kennedy puts it, we are divided within ourselves when it comes to individualism and altruism.[28] There is no reason to think that Hutchinson, or any other major CLS figure, would dissent from Kennedy on that score.

Dworkin's second point comes closer to the heart of the issue. It is true, as Dworkin charges, that Hutchinson does not show that the legal principle and counterprinciple in question are contradictory. That Hutchinson does regard the two as contradictory is made plain in another piece of his, where he writes that "doctrine contains . . . its own contradictory self-image."[29] Yet the only argument that can be reconstructed from his articles for the claim of contradiction is unconvincing. The core of the argument is the idea that principle and counterprinciple are logically incompatible because they are derived from logically incompatible moral and political visions. Let us assume for the moment that individualism and altruism are logically incompatible and therefore, as Kennedy asserts and Hutchinson assumes, that there is no higher-order normative viewpoint from which they can be reconciled. The key question then hinges on the precise relationship between those two conflicting ethical viewpoints and the two legal principles in question.

Hutchinson says that each of the legal principles "derives from

[28] Kennedy, "Form and Substance," pp. 1685, 1776.

[29] Allan Hutchinson, "Part of an Essay on Power and Interpretation," *New York University Law Review* 60 (1985): 871.

and is empowered by" the associated ethical viewpoint.[30] But what exactly does that mean? The best interpretation I can come up with is this: The foreseeability principle can be plausibly defended only on the basis of the individualist morality, while the direct-consequences principle can be plausibly defended only on the basis of the altruist morality. But such a contention lacks conviction. There are no grounds for believing that restricting liability as the foreseeability principle does can be plausibly defended only on the basis of an ethical view that, for example, restricts the law to the protection of private property, the enforcement of bargains, and the other functions of the minimal state. It is perfectly consistent to reject such a minimalist role for the state, yet to defend the foreseeability principle on the ground that when an instance of minor negligence produces extensive losses for the plaintiff due to some freak causal chain, it is typically unfair to hold the defendant liable for the full extent of the plaintiff's losses. Of course, one could argue as well that it is equally unfair to require the plaintiff to absorb the vast bulk of the losses, but even if that argument were granted, rejection of the foreseeability principle would not follow. The conclusion one might well draw is that while the foreseeability principle should govern negligence cases, there should also be some special social fund from which those injured in the freak-causal-chain cases could draw by applying to a state administrative agency. Such a view would combine the foreseeability principle with an altruist principle of sharing. Dworkin is, then, correct in claiming that Hutchinson fails to give us good reasons to believe that the legal principle and counterprinciple in question are contradictory or logically incompatible.

The Flaw in the CLS Argument

Hutchinson's work accepts the patchwork thesis but does not provide any cogent argument in its favor. Yet there are many other pieces in the CLS literature that endorse and/or rely on the patchwork thesis. Is there, somewhere in the literature, a good argument for the thesis? I think not. Virtually all of the arguments adopt the basic strategy used by Hutchinson: (1) to specify a principle and a counterprinciple in some area of doctrine, (2) to formulate (or invoke) two models of ethical thinking that are presumed to be logically incompatible, (3) to claim that there is a link

[30] Hutchinson, "Of Kings and Dirty Rascals," 282.

between the principle and one model and the counterprinciple and the other model, and (4) to conclude that the principles must be contradictory, since they are associated with incompatible ethical viewpoints, and that doctrine must therefore be unamenable to rational reconstruction in terms of any consistent set of principles.

There are several ways to attack this sort of argumentative strategy. One is to claim that the ethical models that are relied on are distortions of the views that are actually held; they are the positions of straw men. Dworkin makes such a claim in the course of arguing against Hutchinson.

The deeper problem with the strategy, however, concerns steps (3) and (4), the claim of a link between the legal principles and the ethical models and the inference of a contradictory relationship between the principles. The strategy will not work unless one can show that for each pair of principle and counterprinciple, one member of the pair can be defended only on the basis of one model and the other only on the basis of the other model. If a given principle or counterprinciple (or both) could be defended on either model or on the basis of some third model, the argumentative strategy would fall apart; it would then be possible to argue that doctrine derived from the consistent application of a single ethical model and to accept consistently both principle and counterprinciple.

The crucial problem with the argumentative strategy for the patchwork thesis is that legal principles and counterprinciples can be defended on either of the contrasting models developed by CLS theorists. This point is in fact conceded by Kennedy with respect to his models of individualism and altruism. In "Form and Substance" and later pieces, he says that the principles that constitute these opposing ethical viewpoints are sufficiently abstract so that with appropriate auxiliary assumptions, one could derive from individualism any of the doctrinal norms that appear to be direct expressions of altruism, and vice versa.[31] Thus, the doctrines of fraud and unconscionability can be construed as conforming to the altruist demand that those who are cunning should not be allowed to take advantage of the uninformed, but it can also be construed as conforming to the individualist demand that bargains be enforced only when they are voluntary. Kennedy also insists that the concept of voluntariness (individual free will, etc.) is sufficiently

[31] See Kennedy, "Form and Substance," pp. 1737, 1762, 1766, and "Distributive and Paternalist Motives," pp. 577, 580–82.

abstract that, given suitable auxiliary assumptions, any of the contract principles that require altruist sharing (e.g., the sharing of information) can be seen as marginal but coherent elements of an individualist order that demands self-reliance.

Kennedy's points here destroy the CLS argument for the patchwork thesis. If the ethical models that he and other theorists employ are sufficiently open that it is possible to derive from each of them the legal principles and counterprinciples found in doctrine, then the argument that those principles and counterprinciples are logically incompatible fails. And if it cannot be shown that they are incompatible, then the argument for the patchwork thesis fails as well.

Empirical and Logical Connections

There can be little doubt that incompatible ethical viewpoints in our culture do influence the content of legal doctrine. In a pluralist society such as ours, with a relatively open political process, it would not be reasonable to expect anything else. Moreover, it can be persuasively argued that there are logical links between the incompatible ethical views that make up our pluralist society and different aspects of legal doctrine. However, it is important to see that neither of these links, empirical or logical, establishes the truth of the patchwork thesis.

Consider the legal duty to aid a person to whom one owes no contractual or statutory obligation. The traditional common law rule is that there is no legal duty to aid such a person (a "stranger"). But there are a series of rules that qualify and carve out exceptions to the traditional rule. Thus, there is a rule that if the actions of the defendant helped to create the dangerous situation in which the plaintiff found himself, the defendant may have had a duty to render aid.[32] There is a rule that if the plaintiff and the defendant stand in some "special relationship," there may be a duty to render aid, even if there is no statute or valid contract between the two requiring the aid.[33]

There are significant logical links between the common law rule, its various qualifications and exceptions, and the ethical models of individualism and altruism. The altruist model provides reason to favor an expansive reading of the qualifications and exceptions—

[32] See *Montgomery v. National Convoy & Trucking Co.*, 195 S.E. 247 (1937).

[33] See *Tarasoff v. Regents of University of California*, 551 P.2d 334 (1976).

for example, a broader interpretation of what counts as a special relationship or what counts as action creating a dangerous situation. Individualism tilts in the opposite direction; it provides reasons for giving an expansive reading to the common law rule and very restrictive readings to the exceptions and qualifications. There are no grounds for holding that the exceptions to the common law rule are logically inconsistent with individualism, but individualism would give one reason to restrict the scope of their influence, lest they unacceptably undercut individualist self-reliance.

In addition, it is eminently plausible to argue that the presence in our law of both the common law rule and its exceptions is due to the cultural influence of individualist and altruist thinking. A purely individualist culture might include our exceptions to the common law rule, but it also might not. And even if it did, the exceptions probably would not play as significant a role in the system. Moreover, the best explanation for why our legal culture has such exceptions is the influence of the idea that people have duties to strangers that go beyond refraining from violating the rules of peaceful coexistence among self-interested and self-reliant selves.

The claim of both logical and empirical links between legal doctrine and incompatible ethical viewpoints, then, is a persuasive one for at least some elements of the law. However, the links that have been examined provide no grounds on which to assert the patchwork thesis. With regard to the empirical link, the fact that our legal system includes both rule R and exception E because of the influence of contrasting ethical models X and Y, respectively, does not show that the inclusion of R and E make the patchwork thesis true. Ethical model X may yet give some reason to include E—though perhaps not as strong a reason as Y gives—and the contingent fact that it was the acceptance of Y rather than X that was the cause of the inclusion in doctrine of E fails to give good reason to say that its inclusion renders doctrine unprincipled in the manner claimed by the patchwork thesis. With respect to the logical link, the fact that rules and exceptions will receive a more or less expansive interpretation, depending upon which of two incompatible ethical models one adopts, does not show that certain doctrinal norms are themselves inconsistent with the principles required to provide a reconstruction of other doctrinal norms.

The CLS effort to establish the patchwork thesis by arguing for various links between legal doctrine and incompatible ethical models fails. The kind of strong logical link that would be needed for the argument to work does not exist, as Dworkin claims in his criticism of Hutchinson. And the kind of empirical link that can be cogently argued for provides no grounds for accepting the thesis. However, a distinct CLS thesis regarding the connection of doctrine to incompatible ethical viewpoints, the duck-rabbit thesis, is not defeated by the arguments which have been given against the patchwork thesis.

The Duck-Rabbit Thesis

In a number of passages by Kennedy and Unger, they suggest that there would be a radical shift in our legal culture's understanding of the structure of private law if the culture reversed its ethical polarities from the dominance of individualism to the dominance of altruism.[34] As they see it, doctrine is interpreted and applied in a way that is largely a function of which norms are taken to be part of the core of doctrine and which norms are taken to be part of the periphery. And this structuring of doctrine in terms of core and periphery is tied logically and empirically to what is regarded as an underlying dominance of individualism in our legal and political culture. In this view, the difference between individualism and altruism reveals itself in the law, not in the incompatibility of particular doctrinal norms with one or the other of these two ethical viewpoints but in how those norms are structured in terms of their relative centrality to the department of law in question. In short, the battle between individualism and altruism is one over the structure of doctrine, not over its contents.

Individualism entails a certain way of structuring the doctrinal norms; altruism entails the inverse structuring of those same norms. Thus, law is viewed not as a patchwork of conflicting norms derived from incompatible ethical viewpoints but as analogous to the duck-rabbit figure which, without any alteration in the lines that compose it, can change its overall appearance, depending on how one perceives it. The duck-rabbit metaphor can be misleading, at least with regard to the way Unger understands the thesis, but it does provide a vivid way of distinguishing this claim from the patchwork thesis criticized in the previous section.

Kennedy and Unger suggest that the structure that most legal professionals see in private law stems from an ethical view domi-

[34] Unger provides somewhat different versions of the individualist and altruist models than does Kennedy, but those differences are not important at this stage.

nated by individualism. In this regard, Kennedy claims, "Individualism is the structure of the status quo."[35] But both he and Unger see the opportunity for flipping the structure inside out. Unger's "deviationist doctrine" involves the practice of moving peripheral doctrines toward the center and core doctrines toward the periphery. This is possible without making dramatic changes in the specific rules that constitute private law doctrine. What needs to be changed is not the rules themselves but the position within the overall structure of doctrine that the existing rules are regarded as holding.

Unger and Kennedy do appear to disagree on one crucial point. In several important passages, Kennedy seems to suggest that doctrine has no structure independent of an individual's view of it: Doctrinal structure is in the eyes of the beholder. Thus, he criticizes the view that doctrine is structured in terms of a fixed core of rules and a periphery of limited exceptions by claiming, "What distinguishes the modern situation is the breakdown of the conceptual boundary between the core and the periphery. . . . There is no core. Every occasion for lawmaking will raise the fundamental conflict of individualism and altruism."[36] Referring to our private law, he adds:

> Certainly it falls far short of imposing the altruist's vision of social duties of sharing and sacrifice. Yet it is possible to argue that *all* of its doctrines point in that direction. . . . The trouble is that the glass may be half empty rather than half full. It is just as plausible to see the common law, as we have inherited it, as the manifesto of individualism against feudal and mercantilist attempts to create an organic relationship between state and society. There is nothing left [of doctrinal structure] but a field of forces. In order to decide cases, the judge will have to align herself one way or the other. But there can be no justification for her choice—other than a circular statement of commitment to one or the other of the conflicting visions.[37]

There are many ideas embedded in the above passage, but its focal point is the notion of a collapse of any objective doctrinal

[35] Kennedy, "Form and Substance," p. 1775.

[36] Kennedy, "Form and Substance," pp. 1737, 1766. The context in which these words appear shows that when Kennedy writes of "lawmaking," he has in mind caselawmaking by judges who are deciding civil cases.

[37] Ibid., p. 1762.

structure.[38] To the extent that one adopts individualism, doctrine takes on one structure; to the extent that one adopts altruism, it takes on another. But there is no structure to doctrine independent of the particular ethical position of a given individual. The structure exists only relative to the person and his choice of ethical viewpoints, though most legal professionals accept a view dominated by individualism, leading to the illusory appearance of an objective structure.

Unger suggests, to the contrary, that doctrine does have an objective structure. The dominance of individualism is part of existing doctrine, not simply the way most legal professionals have chosen to look at doctrine. To this extent, the duck-rabbit metaphor is more appropriate for Kennedy's interpretation of the structure of doctrine than Unger's. The duck-rabbit figure is not in itself a picture of a duck or a rabbit; its status as one or the other is merely relative to the way a given individual is looking at it, at a particular moment. Similarly for Kennedy, doctrinal structure is not in itself one way or another; it is merely relative to the set of ethical lenses through which a given individual happens to look at doctrine.

This difference between Unger and Kennedy implicates the deepest issues that divide the CLS camp. It stems ultimately from conflicting conceptions of social reality. Those conceptions have crucial implications for the possibility of the rule of law and the extent to which a radical departure from liberal legal and political philosophy is needed. A full-scale examination of these conflicting conceptions must await the next chapter. For now, let us explore in more detail the different versions of the duck-rabbit thesis defended by Unger and Kennedy.

Unger v. Fried: Contract Doctrine

In his analysis of contract law, Unger attempts to show that the structure of doctrine should and would be radically modified by replacing the dominant ethical view that he claims underlies it with an incompatible view.[39] He contends that existing contract

[38] It should be noted that there are passages in other pieces by Kennedy in which he seems to take precisely the opposite position, viz., that legal doctrine does have an objective structure. Thus, he describes the structures of legal thought as having "a life of their own." See "The Structure of Blackstone's Commentaries," *Buffalo Law Review* 28 (1979): 215–16.

[39] Roberto Unger, *The Critical Legal Studies Movement* (Cambridge: Harvard University Press, 1986), pp. 58–90.

doctrine is structured in terms of two dominant principles and two peripheral counterprinciples. The dominant principles are (1) that individuals are legally free to choose with whom to enter into a binding contract and (2) that the individuals who enter into a contract are legally free to specify its terms. The counterprinciples are (1) that "freedom to choose the contract partner will not be allowed to work in ways that subvert the communal aspects of social life"[40] and (2) that there are substantive principles of fairness which will legally nullify certain contractual terms.

The first counterprinciple is formulated in such vague terms that it is not especially informative, but it can be read as an effort to capture the common rationale behind three more definite, subsidiary counterprinciples: There are duties between individuals that arise out of their dealings with one another, even when those dealings do not involve any completed bargain; there are duties between individuals arising out of their completed bargains that go beyond the terms explicitly agreed to as part of their bargains; and there are social ties between individuals, such as family ties, that should be legally protected from subversion by the efforts of individuals to enter into binding contracts. Unger's idea seems to be that the common justification for these three subsidiary counterprinciples is that they serve to protect ties of social solidarity that help to hold the social order together.

What is the relationship of the principles to the counterprinciples? There are two views of the matter, says Unger, a dominant view and deviationist one. In the dominant view, "the counterprinciples are anomalies. They prevent the principles from doing injustice in unusual if not extreme cases."[41] In other words, the principles represent the operational and conceptual core of doctrine; they play the central role in the operation of our law, and there is a strong presumption that they are the principles to be applied in any given case. The counterprinciples represent the conceptual and operational periphery; they can come into play in exceptional instances, but there is a presumption against their applicability, and they have a relatively marginal role in the operation of the law. Moreover, the dominant position does not consist of merely the descriptive claim that in the structure of current contract law, the principles are central and the counterprinciples are peripheral. Rather, the heart of the position is the ethical claim that

[40] Ibid., p. 61.
[41] Ibid., p. 74.

the structure should be this way because it reflects the structure of sound moral thinking. (The grounds for this ethical claim are examined later.)

There is, however, an alternative conception of the relationship of principles to counterprinciples. Unger writes, "Although the counterprinciples may be seen as mere restraints upon the principles, they may also serve as points of departure for a different organizing conception of this whole area of law."[42] In this alternative deviationist view, the counterprinciples "serve as the points of departure for a system of law and doctrine that reverses the traditional relationship and reduces the principles to a specialized role."[43] This is not to say that the reversal can be produced overnight. In Unger's view, there is simply not enough to work with in the doctrinal materials to argue cogently for such an immediate reversal within our existing standards of doctrinal argumentation. However, there is enough to work with to start moving in the direction of reversal.

The eventual goal of the deviationist view is to alter the structure of contract doctrine, so that the counterprinciples are central and the principles are special peripheral cases. At the heart of the deviationist position is the ethical claim that the structure of doctrine should be so reversed because only then would it reflect the structure of sound moral thinking. The grounds for this ethical claim will be examined momentarily.

There are, then, incompatible ethical viewpoints underlying the dominant and deviationist positions. The basic differences stem from conflicting normative conceptions of social life. Underlying the dominant view, says Unger, is a conception that sharply divides (the relevant portions of) social life into two arenas, with starkly different principles governing each. First, there is the sphere of family and friends, which ought to be governed by considerations of altruism, solidarity, and forgiveness. Second, there is the sphere of economic activity and exchange, which ought to be governed by a principle of self-interest that licenses the individual to pursue his own interests without giving any intrinsic weight to the interests of those with whom he or she has dealings. The central position of the two principles of contract law guarantees that outside the family, individuals will be largely free to pursue their own interests without the constraint of giving intrinsic

[42] Ibid., p. 59.
[43] Ibid., p. 75.

weight to the interests of others. This is how it should be in the view of the position that underlies the dominant mode of organizing contract law; that, at any rate, is Unger's reconstruction of the position.

Underlying the deviationist view, says Unger, is a conception that repudiates the sharp contrast between spheres of social life that is drawn by the dominant view. Rather than a sharp division between different spheres operating on starkly different principles, the deviationist view envisions a continuum of social relationships, from those that would allow the participants to be largely (though not entirely) self-interested to those that would require a considerable degree of sharing (though not saintly sacrifice). Some business dealings would fall at the former extreme, but by no means all.

Essential to the deviationist view is the idea that duties arise between people as a result of their particular relationships, interactions, and dependencies. The specific duties arising from completed bargains or the general duties imposed by the state on its citizens are merely special cases. In one case, the duties arise from the quite specific relationship worked out by contract partners; in the other, from one's status as a member of a political community that has decided to impose certain obligations upon its members or a certain class of them. But between those two cases is a large spectrum of relationships and associated duties. By working to move the counterprinciples toward the center of doctrine, the deviationist program regards itself as making our legal duties a more faithful reflection of our moral duties.

Charles Fried has rejected Unger's account of contract law. He believes that Unger identifies liberalism with the ethical position that underlies the dominant view of the structure of contract law, and he regards Unger's portrait of that position as a severely distorted picture of liberalism. While Unger insists that the dominant conception of contract law rests on a vivid contrast between the sphere of family and the sphere of economic dealing, Fried responds that the "contrast is false through and through."[44] He means not only that the contrast is ethically indefensible but also that there is no commitment to such a contrast in liberal moral or legal thinking. While the family may be based on a principle of sharing, liberalism holds that the sharing must be voluntary, for,

[44] Charles Fried, *Contract as Promise* (Cambridge: Harvard University Press, 1981), p. 90.

Fried tells us, coerced sharing is tyranny within the family as much as within the political community at large. Individual freedom is essential in family relationships as well as in economic dealings, and the liberalism that underlies the dominant conception of contract law can and does easily incorporate this idea.

On the other side, Fried continues, there is no liberal principle that prohibits contract partners from sharing the benefits and burdens that ensue from their dealings in ways that are not required by the terms of the contract. "Nothing in the liberal concept of contract, nothing in the liberal concept of humanity and law makes such altruism improbable or meaningless."[45] Indeed, the moral goodness of sharing and sacrifice can and should be affirmed. The liberal view is only that, exceptional cases aside, the law should not demand such sharing and sacrifice of contract partners.

Part of Fried's response is off the mark. It is irrelevant that liberalism is not committed to the prohibition of sharing and sacrifice by contract partners in ways that are not called for by their contract. The relevant point that Unger is making is that, exceptional cases aside, the moral view underlying the existing structure of contract law is committed to denying that there are any moral duties between such parties, except for those requirements set forth in the contract and the duties the state imposes on them through statutory law.

More to the point is Fried's claim that liberal legal theory concerns the duties that the state should enforce, not all moral duties whatsoever. It is perfectly consistent to assert that there is a certain moral duty but that the state should not enforce it. Such a claim is, indeed, part of the very lifeblood of liberal political and legal philosophy. Unger's account of contract doctrine does slight the distinction between asserting the existence of a moral duty and asserting that there should be a legal duty, and Fried is surely right to bring that to our attention. Unger has also overstated the contrast drawn by the dominant view between the normative principles that govern the family and those that govern business and commercial relationships. But to focus on these criticisms misses three essential points that Unger is making, points to which Fried has no counterargument and with which he may well agree.

The essential points concern the connection between the structure of contract doctrine and the scope of a person's moral and

[45] Ibid., p. 91.

political duty to share the benefits and burdens of life with his or her fellow citizens. (By *political duty*, I mean a moral duty that should be legally enforced.) The first of Unger's essential points is that the relationship between principle and counterprinciple in contract law that is most defensible from the perspective of political morality is a function of the scope of a person's political duty to share; the wider the scope of such a duty, the stronger the reason for the counterprinciples to be shifted more toward the center of doctrine. Unger's second main point is that standards of doctrinal argument are sufficiently flexible, and legal cases sufficiently ambiguous, for lawyers and judges who have a relatively expansive view of our political duty of sharing to shift the structure of doctrine toward greater centrality for the counterprinciples. And his third main point is that deviationist doctrinal argument could eventually produce a structure for contract law that is an inversion of the present structure.

None of Fried's arguments against Unger touch these points, and I believe that Unger has made a good case for them. What Unger fails to make clear, though, is that the points are fully consistent with liberal legal philosophy. Liberalism requires that contract doctrine have some kind of discernible structure independent of a particular person's perception of it; that is, there be some objective and determinate relationship between principles and counterprinciples, but it does not entail that the structure must be identical or similar to the current one or that it must be a structure that is unyielding under the impact of doctrinal arguments of any kind.[46] The significant level of indeterminacy acknowledged in chapter 2 to be a part of our legal system allows sufficient play in the system for doctrinal argument to shift the structure of doctrine

[46] It is undoubtedly true that Fried would reject, on grounds of his version of liberal political morality, the effort to shift the structure of doctrine along the lines attempted by Unger's deviationist doctrine. But the issue on which I have focused is not whether it is a morally defensible idea to pursue deviationist doctrine but whether the assumptions about law that underlie the deviationist program are consistent with liberal legal theory. Shifting the structure of doctrine in the way the deviationist position seeks would surely expand the scope of an individual's legal duty to others, but by itself, it would not be inconsistent with the liberal commitment to the rule of law. Fried's version of liberalism lies toward the individualist pole of Kennedy's individualist-altruist contrast, but there are other versions, such as Rawls's, that lie toward the altruist end. If altruism were taken to the extreme of denying any role to the principle of freedom to choose contract partners and terms, it would be difficult to see how that could be rendered consistent with any version of liberalism (cf. Fried, *Contract as Promise*, p. 77). But deviationist doctrine is not committed to such an extreme.

over time. Finally, liberal theory does not deny that one's view regarding how doctrine ought to be structured will be a function of one's beliefs about the scope and intensity of a person's moral and political duties to others. It does deny that all moral duties should automatically be legal duties, but that is not to cut all ties between moral and legal duty; it is only to see the connections in a more complicated light.

Kennedy: Antistructure

Kennedy seems to go further than Unger, to make claims about doctrinal structure that are starkly inconsistent with liberal legal philosophy. He asserts that every legal case and every piece of legal territory is disputed ground between the warring armies of individualism and altruism.[47] Unlike Unger, who believes that there is an objective and definite—though not wholly determinate—structure to contract law, Kennedy appears to regard the norms of contract doctrine as an unarticulated mass that assumes a structure only from the ethical perspective of the particular observer. The conflict of individualism and altruism over each spot of legal ground is a conflict over the position that ground is to hold in the overall structure of doctrine. But neither side can be "correct," in the sense of portraying the structure of doctrine as it really is. Doctrine really has no particular structure.

We are thus left with two interpretations of the duck-rabbit thesis: the more modest one defended by Unger and the more radical one proposed by Kennedy. The former is consistent with the requirements of liberal legal theory and so provides no special problem for my effort at defending liberal theory from CLS attack. But the duck-rabbit thesis under the latter interpretation is inconsistent with liberal theory. The rule of law can be only a fiction if the radical version of the thesis is true. Given the thesis, the law can determine decisions only if some structure is imposed on it from the outside, but different people with different ethical views will impose radically conflicting structures. The law as it is in itself lacks the articulated structure it needs to determine legal outcomes. But the law as structured by individualist principles will be very different from the law as structured by altruist ones.

Thus, the radical duck-rabbit thesis, like the radical indeterminacy position, rests on the crucial idea that there is no objective

[47] Kennedy, "Form and Substance," p. 1766.

structure to the law. But does law really lack any objective structure? Is it wrong to suggest, as Unger does, that certain principles are actually central to the structure of contract doctrine and that others are peripheral? Is legal structure only in the eyes of the beholder?

It is far from self-evident that the radical CLS answers to these questions are correct. Indeed, the typical experience that lawyers and judges have of the law, quite the opposite of these radical claims, is that law does have an objective structure and that one must know that structure in order to practice law competently. The experience is that the law does have an objective structure and that it takes time and a collective effort to change that structure. Of course, these experiences could be illusions, appearances that hide a different reality. But the defenders of the radical CLS view need to provide some ontology of law in order to sustain their highly controversial claims regarding legal structure. Some CLS thinkers have sketched such an ontology, and in the next chapter, I will examine and criticize it.

The Truncation Thesis

The third and final thesis connected with the claim that doctrine is riddled with contradiction is the truncation thesis. It holds that the ethical principles underlying legal rules and doctrines are not consistently carried through to cover the full range of cases over which, in the eyes of their proponents, they exercise moral authority. In this sense, legal rules and doctrines represent truncated expressions of the ethical principles which underlie them.

As we will see shortly, the truncation thesis is virtually a corollary of the patchwork thesis. But the truth of the latter is by no means a necessary condition for the truth of the former. Moreover, unlike the patchwork thesis, the truncation thesis is fully consistent with the duck-rabbit thesis, at least under Unger's more moderate interpretation.

The key problem with the patchwork thesis was its insistence on the idea that different rules and doctrines could only come from (i.e., be defended on the grounds of) incompatible ethical positions. But the case for this idea could not be made. And the argument for the duck-rabbit thesis explicitly jettisoned the idea in favor of the notion that virtually all the rules of legal doctrine could be derived from each of the incompatible ethical viewpoints sketched by Kennedy and other CLS theorists. The contrast between these incompatible ethical views would not manifest itself in the particular rules and doctrines included in the law but in the relationships that the rules and doctrines would have to each other within the body of law. What individualism would regard as central altruism would regard as peripheral, and vice versa.

Since individualism tends to dominate our liberal legal and political culture according to CLS, the structure of doctrine tends toward what it would be in a purely individualist culture. But since altruism has not been (and perhaps never will be) entirely vanquished, certain "altruist" doctrines play a more significant role in the law than would be the case in a system of pure individualism. These doctrines can be regarded as "altruist," but not in the sense that they are logically incompatible with individualist principles—that is the mistake behind the patchwork thesis. Rather, they are altruist in the sense that, while individualism would regard them as peripheral exceptions, an altruist system of ethical thinking regards them as central.

The truncation thesis is consistent with the argument I have given against the patchwork thesis. Legal rules might be truncated manifestations of underlying ethical principles for a variety of reasons. If the patchwork thesis were true, one would expect legal rules to be truncated, because each of the clashing ethical viewpoints would prevent the principles of the contrasting viewpoint from being carried through to their morally authoritative conclusions. But rules might be truncated when an ethical principle clashes not only with an incompatible principle but also with the forces of factional interest or self-interest. Moreover, rules may be truncated by clashing ethical ideas about which principle should be regarded as part of the (moral and legal) core and which part of the periphery. In short, the truncation thesis may be true, even if the patchwork thesis is false.

Unger: Truncation and Equal Protection

There are two complementary kinds of arguments in the CLS literature for the truncation thesis. One revolves around the general point that in our culture, the settled law is the transitory and contingent outcome of ideological and political struggles among social factions in which the positions of each contending force are compromised, truncated, vitiated, and adjusted. The other supplements and reinforces the first by focusing on specific rules and doctrines and trying to show that none of the ethical principles that can be plausibly thought of as underlying them is consistently carried through in the law so that it applies in all areas over which a proponent of the principle would claim that it has moral authority.

Unger uses both arguments; along the lines of the first, he claims:

> [I]t would be strange if the results of a coherent, richly developed normative theory were to coincide with a major portion of any extended branch of law. The many conflicts of interest and vision that lawmaking involves, fought out by countless minds and wills working at cross-purposes, would have to be the vehicle of an immanent moral rationality whose message could be articulated by a single cohesive theory. The dominant legal theories in fact undertake this daring and implausible sanctification of the actual.[48]

Several comments are in order on this important passage. First, it can be regarded as an argument for either or both the patchwork thesis and the truncation thesis. In fact, it seems to be commonly interpreted as an argument primarily for the patchwork thesis (and so derivatively for the truncation thesis). But since we have rejected the former thesis, let us construe it as an argument solely for the latter. Second, the argument clearly invokes the clash of ethical principle with the forces of factional interests and self-interest as a reason for truncation and not merely the clash of principle with competing principle. Third, the passage suggests that the truncation thesis is incompatible with liberal legal philosophy (the "dominant legal theories").

Let us examine the cogency of Unger's argument. On the surface, it appears to suffer from the same fatal flaw as the empirical argument for the patchwork thesis, rejected earlier, but this appearance is deceiving. It is true that Unger's current argument attempts to draw conclusions about the logical structure of doctrine from premises regarding its origin, as did the flawed argument for the patchwork thesis. But the latter argument came apart specifically because it needed to show, but could not, that there were doctrinal norms inherently inconsistent with one or another of the incompatible ethical views needed in a rational reconstruction of the various areas of doctrine. Thus, the possibility could not be ruled out that each of the views was consistent with virtually all

[48] Unger, *Critical Legal Studies*, p. 9.

the doctrinal norms and that where the views collided was on the question of the relative centrality the different norms should have within the body of the law. Our examination of the patchwork and duck-rabbit theses strongly suggested that such a possibility was in fact realized in our law.

On the other hand, Unger's argument for the truncation thesis does not need to show that any doctrinal norms are inherently inconsistent with the warring ethical viewpoints. It is fully compatible with the contention that ethical disputes are manifested in disagreements over the structure of doctrine rather than over which norms are, or should be, part of the law. The argument hinges on the inductive inference that, given an empirical situation where legal doctrine is the outcome of conflicts among incompatible ethical positions in which no one position can vanquish its competitors, it can be expected that many (though not necessarily all) of the ethical principles that underlie doctrinal rules will have their range of application truncated. Why can this be expected? Because principles regarded as central by one ethical viewpoint are likely to be confined in their scope of application by counterprinciples from an incompatible viewpoint.[49]

This is true even if the principles are accorded a place in the doctrinal core; they simply will not be as dominant as those who take them to be central think that they should be. (Consider the common law rule regarding duties to strangers and how it is somewhat confined in its scope by the special-relationship exceptions: the common law rule may be part of the core, but it is not as dominant as a hard-core individualist would prefer.) Of course, from the perspective of those who take the opposing ethical position, their counterprinciples will be even more severely truncated. While it is logically possible that there is some Hegelian alternative that provides a consistent set of principles that accounts for the doctrinal norms just to the extent to which the existing law takes them, it is difficult to see what the grounds for believing in such an alternative could be. I thus regard this argument of Unger's to be a cogent one. But it can be reinforced by turning to a specific example of truncation within the body of our law.

Unger provides an account of equal-protection doctrine that is

[49] Thus, the truncation thesis, like the patchwork thesis, asserts that the body of legal doctrine fails to be amenable to rational reconstruction. But the explanations that each thesis provides for this failure are not the same. The former, unlike the latter, does not claim that it is due to the fact that any set of principles from which certain doctrinal norms could be derived would be inconsistent with other doctrinal norms.

designed to highlight its truncated character.[50] He finds two distinct principles operating. The first mandates that laws must apply to sufficiently general classes of people to insure the difference between legislation and adjudication. This mandate is, in effect, a requirement of the rule of law, needed to prevent the legislature from turning itself into an organ for the administration of society. It is the *generality-requiring* principle.

Another principle prohibits the legislature from enacting laws that impose on social groups disadvantages that either prevent their members from having an equal voice in the democratic political process or that take unfair advantage of the less-than-equal voice that such groups have. This is the *generality-correcting* principle, and Unger finds it seriously truncated.

In equal-protection doctrine, the generality-correcting principle is put into effect, in part, through the concepts of suspect classification and strict and intermediate scrutiny. When a law allocates a burden on the basis of a highly suspect category (e.g., race), equal-protection doctrine imposes strict judicial scrutiny on the law. To pass constitutional muster, the law must be necessary for the accomplishment of some compelling government interest. Current constitutional doctrine is extremely suspicious that racial classifications will violate the principle that people should have an equal chance of being heard and counted in the democratic political process, so it imposes a heavy burden on such classifications. Gender classifications are handled differently. Current doctrine is somewhat suspicious that gender classifications involve the violation of basic democratic principles, but the suspicion is not as great as with racial classifications, so a less-than-strict form of judicial scrutiny ("intermediate scrutiny") is demanded. On the other hand, doctrine does not regard with any significant suspicion laws that explicitly or implicitly classify by economic terms such as income or wealth. Such laws need to meet only the most relaxed judicial standards, not much more rigorous than the generality-requiring principle.

Unger finds the law's way of handling equal protection seriously deficient. Of course, he does not question the proposition that the political process has often been unfairly biased against blacks and women. But, he asks,

> what about all of those legislative categories that, directly or indirectly, mention or reinforce entrenched positions in the social division of labor and systematic, discontinuous differ-

[50] Unger, *Critical Legal Studies*, pp. 44–56.

> entials of access to wealth, power, and culture? These inequalities can certainly not be said to be exceptional. Yet their existence and their tenacity in the face of political attack are matters of common observation. . . . To defend the thesis that racial and sexual advantages count most because they are in fact more severe than other forms of social division and hierarchy would involve the established doctrine in controversies that it could not easily win.[51]

The heart of Unger's critique is that equal-protection doctrine is guilty of an "arbitrarily selective focus upon some sorts of group inferiority (such as race and gender . . .) to the exclusion of others (such as class)."[52] And "the characteristically makeshift quality of conventional legal analysis . . . is a direct consequence of the troubled and stunted relation of doctrine to its own theoretical assumptions."[53] The generality-correcting principle can be stopped short of applying intermediate, or even strict, scrutiny to laws that have differential impact on economic classes only because the courts have chosen to develop doctrine on the basis of a fictionalized account of our social world. Unger's claim is that in any realistic picture of that world, consistency would require the principle to be extended much further.

Notice that although Unger's claim is made in the spirit of a leftist assault on the social status quo, it can be readily accepted by (some) conservatives as well.[54] The latter would see in the claim the reductio ad absurdum of the generality-correcting principle and the lesson that equal-protection doctrine should be limited to the generality-requiring principle. The critical legal scholar sees in the claim the law's stubborn refusal to challenge across-the-board illegitimate hierarchies of power and privilege. The important point is that one need not think that the truncated principle is a good one and should be extended to recognize the existence of the truncation.

[51] Ibid., p. 51.

[52] Ibid., p. 53.

[53] Ibid., p. 50.

[54] In the course of arguing against liberals who invoke the Constitution to combat sexual and racial discrimination but who are silent on matters of economic class, George Will writes with his typical mixture of sarcasm and seriousness: "Where is Karl Marx when we really need him? It is time for American reformers to learn to talk the language of class. Interesting, is it not, that the right to discriminate on the basis of class is the only right so inalienable that it is unquestioned, even unnoticed." See Will, " 'Civil Rights' for the Ruling Class," *Washington Post*, 23 June 1988, A-19.

Although one might quibble with the details of Unger's critique of equal-protection doctrine, it is impossible for me to deny its main point: The doctrine does truncate the principles that animate it. Moreover, similar kinds of truncation are a pervasive aspect of our legal doctrine. For instance, tort doctrine imposes a duty to aid, but it does so in a stunted form. Perhaps it should not impose such a duty, but even those who support such a view can acknowledge that the scope of the duty in the law does not extend as far as its authoritative scope within the moral domain.

Truncation, Liberal Legal Theory, and Dworkin

The final question concerning the truncation thesis is whether truncation is incompatible with liberal legal philosophy. Unger suggests that the answer is affirmative. I believe that he is wrong. Quite to the contrary, liberal theory would lead one to expect that the thesis would accurately describe the legal system of a state functioning in accordance with the demands of liberal legal and political philosophy.

A liberal state will contain incompatible conceptions of justice and goodness and political institutions that require the proponents of these incompatible conceptions to engage in compromise, bargaining, and negotiation if they are to exercise influence over the content of the law. In such a situation, it is difficult to see how one could avoid a legal system with rules that are the truncated expressions of ethical principles. This would be true even if factional and self-interest played no role in the political process—even if what existed were a pure politics of principle. Once a realistic dose of factional and self-interest is thrown into the mix, rather severe and widespread truncation is clearly unavoidable. Acknowledgment of the truth of the truncation thesis is thus perfectly consistent with the demands of liberal legal theory.

The consistency of liberalism with truncation is also a natural extension of its consistency with—indeed its insistence upon—the proposition that not all moral duties ought to be made into legal ones. If a position can consistently hold that the state should refrain completely from imposing certain moral duties, it is not easy to see why it cannot also consistently hold that the state should impose certain duties only in a truncated form.

In the early chapters of *Law's Empire,* Dworkin appears to be endorsing the all-or-nothing approach: Either refrain from imposing a moral duty at all, or impose it to its full scope. He argues that if a moral principle was imposed in truncated form, the state would be guilty of violating the important moral ideal of integrity. But if we look at *Law's Empire* more carefully, we find that Dworkin in fact rejects the idea that, if the state imposes a moral duty, it must do so without truncation. In the final analysis, his view seems to be that, although integrity is an important ethical ideal, it is not the only one and does not impose any absolute requirement on the liberal state. Accordingly, even in Dworkin's theory, truncation is permissible in the law of the liberal state. Moreover, in the last chapter of *Law's Empire,* he explicitly accepts the accuracy of the truncation thesis as applied to our legal doctrine and concedes that his reconstruction of the law of accidents construes it as relying on a certain egalitarian principle that our law seriously truncates.[55]

On the other hand, Dworkin goes astray when he suggests that our goal should be a system of law that is purified of truncations.[56] A crucial part of his rationale for such a suggestion is that to purify law of its truncations would be to realize integrity in its purest possible form. However, his argument fails to take account of the implications of the fact that our liberal society is one in which there is a robust pluralism of moral, religious, and political positions. In such a society, there will be vigorous disagreement, not only about the good but also the right and the just. And where there is such pluralism, it would be a mistake for any liberal to advocate a law that has no truncations. For the only plausible scenario on which a law without truncations could be established is if one of the groups in society was able to inscribe its normative conceptions into the law without having to engage in compromise and negotiation with groups holding incompatible moral and political views. The liberal devotion to the protection of pluralism requires that pure Dworkinite integrity be subordinated to the demand that government not fall under the sway of any single faction that can work its will, unhampered by the need to negotiate and compromise.

It is true that one can imagine a scenario in which political negotiation and compromise involved no truncations; each group would get some of its principles into the law in an untruncated form but only by means of compromises that would enable other groups to get some of their principles into the law in a like form.

[55] Dworkin, *Law's Empire,* p. 407.
[56] Ibid., pp. 406–08.

There would be no compromises that involved an agreement between a group and its competitors to endorse laws that embodied their competing principles but in a truncated form. Dworkin appears to have such a scenario in mind when he advocates a law purified of truncations.

The problem is that such a scenario could not be realized without seriously violating the liberal demand to respect the robust pluralism of moral and political views within liberal society. In a liberal pluralist society such as ours, there are quite conflicting assessments of the importance of integrity in the law, particularly its importance relative to the value of respecting the results of a democratic political process. Dworkin might so value integrity that he is willing to confine the democratic process so that it is unable to inscribe moral principles into the law in a truncated form. But many others would judge such constraints on the political process to be highly objectionable. While all liberals must agree to substantial constraints on the political process, many would object that the constraints required to purify law of any truncations would be going much too far. The basis for their objection can perhaps be seen more clearly when we realize what the likely institutional mechanism would be to enforce Dworkinite integrity: Courts would be authorized to declare all truncations unconstitutional. Given the powerful opposition that is likely to exist to any such judicial authority, pure Dworkinite integrity could be accomplished only by imposing it on the population in an antiliberal fashion. Of course, Dworkin can deploy his argumentative skills to advocate pure integrity in the law, but it would be an understatement to say that his chances of creating a consensus on the issue are miniscule. Perhaps he can move our political culture toward a greater appreciation of the value of integrity in law, but in the end, he will have to settle for something less than the full implementation of the principle that the law should be free of truncations. As a good liberal, he will have to accommodate his views to a process of political negotiation and compromise that will truncate that principle.

Truncation, then, is an essential phenomenon in a liberal system of law, and CLS has provided some important insights into the character of liberal legal doctrine by highlighting and analyzing the phenomenon. Dworkin and other legal liberals certainly should acknowledge the CLS contribution on that score. But critical theorists go seriously wrong when they take the existence of truncation to undermine the legal theory of their liberal antagonists.

Summary

In this chapter, we have discovered some significant truth to the CLS claim that liberal legal doctrine is filled with contradiction. Two of the theses associated with that claim—the moderate version of the duck-rabbit thesis and the truncation thesis—were found to be convincing and important. The theses revealed significant aspects of the relationships between legal doctrines and the ethical principles that underlie them. But neither of the theses proved incompatible with liberal legal philosophy. Moreover, those CLS claims regarding doctrinal contradiction that are incompatible with the liberal theory of law proved to be unpersuasive or to rely on questionable ideas about the structure of law. Those questionable ideas are examined and criticized in the next chapter. Although the CLS literature contains some important insights into the character of liberal law in its charges of doctrinal contradiction, it fails in its principal aim of subverting the liberal view of law.

FIVE

LAW AND SOCIAL REALITY

Some of the most fundamental claims within the CLS literature concern the character of social reality. These claims are connected in important ways to the CLS positions examined in previous chapters on the liberal conception of the rule of law and the nature of legal doctrine in contemporary liberal states. The claims also expose the deepest divisions within the CLS movement itself. A liberal critique of CLS must come to grips with these claims about the character of social reality. In this chapter, I complete my critique by examining certain key CLS contentions regarding social reality.

Rules and Social Reality

A useful way to gain access to CLS claims about social reality is to begin with an approach to the study of society that was widely influential in the social sciences from before World War II until the early 1960s.[1] The CLS claims about the character of social reality are part of a broader movement in social theory that rejects that approach and should be understood in that context.

The approach in question regards societies as systems whose basic building blocks are rules. Such rules mold, channel, and constrain individual action, thought, and desire. Moreover, rules are regarded as having explanatory primacy within social theory in this sense: The social behavior of individuals must be explained by reference to the rules that constitute their society. Of course, behavior in violation of a rule is possible, but insofar as it has a social meaning, such behavior must be explained by reference to some rule or other (e.g., a rule of some subculture within the society). Social reality is thus taken to be fundamentally constituted by

[1] My account of this conception and the reaction against it in social-scientific circles is indebted to Robert Edgerton, *Rules, Exceptions, and Social Order* (Berkeley: University of California Press, 1985), pp. 8ff.

rules, and social behavior is to be explained with reference to such rules. Let us call this view the *rule conception* of society.

This conception of social reality and social behavior is not limited to its most obvious manifestation in the work of those theorists who adopted some version of structural-functionalism. The elements of this conception can be separated from functionalist ideas about social equilibrium and can be incorporated into a theory that allows more room than traditional functionalism did for social conflict. Indeed, structuralist Marxism proceeds on the basis of a rule conception of society. Moreover, ethnographic accounts of alien cultures, largely innocent of explicit social theorizing, often appear to presuppose the rule conception by focusing their inquiry on the norms which presumably constrain and channel the behavior of individuals and mold their thoughts and desires. A methodological corollary of the rule conception is that the fundamental aim of social inquiry should be the discovery and understanding of the rules constituting a society, since neither rule-abiding nor rule-breaking behavior can be explained unless the rules are understood. In the philosophical literature, the classic postwar presentation of the rule conception of society is in Peter Winch's *The Idea of a Social Science*.[2]

There have long been students of society who have had their doubts about the rule conception and/or its methodological focus on discovering and understanding social rules. Malinowski argued vehemently against the methodological focus on rules, pointing out that in the cultures he studied, the rules were often bent, stretched, evaded, and even blatantly disregarded without social sanctions being visited upon those who treated the rules in that way. Freedom from the prescriptions of the rules, he argued, was as important an element of social reality as conformity to rules, and a culture could not be understood without giving both phenomena a central place in any ethnographic account.

In *Crime and Custom in Savage Society*, Malinowski subjected to devastating criticism the then prevalent view that individual members of primitive cultures automatically and effortlessly obeyed the dictates of their culture's norms.[3] He insisted that norm breaking was a central element of cultural life and could not be marginalized by ethnographic studies without seriously distorting the cultural

[2] Peter Winch, *The Idea of a Social Science and Its Relation to Philosophy* (London: Routledge and Kegan Paul, 1958).

[3] Bronislaw Malinowski, *Crime and Custom in Savage Society* (London: Routledge and Kegan Paul, 1926), pp. 9–16.

picture. However, in the final analysis, Malinowski's methodological prescriptions are not at all incompatible with the rule conception of society. It is perfectly consistent to point out that rule-breaking behavior is pervasive in all cultures and that no good ethnographic account can ignore or marginalize the extent of such behavior while claiming that such rule-breaking behavior, like all socially meaningful behavior, must be explained by reference to a rule. The former point is Malinowski's; the latter claim is that of the rule conception of society.

To join the issue with the rule conception, one must deny the claim that socially meaningful behavior must be explained by reference to social rules. This denial became more and more frequent in the 1960s and 1970s. The view became widespread that social rules must be explained by reference to individual presocial motivation. According to this view, rules do not constrain and channel individual behavior at all or do so only in sporadic and marginal ways. By and large, rules are resources and instruments that individuals manipulate to get what they want or think good, and what they want or think good, at the most fundamental level, is not determined by social rules. Rules exert no power (or little power) of their own over individual thought, desire, and action; they are mere words. Nonetheless, rules can be invoked by those who wield power to rationalize their actions and even to convince those over whom they exercise power that their subordination is right and proper. Let us call this the *instrumentalist* view of social rules. Edgerton summarizes the influence of this view on contemporary thinking:

> In most social theory today, rules are seen as ambiguous, flexible, contradictory, and inconsistent; they are said seldom to govern the actions of people, much less to mold these people by being internalized by them. Instead, they serve as resources for human strategies.[4]

The CLS literature is united in rejecting the rule conception of society, and one important strand of the literature consists of the instrumentalist view applied to the formal legal institutions of our culture and carried out in a manner designed to expose the implications for the rule of law. If rules cannot constrain and channel conduct, the rule of law must be a fiction. If rules are just instru-

[4] Edgerton, *Rules, Exceptions,* p. 14; see also p. 178. Edgerton uses the term *strategic interactionism* to refer what I am calling the instrumentalist view.

ments of manipulation, then liberal legal philosophy, by its stubborn insistence that legal rules protect us from the state and from one another, is responsible for helping to hide the manipulation of law by judges and other powerholders.

There are numerous passages in the works of leading CLS authors that exemplify the instrumentalist approach. Kairys's account of the rule of *stare decisis* (the prescription that precedents are to be followed) is representative:

> While seeming to limit discretion and to require objective and rational analysis, *stare decisis* in fact provides and serves to disguise enormous discretion. . . . Precedents are largely reduced to rationalizations, not factors meaningfully contributing to the result; they support rather than determine the principles and outcomes adopted by judges.[5]

In other words, judges manipulate the doctrine of precedent and the rules that can plausibly be attributed to precedents in order to provide legal rationalizations for decisions reached on other grounds. This is the instrumentalist view applied to the judge.

The presence of the instrumentalist approach in CLS stems in part from the influence of the law-and-society movement, a movement devoted to the empirical study of legal behavior and part of the social scientific rejection of the rule conception of society. But the crucial influence on CLS, and on the law-and-society movement itself, stems from American legal realism of the 1920s and 1930s.

Part of the realist view of law is a position known as *rule skepticism*. The label actually covers two distinct theses, one quite moderate, the other quite radical. The moderate thesis is that legal officials often do not behave in the way called for by the rules inscribed in the authoritative legal texts. This position was articulated by a leading spokesman for realism during its heyday in the 1930s, Karl Llewellyn:

> We know that precedents have no [absolutely binding] force. But force they have. We know the doctrine of precedent, and the effect of rules, as studiously ambiguous. Yet ambiguous within margins which in the main are reasonably defined. Rules guide, although they do not control, decision. The rule

[5] David Kairys, "Legal Reasoning," in *The Politics of Law*, ed. D. Kairys (New York: Pantheon Books, 1982), p. 15.

of the case or the code does lay its hand upon the future, though one finger or several may slip or shift position.[6]

The radical thesis associated with rule skepticism challenged the very existence of legal rules, at least when they were thought of as capable of constraining and channeling individual behavior. The thesis denied that rules were capable of exercising such constraint. Of course, the radical realists would acknowledge the existence of verbal formulations that could be found in legal materials and identified semantically as *rules*. Their point was that rules were simply such paper formulations and could exercise no power over individual behavior. Jerome Frank, the most prominent of the defenders of this radical view, argued that legal rules were just summaries of past judicial decisions; they were "merely words" that aided in the prediction of decisions but were incapable of exercising any constraint over them.[7]

Legal realism's radical version of rule skepticism was an early and undeveloped form of the instrumentalist view of rules. Those realists who accepted the radical position were quite prepared to agree that people in robes could incant the words of some paper rule and other legal mumbo jumbo, and thereby convince some poor soul that the law required that x be done. But this was simply the employment of the rule as a tool to produce the desired effect. It was not the rule that exercised power but the judge who exercised power and who used the rule both to help him do it and to hide the fact of his power.

The implications for the rule of law of radical rule skepticism are not difficult to fathom. If radical rule skepticism was true, then the rule of law would be impossible. People would always govern; the law never could.[8] Our faith in the law as a protection against overweening power would be groundless. Our legal rights could no more stop government officials or private centers of power from wreaking havoc with our lives than a toy gun could destroy a tank.

[6] Karl Llewellyn, "*Law and the Modern Mind*: A Symposium," *Columbia Law Review* 31 (1931): 90.

[7] Jerome Frank, *Law and the Modern Mind* (Gloucester, Mass.: Peter Smith, 1970), pp. 135, 297–98. The earliest realist statement of the radical view of legal rules is in Joseph Bingham, "What is Law?" *Michigan Law Review* 11 (1912): 8.

[8] Despite the fact that the CLS literature typically classifies Hobbes as one of the founding fathers of liberalism, he rejected the rule of law as a fiction, and he did so precisely because he believed that it was impossible for laws to govern: "And therefore this is another error of Aristotle's politics, that in a well-ordered commonwealth, not men should govern, but the laws." Hobbes, *Leviathan*, ed. M. Oakeshott (London: Collier-MacMillan, 1962), pp. 490–91.

The radical realists, however, did not explicitly draw these conclusions. Along with their moderate colleagues, the radical realists were largely content with liberating state power from the stranglehold of judges and other powerholders who were opposed to the growth of the administrative-regulatory state. Those judges and powerholders had rationalized their opposition by invoking the requirements of the existing legal rules. The basic legal rules of property, tort, and contract, they argued, did not allow for the sort of policies favored by those intent on creating a full-fledged administrative-regulatory state. The realists, both radical and moderate, aimed to defeat these arguments, but the radicals avoided the implications of their rule skepticism for the very idea of the rule of law and the viability of the liberal legal tradition.

In sharp contrast to the realist strategy of avoidance, an important part of the CLS project has been an insistence not only on radical rule skepticism but also on its implications for liberal legal thought. Tushnet, who accepts radical rule skepticism, summarizes the CLS view of the implications of that position for liberalism and the rule of law. He tells us that, given liberal premises about the human tendency to oppress and exploit others, "if the Realists were right, nothing stood between us and the abyss in which the strong dominated the weak, for the law, which liberals thought was our guardian, provided only the illusion of protection."[9]

However, not all CLS figures have adopted radical rule skepticism. Unger, for example, has clearly rejected the radical realist view and has recently formulated the main points of a social theory that rejects both the instrumentalist conception of rules and the rule conception of society. He suggests that neither approach can do justice to both the power of norms to constrain individual thought, desire, and action and the power of individual thought, desire, and action to transcend, break, and create norms.

As we will see, Unger's social theory is fully consistent with the rule of law and the liberal idea that the law can protect us from the power of the state and from one another. This represents a significant departure from his earlier arguments for the impossibility of the rule of law. Even more striking, the political program that he has proposed as the complement to his social theory relies on the implementation of the rule of law for its success and utilizes the rule of law for the liberal aim of protecting individuals from op-

[9] Mark Tushnet, "Critical Legal Studies and Constitutional Law: An Essay in Deconstruction," *Stanford Law Review* 36 (1984): 625.

pression and persecution. In addition, there are a number of other thinkers associated with CLS who have formulated proposals for legal reconstruction that similarly rely on the rule of law and so tacitly presuppose the falsity of both rule skepticism and the instrumentalist view of social reality.[10]

There is, then, a central dispute within CLS about the character of social reality and the place of rules within it. But it would be a mistake to think that the dispute is just a replay of the disagreement between the moderate and radical realists or between social-scientific advocates and opponents of the rule conception of society. As it has proceeded in CLS, the dispute has revolved around both the logical and the political implications of the idea that society is a human artifact. Both sides of the CLS dispute have accepted the idea; they have disagreed over its meaning and implications. The dispute has revealed facets of the issue of the place of rules in social reality that lay unexposed by the previous debates in law and social science.

Unger has contributed more than any other scholar to the task of formulating the issues that divide CLS thinkers in terms of the idea that society is a human artifact. He has also provided the most sophisticated explication and defense of the idea to be found in the CLS literature. Let us turn, then, to his treatment of the idea of society as a human artifact.

Unger: Society as an Artifact

The idea of society as an artifact can best be understood in relation to the thesis it opposes. The *naturalistic thesis*, as Unger calls it, holds that there is a well-defined social order programmed into human nature. In this respect, humans are regarded as no different from any of the other living creatures who lead a social life:

[10] See, e.g., Staughton Lynd, "Government without Rights: The Labor Law Vision of Archibald Cox," *Industrial Relations Law Journal* 4 (1981): 483–95. Lynd advocates stronger rights under law than currently exist for the protection of workers' efforts at union organization and activity, and he presumes that such laws could effectively strengthen worker self-determination and confine the power of management. British critical theorist Alan Hunt is quite explicit about his commitment to the rule of law when he writes that "the most important lesson for legal politics that may be drawn from our experience of 'actual socialism' in the Soviet Union and other states is the necessity of retaining formalized and entrenched rights, the core of the rule of law, to protect citizens and social institutions against political usurpation by the state and the bureaucracy." Hunt, "The Ideology of Law: Advances and Problems in Recent Applications of the Concept of Ideology to the Analysis of Law," *Law and Society Review* 19 (1985): 30.

ants, monkeys, and so forth. Although the thesis of a natural social order does not by itself carry with it any implications for the precise kind of social order natural for humans, there is a thesis that has virtually always accompanied it that ascribes one important characteristic to the natural human order. According to this second thesis, the natural social order for humans is a fixed and all-encompassing hierarchy. To describe a hierarchy in such terms is to ascribe to it the following features: people are born into their rankings in the stratification system; the lines between the rankings are sharp and stable; and there is a single comprehensive and consistent stratification system that determines where a person falls with respect to all of the major cultural categories that determine status and privilege.

The idea of society as an artifact repudiates the doctrine of a natural social order for human beings. Unger writes, "Modern social thought was born proclaiming that society is made and imagined, that it is a human artifact rather than the expression of an underlying natural order." Yet, he continues, "no one has ever taken the idea of society as artifact to the hilt."[11] Unger's project is to take the idea to the hilt and to criticize other modern social theories for failing to do so.

Before turning to these other modern theories, it is appropriate to point out that Unger sees the idea as having important political implications. The naturalist thesis, in conjunction with the idea of a natural social hierarchy, provides the beginnings of an answer to a central question of political philosophy: Why are some adult humans entitled to the power to rule over other adult humans? The beginning of the answer is, They are the persons whose rank in the natural social hierarchy is highest. No such answer is available to those who accept the idea of society as an artifact. For the moderns who did accept it, then, the idea reopened the question of what justifies the exercise of political power by some humans over others, and it is precisely this question that occupied the great theorists of the seventeenth century such as Hobbes and Locke.

In Unger's account, the theories of modern social thought dilute, but do not eliminate, the notion of a natural human social order. He tries to show that this is so by dividing modern theories into two main types and then demonstrating how each type retains the naturalist thesis in diluted form.

[11] Roberto Unger, *Social Theory: Its Situation and Its Task* (New York: Cambridge University Press, 1987), p. 1.

The first type consists of the *deep structure* social theories. These theories proceed on two main ideas and an underlying premise. The underlying premise is that in every social world, one can distinguish a framework (or "formative context," as Unger sometimes calls it) that channels and constrains the routine activities of life, on the one hand, and those routine activities themselves, on the other. The framework consists of the rules and roles that constitute the major institutions of society. The routines consist of the behavior of individuals filling the roles and following the rules.

Proceeding from this premise, the first main idea of deep structure theory is that there are powerful constraints that limit the kinds of possible social frameworks. These constraints rule out all but a handful of ways to organize human social life. Different deep structure theories invoke different kinds of constraints as the crucial ones. Some focus on psychological constraints, typically claiming that egoism is the principal constraining force; others focus on economic constraints, typically invoking considerations of productive and distributive efficiency; still others focus on organizational constraints that are neither economic nor purely psychological. An example might be Michel's *iron law of oligarchy*.[12] But whatever the character of the constraints invoked, deep structure theories claim that the constraints are compatible with only a severely limited number of types of social world.

The second main idea of deep structure theory is that in each of the possible social worlds, the different elements that make up the framework (i.e., the different subsystems of rules and roles) form an indivisible package. The elements of the framework not only work together but could not function if an element from another social framework was substituted. This idea is not to be equated with the claim of functionalism that the subsystems work in harmony, preventing social conflict and maintaining social equilibrium. There are "conflict versions" of this second idea. The most notable is Marxism, which holds that the different elements of any class society form an indivisible whole, but a whole through which run the fault lines of class conflict.

One version of deep structure theory, the *evolutionary*, adds to the aforementioned two ideas a third: Recorded human history has seen the emergence of new and unprecedented social worlds, but they are generated in accordance with a strict predefined se-

[12] Robert Michels, *Political Parties* (New York: Free Press, 1962), pp. 342–56.

quence. Marxism is, of course, the major example of evolutionary deep structure theory.

The other main category with which Unger classifies the various approaches of modern social science is *positivist social science*. In contrast to deep structure theory, it does not rely on the idea that societies are constituted by frameworks of rules and roles that channel and constrain individual behavior, and it thus makes no claims about limits on the kinds of social worlds that are possible. Positivist social science does seek to formulate and confirm empirical generalizations regarding social behavior, but there is no claim that these generalizations are valid across societies and historical epochs.

From Unger's point of view, positivist social science does not so much embrace the naturalistic thesis as duck the whole issue raised by the thesis and the opposing idea of society as an artifact. It fails to carry the artifact idea to its logical conclusion because it avoids any explicit acceptance, or rejection, of the idea. Unger believes that this strategy of avoidance leads positivist social science to results that are not so much wrong as impoverished. Its empirical generalizations may hold for particular societies at particular times, but they begin to disintegrate as soon as people start fighting over the ground rules of social life, the basic social rules that determine access to power and privilege. Positivist social science provides us with no conceptual resources for thinking about these periods of struggle over the fundamentals of social life or for understanding why these struggles break out or produce certain outcomes rather than others. A social science capable of dealing with these crucial problems must take seriously the issues raised by the conflict between the naturalist thesis and the idea of society as an artifact. Positivist social science fails to do so.

However, deep structure theory does take such issues seriously, and it is important for us to examine Unger's critique of the deep structure approach. According to Unger, deep structure theories retain in diluted form the idea of a natural social order because they retain the idea that there are a severely limited number of possible kinds of social world. To be sure, such theories reject the notion that there is only one natural order for human society, yet they are, in effect, contending that there are only a handful of natural orders—those few orders that the constraints of psychology, economics, or organization do not rule out.

At one time, Unger himself accepted the idea of a natural social order. In *Law in Modern Society*, he wrote of the connection between that idea and the question of what justifies political power: "Unless people regain the sense that the practices of society represent some sort of natural order instead of a set of arbitrary choices, they cannot hope to escape from the dilemma of unjustified power."[13] Moreover, in Unger's view at the time, there was a deep connection between the practice of law and the naturalistic idea: "Throughout history there has been a bond between the legal profession and the search for an order inherent in social life."[14] It is not difficult to discern in these statements a commitment to the idea of a natural social order.

What led Unger to change his mind and to repudiate the naturalist thesis, even in its diluted deep structure version? In his later work, Unger comes to the conclusion that human history has generated certain "surprises" that, when fully appreciated, defeat the two main ideas of deep structure theory (but do not defeat the underlying framework-routine distinction). His earlier endorsement of the naturalistic thesis was presumably predicated on an insufficient appreciation of these surprises. In Unger's current view, the best interpretations of the facts of human history defeat all efforts to specify a strict historical sequence of social worlds, to see social frameworks as indivisible packages, or to specify the constraints that allegedly place severe limits on the kinds of social worlds that are possible. For example, in this century, nations outside of North America and Western Europe (Japan, to take a notable case) have combined elements of Western economic and political organization with elements from their native cultures, producing social frameworks substantially different from anything proponents of deep structure theory thought possible earlier. For Unger, such unexpected developments not only destroy Marxist theories of historical development but also destroy the most vigorously anti-Marxist versions of deep structure theory.[15]

Unger does not pretend that a simple recitation of the facts of history can, by itself, conclusively prove that the success of deep structure theory is impossible. Even if we grant that the simple facts of history have defeated all deep structure theories formulated up to now, a successful deep structure theory could be one of the surprises of the next century or the subsequent one. Indeed,

[13] Roberto Unger, *Law in Modern Society* (New York: Free Press, 1976), p. 240.

[14] Ibid., p. 242.

[15] For an anti-Marxist theory that Unger takes to have been defeated by the surprises of history, see W. W. Rostow, *The Stages of Economic Growth: A Non-Communist Manifesto*, 2d ed. (Cambridge: Cambridge University Press, 1971).

one might regard the historical argument against deep structure theory as relatively weak. A few centuries of deep structure failure do not, by themselves, seem to be a particularly powerful argument for condemning the theoretical project to eternal futility. Moreover, the simple fact that something (a theoretical project, a piece of technology, a plan of social action) has often gone wrong is, by itself, weak evidence of a fundamental and irremediable flaw. What is needed is an explanation of why it has gone wrong and some confirmation of the truth of the explanation that is not merely a recounting of the episodes when the thing has gone wrong. As I interpret his work, Unger does attempt to provide such an explanation and confirmation.

Unger's explanation for the failure of deep structure theories resides in his account of human nature, and it is this account that provides the lenses through which Unger interprets the surprises of history. Humans are *context-dependent* and *context-transcendent* beings. Unger insists that both aspects are essential to our nature. The former means that humans will always ultimately settle down to live within some social framework. The latter means that no social framework (or finite sequence of them) will fully satisfy humans and that they always possess the power to step outside of their framework. Humans will always find that they can imagine worthwhile possibilities for personal and political life that cannot fit within the boundaries of any past or present social framework. Indeed, they will always find that they can imagine an inexhaustible supply of such possibilities. The surprises of history that defeat deep structure theory are manifestations of the human context-transcending power. They are the epiphanies of the infinite human personality erupting into the finite world of human history. In Unger's view, it is our context-transcending power that ultimately explains why deep structure theories have been continually embarrassed by the surprises of history and why any future deep structure theory will meet with some future surprise to embarrass it.

But what is the independent confirmation of this context-transcending power? I believe that Unger appeals to the subjective experience that the individual has of himself and of his social world. Unger suggests that the individual's experience of social frameworks is (in part) an experience of constraint, but his experience of himself is one of inexhaustible, worthwhile possibilities. As Unger sometimes puts it, each individual experiences himself as an infinite personality trapped within the finite boundaries of his social world.[16] For Unger, deep structure theories belittle the infinite human personality and inevitably fall victim to the inexhaustible creativity of the human context-transcending power.

One approach to criticizing Unger's argument against deep structure theory is to claim that the experience of context-transcendence is not the universal human phenomenon that Unger takes it to be. William Galston makes this claim in the course of a critique of Unger's theory of human nature. Galston suggests that the experience of context-transcendence that Unger invokes is characteristic only of certain modern personality types:

> [T]he impulse to imagine and act out context-smashing transgressions is indeed characteristic of modernist artists, authors, and revolutionaries. But Unger mistakes the part for the whole. His critical error is to assume that the motives and satisfactions of a tiny elite somehow constitute the (hidden) essence and desire of all human beings. . . . Most human beings find satisfaction within settled contexts and experience the disruption of those contexts not as empowerment, but rather as deprivation.[17]

In Galston's view, then, Unger's account of human nature is fundamentally flawed by the mistake of taking the experience of the few to be representative of human experience in general.

Much of Galston's criticism is vitiated by the fact that it rests on a distorted picture of Unger's theory. Unger never denies that most people find satisfaction within their settled contexts; that is one side of human nature, and Unger does not blink it. The other side is that humans also experience dissatisfaction stemming from the constraints imposed by those contexts, so they seek to transcend such constraints. Moreover, Unger is quite prepared to concede that as a historical fact, the serious disruption of contexts is typically experienced as disempowering, because such disruptions typically pose grave threats to personal safety and security. One of Unger's key points is that context-revising activity, even when it is very extensive, need not pose such threats, and as we will see, one of his main programmatic aims is to describe a set of political

[16] Roberto Unger, *False Necessity* (New York: Cambridge University Press, 1987), p. 12. But for a caution on the use of the phrase "infinite caught within the finite," see Unger, *Passion* (New York: Free Press, 1984), p. 4.

[17] William Galston, "False Universality: Infinite Personality and Finite Existence in Unger's *Politics*," *Northwestern Law Review* 81 (1987): 759.

arrangements that breaks the historical link between context-revision and personal insecurity.

In addition, the idea that context-transcendence is a universal human capacity is not so wrongheaded as Galston suggests. The anthropological evidence strongly suggests that there is an important context-transcending element in all human cultures. All cultures have rules, but as Malinowski emphasized, in all cultures the rules are often bent, broken, and ignored. Such rule-disregarding activity is hardly limited to an elite few in modern culture. And in all cultures, at least some of the rules are experienced by individuals as uncomfortable constraints that limit the worthwhile possibilities of personal and political life, suggesting again that people "overflow" the rules of their social framework in important ways.[18]

Yet Unger's appeal to his theory of human nature in order to defeat deep structure theory ultimately does not work. In describing our context-transcending side, Unger stresses the discomfort of the constraints we feel in living under the social rules we do and the apparently inexhaustible powers we have to imagine different social worlds. Even if Unger's portrait of human nature in these respects is accurate, the argument against deep structure theory will not be successful unless an additional claim is made regarding the kinds of social worlds in which humans can feel sufficiently satisfied that such worlds can avoid immediate disintegration and stabilize.

Unger assumes that the number of kinds of social worlds capable of providing such satisfaction is too great to fit on any deep structure list. Such an assumption appears to be an implicit part of Unger's understanding of the context-transcending side of human nature and seems to be a pivotal factor in Unger's quick inference from the surprises of history to the futility of the deep structure theoretical project. However, once the assumption is articulated, it easy to see that it is question-begging. Moreover, the assumption is not entailed by the premise that humans never feel fully at home in any social world and/or the premise that humans can imagine an inexhaustible list of social worlds. My conclusion, then, is that Unger's argument against deep structure theory falls short. The naturalistic thesis has not been defeated. The idea of society as an artifact has not been established.

However, there is a different sort of antinaturalist argument that

[18] See Edgerton, *Rules, Exceptions*, pp. 14–15, 22, 28.

can provide much of what Unger and his CLS colleagues are after when they attack the naturalistic thesis in favor of the idea of society as an artifact. A more chastened antinaturalist argument than Unger's would be aimed not so much at deep structure ideas as hypotheses of social theory as at deep structure ideas as they often function in political discourse and argument. In particular, the argument would seek to defeat the use of such ideas to brand as "unworkable" or "impossible" programs of political action and social reconstruction, especially programs dedicated to dismantling or diminishing social hierarchies and/or to decreasing the extent to which egoism operates in social life. Such an argument need not aim to show that no deep structure theory can possibly succeed. It need show only that no such theory can yet claim sufficient success to provide a basis for concluding that some program of social and political reconstruction violates natural constraints on social invention. Such an argument would be important for CLS thinkers because it would defeat objections that are often raised to paralyze the kind of radical political action to which virtually all of the critical theorists are committed.

This antinaturalist argument would actually be a series of related arguments, each aimed at a different effort to deem impossible some scheme of social reconstruction. In each case, the argument would be that there is insufficient evidence to support the contention that the scheme violates a natural constraint on human social organization. Such arguments would, for the most part, be quite powerful.[19] They would rest on the failure of deep structure theories to specify and confirm, with anything approaching sufficient epistemic rigor, the constraints that allegedly limit the kinds of social frameworks that are possible and that thereby render various schemes of radical reconstruction impossible. Although I cannot establish the point here, an examination of arguments that invoke any interesting natural constraint on social life will, I believe, show that they hide their lack of empirical evidence by making claims that are ambiguous between "A society of type x is impossible"

[19] There are some limits on social possibility that can be specified with a high degree of confidence. For example, a society must be organized so as to provide a certain level of caloric intake for enough of its members to survive and reproduce, and a society must have some rules that prescribe behavior. For the most part, though, limits such as these do not by themselves entail the impossibility of even the most radical models for social reconstruction. But for one possible exception, see "Abstraction and the Law" in this chapter where I examine and reject a radical position that seems to presuppose that there can be societies without prescriptive social rules.

and "A society of type x is morally objectionable." When the lack of evidence is raised, the arguments shift from the former to the latter claim.

If there is no convincing argument against the possibility of a successful deep structure theory, at least there are convincing arguments against the current use of deep-structure–naturalistic claims to dismiss radical political ideas as unworkable or impossible. There is no good reason to conclude that the naturalistic thesis is, as a matter of social theory, false. We just do not know whether it is true or false. But it is generally unfounded to attempt to paralyze radical political action with ideas born of the naturalistic thesis. I believe that this is the most that can be saved from Unger's antinaturalist argument, and it is by no means insignificant.

Ultra-Theory v. Super-Theory

Unger suggests that there are at least two quite distinct programs for taking the idea of society as an artifact to its logical conclusions. He calls one of them *ultra-theory* and the other *super-theory*. Within the CLS movement, there is an important group that adopts a certain version of ultra-theory. This group includes Mark Tushnet, Peter Gabel, Duncan Kennedy, and Robert Gordon.[20] The most notable CLS proponent of super-theory is Unger himself. The form of ultra-theory adopted by Tushnet and company is an extension of the rule skepticism of the radical wing of legal realism. Super-theory is a sophisticated elaboration of the view that a complete account of social reality must include room for the idea that rules can constrain and mold individuals and the idea that individuals can meaningfully transcend any body of rules that govern their present social life.

Conflicting Theories

Unger's super-theory rests on two crucial generalizations about society: (a) all social worlds result from conflicts and struggles among individuals, and (b) all stabilized social worlds consist of two main elements—a framework that constrains and channels in-

[20] The term *ultra-theory* is Unger's. These theorists do not describe themselves with the term, but the ideas they endorse can be seen as representing a form of what Unger calls ultra-theory. As we will see shortly, this form of ultra-theory is somewhat different from the version on which Unger focuses, but it is a dialectical outgrowth of that version.

dividual behavior and thought and the routine activities and thoughts that occur within the framework. A framework is a structure of social rules, an articulated system of norms. For Unger, it is the existence of frameworks that sets the central tasks of super social theory, providing a general account of how frameworks are formed, how they hang together, how they can be modified, and how they break down. Super-theory holds that frameworks are formed when fighting and conflict over the ground rules of social life stop and people start thinking of the rules that have been put into place as good and natural; frameworks break down when the truce lines represented by the existing ground rules are no longer respected and the fighting breaks out again. The theoretical task is to develop some general account of how and when these processes take place. The account must show the cash value of these military metaphors but avoid relapsing into deep structure naturalism.

Unger portrays ultra-theory as accepting the two basic generalizations of super-theory. However, it rejects the effort to develop any general account of the formation, operation, or breakdown of social frameworks. The basis of the rejection is the contention that such an effort will invariably relapse into deep structure naturalism. In the view of ultra-theory, then, super-theory has not taken the artificial character of social worlds seriously enough; it has not carried the idea of society as an artifact to the hilt.

The version of ultra-theory described by Unger is unstable in the following way: If social frameworks really exist, then it is sensible to ask how the various norms that constitute them coalesce to form articulated systems. If frameworks really constrain and channel individual behavior and thought, then it is sensible to ask what the principles are in accordance with which they accomplish this. This is not to deny an element of chance in the creation of a social framework but to suggest that if there are persisting frameworks capable of channeling individual behavior and thought, there are reasons why they are capable of doing so. So if we take the existence of such frameworks seriously, we must ask, "What are the principles that account for why social frameworks are able to persist and to channel individual behavior and thought?"

But it is precisely this sort of question that ultra-theory refuses to address when it rejects the possibility of any general account of social frameworks. Of course, different kinds of social frameworks may operate according to different principles, but any set of operating principles will be generalizable to some extent—will be potentially applicable to more than one particular framework. Ultra-theory insists that we remain at the level of the particular framework and rejects any move toward a generalizable account as a betrayal of the insight that society is an artifact.

The version of ultra-theory described by Unger is thus unstable insofar as it accepts the existence and persistence of frameworks that channel and constrain individual behavior and thought but rejects any general account of how frameworks form or how they accomplish the channeling of behavior and thought. Unger is, I think, aware of this dialectical instability when he suggests that it is a short move from rejecting any general theory of frameworks to rejecting the existence of frameworks themselves.[21] Indeed, I believe that the ultra-theory strand in CLS has made precisely this move. It rejects the existence of frameworks, at least when one conceives of frameworks as having an objective existence and as capable of constraining and channeling individual behavior and thought. If one wishes to speak of frameworks at all, from this point of view, they can amount to nothing more than the patterns which a person cognitively imposes upon the past flow of actions and thoughts. Such patterns do not exist in the events themselves but are imposed by the subject upon the undifferentiated flow of past events. Moreover, the current version of ultra-theory would reject any Kantian idea that there are fixed and universal structures in terms of which human subjects impose cognitive order on the flow of events. Frameworks thus exist only in the eyes of the particular beholder, and lacking any objective existence, they also lack the power to exert any objective control over the thoughts, actions, or desires of a population. Such is the view embedded in the ultra-theory strand of CLS, at any rate.

This version of ultra-theory is internally more stable than the one that Unger describes. Since frameworks do not channel individual behavior and thought, there is no need for a theory to explain how they do so. Since the patterns composing frameworks are merely imposed upon actions and events by the individual perceiver, there is no logical compulsion to develop a general theoretical account of them as though they had an objective existence. I will refer to this more stable version as *CLS ultra-theory* (or simply *ultra-theory*, for stylistic variation, but I mean this CLS version and not the unstable version described by Unger). It is, in effect, the

[21] Unger, *Social Theory*, p. 168.

rule skepticism of legal realism expanded and generalized to cover not just legal rules but social rules of any sort.

CLS ultra-theory is radically at odds with Unger's view of social theory. Unger fails to acknowledge the radical nature of these differences regarding the nature of social reality and the relationship of the social past to the social future. CLS ultra-theory rests on a radical existentialist vision: There are no social institutions or rules that have the power to control individual choice, action, and thought; the social future is entirely open, entirely free from the control of the social past.

Of course, CLS ultra-theorists acknowledge that the belief in social structures capable of controlling individual behavior is part of our social reality, but from their point of view, the belief is necessarily false. Indeed, the belief is a kind of self-deception that we practice in order to relieve ourselves of the existential anxiety that comes from recognizing the openness of the future. Peter Gabel puts the point this way:

> [W]e conspire to generate a "belief" . . . that there exist what could loosely be called a "sovereign" and a body of rules . . . and that these rules "govern" what I am calling the next moment, ridding this moment of its contingent character.[22]

The belief is a false one according to Gabel. The law and the state, like all other social institutions and structures, have no reality that enable them to exert power over the individuals who constitute a population. It is not that there is no social reality; rather, social reality simply consists of those choices that people have already made, and such choices lack the power to control choices not yet made.

Tushnet expresses the ultra-theoretical view thus: "[T]he social world is entirely constructed. Every time one thinks about it, the social world dissolves into a set of choices that one has made."[23] These choices, Tushnet tells us, are always contingent, never necessary, and can never control choices yet to be made. Human choices can settle things only for the moment in which they are made; they cannot settle things for future occasions of choice. Moreover, Tushnet believes that this view of social reality defeats

[22] Peter Gabel, "The Phenomenology of Rights-Consciousness and the Pact of the Withdrawn Selves," *Texas Law Review* 62 (1984): 1570.

[23] Mark Tushnet, "An Essay on Rights," *Texas Law Review* 62 (1984): 1402.

"the liberal premise that human behavior can be governed by rules that have some supra-individual content."[24]

Robert Gordon, another CLS figure who expresses the viewpoint of ultra-theory, writes that "social reality consists of reified structures. . . . Though the structures are built, piece by interlocking piece, with human intentions, people come to "externalize" them, to attribute to them existence and control over and above human choice."[25] Gordon proceeds to criticize particular examples of such externalization, conveying the clear message that social structures cannot control human choice.

Ultra-theorists are fully prepared to concede that individuals can exert power and control over other individuals, and they insist that this control is often accomplished through the use of ideas, including legal ideas such as private ownership. Their point is that it is human individuals, not the law or any other social structure, who exercise control. The very idea of a government of laws, rather than men, rests on the wrongheaded premise that social structures have an objective existence that enables them to exert power over individuals. Ultra-theorists condemn the premise as an instance of the mistake of reification.

Unger's super-theory clearly rejects the idea that there are no social structures that control human choice. In Unger's view, social frameworks constrain and channel the behavior and thought of individuals. Such frameworks are structures that exert an objective control over what people do, think, and desire. But, the differences between Unger and ultra-theory do not stop with their conflicting accounts of the nature of social reality, for the conflicting accounts lead to radically different positions on crucial issues of legal and political philosophy. Let us turn to some of those issues.

Social Theory and the Rule of Law

The CLS ultra-theory is the social theory that lies behind the radical indeterminacy position examined in chapter 3. I argued there that the law would be riddled with indeterminacy if there was no objective structure to the mass of rules and doctrines that compose it. I also provided some reasons from the philosophy of language for thinking that legal discourse did have such a structure. The

[24] Mark Tushnet, "Legal Scholarship: Its Causes and Cure," *Yale Law Journal* 90 (1981): 1207.

[25] Robert Gordon, "New Developments in Legal Theory," in *The Politics of Law*, pp. 290, 288.

argument was couched as one against the deconstructionist position on meaning. But I believe that for those in the CLS movement who adopt the radical indeterminacy position, the last line of argument is not one based on a deconstructionist approach to meaning. Rather, it is based on the theory of social reality embodied in CLS ultra-theory.

The CLS ultra-theorist argues that there is no objective structure to law or legal discourse, because there is none to *any* element of social reality. The rule of law requires that the law provide determinate outcomes for actual and potential cases. But the ultra-theorist argues that the absence of any doctrinal structure independent of how an individual chooses to view the relations among the various doctrinal rules destroys legal determinacy. The meaning and scope of application of each legal norm is largely a function of the role that it plays in the larger system of legal norms. Alter the location of a given norm in the overall system, and its meaning and application can change radically. Carve up the mass of legal norms in a different way, and legal outcomes will be drastically different.

But the ultra-theorist argues that the location of any given norm is not something given, it is, rather, created by how a particular individual chooses to carve up the mass of doctrinal norms. It may be that most legal professionals in our legal culture have thus far chosen to carve up doctrine in very similar ways. This creates the deceptive appearance that there is some objective structure that these choices are merely mapping rather than creating. But there is no such objective structure. There is no aspect of social reality, including the law, that has any structure independent of the choice of any given individual. On that account, there can be no outcomes that the law as such logically requires; it is only the law as someone has chosen to see it structured that can have determinate outcomes for legal cases.

Moreover, for the CLS ultra-theorist, the rule of law cannot serve its vital liberal function of regulating and limiting both private and public power. Such a function would require not only that the law as such entail determinate outcomes in legal cases but also that it consist of a framework of norms capable of constraining and channeling individual behavior. But the CLS ultra-theorist argues that there are no objective social frameworks capable of exercising such powers. Like all other social norms, legal norms cannot objectively constrain. Thus, it is Tushnet's conception of social reality that forms the basis of his rejection of "the liberal premise that human behavior can be governed by rules that have some supra-individual content."[26]

It follows from CLS ultra-theory that it is a mistake for the individual to rely on legal rights for protection from either private or public power. To seek protection in legal rights is to presume incorrectly that social rules can somehow, by themselves, exert power and control over individuals. It is to fail to see that social rules are tools by which individuals exert power and control over other individuals. It is to be taken in by the illusion that rules can and do control us. For CLS ultra-theory, then, the liberal idea that legal rights are vitally important in protecting individuals from public or private power is a fiction. Proponents of CLS ultra-theory do not conclude from this that we should give up trying to protect ourselves from centers of power that can wreak havoc in our lives but that we must find some way of accomplishing such protection that is not rule-based.

The type of social theory represented by Unger's super-theory is, on the other hand, perfectly consistent with the possibility of the rule of law and the reliance on legal rights to protect individuals. For super-theory, social rules can constrain individual behavior. Law can serve to regulate power because it can be an element of the framework of rules that constitute the social world. And like any other part of that framework, it can have a structure independent of the choice or perception of any particular individual. Such a structure is what makes it possible for the law to be more than an undifferentiated mass of norms and to have the determinacy that the rule of law requires.

It should be no surprise, then, that the political program that Unger has recently proposed, the program of *empowered democracy*, relies to a considerable degree on the rule of law to regulate public and private power. Without going into the details of Unger's program, we can convey the relevant points by briefly describing two of its prominent aspects.

First, although property rights are radically restructured from their current form, there is still a precisely defined system of property entitlements in Unger's political order. These new property rights serve to regulate what owners can do with their property and to limit the power of the state to seize it arbitrarily. To be sure, the new rights are designed to do a better job than traditional liberal property rights of preventing owners from building concentra-

[26] Tushnet, "Legal Scholarship," p. 1207.

tions of private power. But just like liberal property, Ungerian property rights establish a well-defined zone of freedom in which the individual has wide discretion to use his property as he sees fit, and the entire system of ownership is underwritten by the rule of law.

Second, the basic liberal rights of free expression, free press, and religious conscience are retained and supplemented by rights that secure a minimum level of material well-being—*immunity rights*. They function to regulate and limit public power and are underwritten by a system of legal norms that meet liberal criteria for the rule of law.

At this point, one may well wonder whether Unger's current position is better described as a form of liberalism than a version of CLS, especially in light of his own description of his political philosophy as "superliberalism."[27] It may appear that while ultra-theory lies squarely within the basic framework of CLS thought, Unger has moved outside that framework with his endorsement of basic liberal rights secured by the rule of law. In order to deal with this issue, we must turn to a fuller discussion of the basic political aims of CLS and the relation of those aims to the liberal rule of law.

Democracy: Empowered and Liberal

Unger and his CLS colleagues are united in the belief that in liberal democratic societies, the scope of overt political conflict and the power of mass political action to effect radical social transformation are unduly restricted. They agree, moreover, that the law (for the ultra-theorist, read "judges and lawyers" for "the law") plays a major part in creating and maintaining such a cramped role for overt and radical politics. It is not that the law can actually reduce the role of politics in setting the terms on which persons live and associate; in CLS eyes, "everything is politics," including the confinement and disempowerment of politics. As Unger explains it, the slogan "Everything is politics" is equivalent to the proposition that society is an artifact, an outcome of the human conflict of interests and ideologies.[28] So neither law nor judges can actually limit the role of politics in the constitution of society, any more than they could actually naturalize human society. But judges and

[27] Roberto Unger, *The Critical Legal Studies Movement* (Cambridge: Harvard University Press, 1986), pp. 41–42.

[28] Unger, *Social Theory*, pp. 10, 145, 172.

lawyers can use the law-politics distinction to hide the pervasiveness of political conflict in setting the terms on which people live and interact. Moreover, the law and legal officials can defuse, discourage, check, and confine any effort at mass political action that aims for the radical equalization of power and privilege in society.

Unger and his CLS colleagues object to the law's latter effect, partly on the ground that a radical equalization is needed to make social life morally tolerable. They object as well on the ground that a society where the power of politics to transform basic institutional arrangements is discouraged and checked is a society that does not do justice to the context-transcending capacities of human beings. It is a society that in self-deception, seeks to naturalize itself, to have its members regard the terms of life and association within it as part of the natural order of things.

Unger and his colleagues also contend that the law-politics distinction is employed to hide the pervasiveness of political and moral conflict. They claim that the net result of this ruse is to help insulate crucial political issues from general public debate and decision. In the legal arena, political issues are translated into the esoteric terminology of legal doctrine, and efforts are made to hide the connections of the legal issues to their political originals. Of course, the law is not always successful in hiding the connections and preventing legal issues from being seen as political ones—witness the debates over abortion, school prayer, and the like. But CLS authors argue that there are many legal issues, in private as well as public law, in which the political stakes are more or less successfully hidden from public view and from which the general public is effectively shut out because of its lack of competence in the esoteric language and arcane procedures of the law. The politics of law is a politics confined to the elite group that has mastered the law's language and procedures.

In light of these objections to the politics of liberal democracy, the aim of Unger and his CLS colleagues is to free democratic politics from the severe constraints it operates under in current liberal societies, to destroy the forces that currently block the potential of mass political mobilization to effect radical social transformation and to remove the obstacles that effectively limit public debate and deliberation over certain important political issues.

But there is serious disagreement between Unger and the CLS ultra-theorists over what would constitute successfully freeing politics from undue liberal constraints. Like the liberal, Unger still insists that politics operate under some significant constraints. Unger's immunity rights remove certain issues from the realm of normal political debate in just the manner that the liberal endorses. Moreover, he insists that politics continue to operate under the rule of law. Thus, Unger believes that not every liberal constraint on politics is undue and that politics can be freed from undue liberal constraints without giving up the liberal idea of individual rights secured by the rule of law. He seeks to integrate certain liberal constraints into a social-political system, that of empowered democracy, where democratic politics would have an increased power to transform basic social institutions and public debate and deliberation would not be confined by turning political issues into esoteric legal ones.

Liberals of a more conventional stripe criticize empowered democracy for unleashing democratic politics to an excessive degree. They argue that social life would become far too unsettled and conflict-ridden for most people, and they stress the dangers, such as fascism, that have historically attended the freeing of politics from its liberal moorings.[29] Unger's rhetoric certainly seems to highlight the quite unsettled character of social life under empowered democracy, although he does attempt to mitigate this aspect of the system by suggesting that people will experience a settled quality to their social world at some very high level of abstraction. Whether Unger can cogently respond to these liberal criticisms of empowered democracy is not an issue into which I delve here. Given the shared commitment of liberalism and superliberalism to certain basic individual rights secured by the rule of law, such an issue would lead us too far astray from the jurisprudential focus I wish to maintain. Yet serious questions must be raised about the logical consistency of Unger's position that bear quite directly on jurisprudential issues.

Consider the much-criticized law-politics distinction. Unger is as critical of the distinction as the CLS ultra-theorists, and despite other important changes in his thinking, he has not given up the criticism. In *The Critical Legal Studies Movement*, Unger had already worked out the basic features of empowered democracy, yet he continued his attack on the law-politics distinction. To acknowledge such a distinction was, according to that manifesto, to be guilty of the jurisprudential sin of legal formalism.

The crucial problem is that Unger never adequately explains

[29] See, e.g., Galston, "False Universality," pp. 759, 762, and Cass Sunstein, "Routine and Revolution," *Northwestern Law Review* 81 (1987): 889–90.

how protection of property and immunity rights by the laws of empowered democracy is consistent with the rejection of the law-politics distinction. Does not the protection of property rights require that officials keep their judgments about whether a plaintiff rightfully owns x distinct from their judgments about whether it would be morally or politically best if the plaintiff was awarded ownership of x? Does it not require the organs of the state to render their judgments based on a mode of reasoning clearly distinct from unrestrained moral or political deliberation? Is not the same true of immunity rights?

It seems to me that the clear answer to these questions is affirmative. Indeed, Unger seems to recognize as much in *False Necessity* by providing his empowered democracy with an independent judiciary: "The adjudication of localized disputes over the boundaries of rights may best be conducted by officials removed from the pressures of conflict over the uses of governmental power and expert in the entire body of law."[30] The point is that the rationale for such an independent judiciary is utterly inconsistent with his attacks on the law-politics distinction and on liberal legal formalism.

I believe that Unger would respond to this criticism by making two related points. First, in an empowered democracy, the authoritative resolution of disputes would be liberated from the esoteric language and arcane procedures that currently render it inaccessible to most people: "The contrast between lawyers and layman would give way to a situation of multiple points of entry into the more or less authoritative resolution of problems that we now define as legal," and there would be a corresponding "disintegration of the bar."[31] Second, under empowered democracy, the general populace would fully appreciate that the norms that govern the authoritative resolution of disputes are expressions of controversial normative visions for human life and would debate and decide the issues raised by such visions. These two points combine to show that under empowered democracy there is a breakdown of the elitist politics of the law; everyone can have an understanding of how fundamental moral and political issues are implicated in the authoritative resolution of social conflicts and disputes, and everyone can have a voice in discussing and deliberating over those issues.

[30] Unger, *False Necessity*, p. 452.

[31] Unger, *Critical Legal Studies*, p. 111.

Let me put to the side the question of how the disintegration of the bar is to be made consistent with the existence of officials who are expert in the entire body of law. Let me also set aside serious questions that might be asked regarding how cogent it is to think that there could be a disintegration of the bar and a destruction of the lawyer-layman distinction under empowered democracy. For the sake of isolating the key jurisprudential issue, I am willing to concede Unger's description of empowered democracy in this regard. The main point to be made in reply to Unger is that, even granting that legal professionals will either disappear or play some greatly reduced role, it does not follow that there is no law-politics distinction under empowered democracy, *as the soundest versions of liberal legal theory understand the distinction*. To be sure, one can argue that there is a sense in which the distinction is undercut, since authoritative doctrines are seen as expressions of controversial political and moral positions. There were once some legal theorists who argued that legal rules (especially in private law) were politically and morally "neutral" because the rules could be derived logically from noncontroversial premises. Those theorists were, in all likelihood, dead wrong, and the operating principles of empowered democracy clearly reject their position.

But the soundest versions of liberal theory can reject their position as well. In such versions of liberalism, to defend the law-politics distinction is to argue that legal reasoning about a person's rights under the law can and should be clearly distinguished from moral or political deliberation unconstrained by any requirement to remain substantially consistent with some body of conventionally accepted norms, decisions, and doctrines. It is this latter version of the distinction that Unger rejects as part of his attack on legal formalism. Yet it is precisely this latter version that must be established and maintained if an empowered democracy is to secure property and immunity rights under the rule of law. This is true, even if it were possible to have a system for protecting such rights that dispensed with the bar and the contrast between lawyer and layman.

CLS ultra-theorists argue that these inconsistencies in Unger's thought arise from his failure to take the rejection of liberal legal theory to the hilt. They contend that politics will never be adequately freed from its undue liberal confinement until we give up the idea that law, or any other system of rules, can objectively control individual action and thought. For the ultra-theorists, the liberal ideas of the rule of law and of individual rights protected by law are fictions that cripple the collective powers of human beings. The liberation of such powers requires the complete repudiation of those liberal ideas. Empowered democracy fails on that score.

It may appear, then, that Unger must choose between liberal democracy and the ultra-theorists' repudiation of law. But that is not right. Unger can still argue in favor of empowered democracy, but consistency requires that its defense demands a defense of the law-politics distinction and of the rule of law as well. And Unger can still claim that the institutions of liberal democracy unduly hamper the power of democratic political action to transform basic social arrangements, but consistency requires that he acknowledge that some significant liberal restraints on politics must be included in an empowered democracy. We can, then, sketch the following rough picture of the relations of liberalism, Unger's superliberalism, and the political philosophy behind ultra-theory. Liberalism defends rather substantial limitations on the power of democratic politics to transform society; it advocates a rule of law that will help stabilize the social order and settle in a relatively fixed manner the basic terms of life and association. Superliberalism defends greatly weakened limitations on the power of democratic politics; it advocates a rule of law that will settle in only a very tentative and provisional manner the basic terms of life and association, leave much of the social order vulnerable to radical transformation, and succeed in "cracking society open to politics."[32] The political philosophy behind CLS ultra-theory rejects all liberal limitations on democratic politics, including those incorporated into empowered democracy, as the product of illusion and mystification. Insofar as the issue is whether liberal democracy unduly confines politics, Unger and the ultra-theorists can make common cause against liberalism. Insofar as the issue is the possibility and/or desirability of the rule of law, Unger and liberals can make common cause against the CLS ultra-theorists. Questions surrounding the latter issue are the focus of the remainder of the chapter.

Criticizing CLS Ultra-Theory

Unger does not mount any sustained criticism of ultra-theory. In fact, he suggests that at present, there are no good grounds for rejecting ultra-theory. This is a puzzling position for him to take in light of the powerful tension between ultra-theory and the po-

[32] Unger, *Social Theory*, p. 48.

litical program he proposes. As we have seen, that program is heavily reliant on the establishment of the rule of law. An ultra-theorist would have to claim that Unger's program rests on a fundamentally flawed view of social reality. Although an ultra-theorist might form a pragmatic alliance with the defenders of empowered democracy for the purpose of transforming liberal democracy and helping to liberate democratic politics from at least some liberal constraints, the alliance could be only a temporary one. At some point and on some important issue, a radical political divergence would divide Unger from the ultra-theorists. For example, there would be a divergence about what steps should be taken next if Unger's program was brought to institutional realization. The ultra-theorist would mount a vigorous critique of the liberal elements that remained in an empowered democracy.

Indeed, the essence of the political program of ultra-theory is perpetual opposition to any settled social order, even the settled elements of the relatively unsettled empowered democracy. Tushnet is not shy about stating this program of permanent opposition. Referring to social changes that he would view as desirable from the perspective of today, he writes: "[W]hen things change all that will be left is to remain in opposition."[33] It is no wonder, then, that he describes his program as one of "interminable critique."[34] Unger, on the other hand, clearly rejects this political program of permanent opposition. His superliberalism is designed as an alternative to the political philosophy of interminable critique, an alternative that political radicals can embrace.

Superliberals and liberals alike thus have good reason to develop cogent criticisms of CLS ultra-theory. In the absence of such criticisms, there will be no convincing response to the CLS ultra-theorist who claims that reliance on the rule of law to constrain power is misguided. There will be no convincing response to the ultra-theorist who claims that any effort to put the social future under the control of the social past is an exercise in self-deception.

Ultra-theory relies, in fact, upon a seriously flawed conception of social reality and rests upon several fallacious inferences. We may begin the criticism of it with a point to which I have already alluded, concerning the issue of whether the social past can control the social future. The CLS ultra-theorist correctly believes that the social past can never guarantee the character of the social fu-

[33] Tushnet, "An Essay on Rights," p. 1402.

[34] Mark Tushnet, "Critical Legal Studies: An Introduction to Its Origins and Its Underpinnings," *Journal of Legal Education* 36 (1986): 516.

ture. It is never a necessary truth that the social world will continue to turn in the way it has been turning up to now. However, ultra-theorists fallaciously infer from this that the social past cannot control the social future, that social rules cannot constrain and channel human social behavior and thought. This inference is a fallacy because control is always a matter of degree; it may never reach the point of constituting a necessary connection between past and future, but it does not follow that there is no control.[35]

CLS ultra-theorists have been led astray here by an ill-conceived reliance on the metaphysical categories of contingency and necessity. They reason that the social future is contingent, that it does not have to be a certain way; in particular, it does not have to be a repetition of the social past. They fallaciously conclude that the social past can exert no control over the social future. Underlying this fallacious inference is the mistaken belief that there can be a relation of control between X and Y only if X's prescription that Y behave in a certain way necessarily leads to Y behaving in that way.

Moreover, the ultra-theorist's view that control requires necessary connections contradicts his own view that one individual can control another. Recall that the CLS ultra-theorist denies that social rules have the power to control the behavior and thought of individuals but that he simultaneously affirms that individuals (e.g., slaveowners) can control other individuals (e.g., their slaves). Yet the ultra-theorist argument explaining why rules cannot control individuals also defeats the possibility of individuals controlling other individuals. Nothing makes it impossible for slaves to revolt, for workers to rebel, for the oppressed to rise up. The ultra-theory argument would force one to conclude that masters exert no control over slaves, bosses no control over workers, the oppressors no control over the oppressed. These conclusions are flatly inconsistent with the claims of CLS ultra-theorists, in addition to being wholly implausible. The conclusion to draw from the fact that the oppressed can revolt at any time is not that the oppressors do not exert control over them but that the control is not total. And exactly the same conclusion should be drawn about social rules: The fact that such rules can be trashed at any moment does not show that they exert no control, only that the control is not total.

The problem for the ultra-theorist is to develop a convincing ac-

[35] Recall Llewellyn's description of a rule as laying a hand on the future, even though a few of its fingers may slip. See note 6.

count of constraint and control in social life that shows why individuals can control other individuals but social rules cannot control individuals. I do not believe that such an account can be developed. In order to see what undercuts the efforts to construct it, we must turn to a premise that ultra-theory shares with a starkly opposing kind of social theory.

At the opposite end of the spectrum of social theory from ultra-theory is the kind that postulates the existence of collective entities that exist over and above individuals, their actions, thoughts, and relations. These collective entities are thought to be the essential elements that constitute social reality and to have a power to control what individuals do, want, and think. For those who adopt this sort of social ontology, the decisive experience testifying to its truth is the experience of constraint exercised by the rules and roles of society, an experience distinct from that of constraint exercised by specific individuals. Durkheim gives clear expression to this view in his claim regarding the existence and character of social facts: "Since their essential characteristic is their power of exerting pressure on individual consciousnesses, it follows that they are not derived from the latter."[36]

As starkly different as this collectivist view is from that of CLS ultra-theory, it shares one crucial premise: If the experience of constraint by social rules, as opposed to constraint by specific individuals, is not an illusion, then society must be constituted by collective entities. Collectivists affirm the antecedent; CLS ultra-theorists deny the consequent. The premise is mistaken, however. It is possible to have constraint by rules, as opposed to constraint by specific individuals, without a collectivist ontology. In other words, Durkheim's inference is a non sequitur.

In order to show that this is so, we must examine the nature of social rules. The aim will be to show that there is an anticollectivist social ontology that can adequately account for the experience of constraint by rules and can account for it as distinct from the experience of constraint by specific individuals. In order to develop the needed account of social rules, I will rely on some of Hart's ideas regarding social rules, which we examined in chapter 2. Hart's account is useful for present purposes because it employs an ontology that contains human individuals, their actions,

[36] Émile Durkheim, *The Rules of Sociological Method*, 8th ed., trans. S. A. Solovay and J. H. Mueller (New York: MacMillan, 1964), p. 101.

thoughts, and relations to one another, but does not contain any collective entities in the Durkheimian sense.

Recall that in Hart's account, a social rule to do x exists in a given population if most people in it do x and adopt a critical internal perspective toward the doing of x. The internal perspective means that there is a disposition to regard the failure to do x as a reason for criticism. Put another way, the rule is regarded as action-guiding, and when the behavior called for by a rule fails to be performed, just about anybody in the population will regard the failure as grounds for criticism. Of course, that is the theoretical ideal. In real life, the internal and external aspects of rules are significantly weakened by rule breaking and by the failure of some to adopt the appropriate internal perspective. There is no clear point at which the rule vanishes. Social reality is not like that. It does not have sharply defined edges and boundaries, but it cannot thereby be excluded from the ontological map.

We now need to account for the experience of constraint by rules in a way that does not collapse it into the experience of constraint by specific individuals. Although the experience of constraint can be connected to all sorts of potential evils, the one in question here is that of being the object of criticism by others. People tend to be averse to criticism. To the extent that the feared agent of criticism is just anybody in the population, the experience is one of constraint by rules rather than by specific individuals. That is, insofar as I do x in order to avoid the criticism of no particular person but just anybody who may find out about it, I have an experience of constraint by rules. To the extent that the feared agent of criticism is a certain individual (or group of identifiable individuals), the experience is one of constraint by specific individual. The constraint is just as real in both cases; the potential undesirable consequence (criticism) is just as real in the two cases. And in both cases, only particular flesh-and-blood individuals can inflict the consequences. The difference is in the level of abstraction at which the agents who have the potential to inflict the undesirable consequences are thought of; in the case of rules, one abstracts from their particularity; in the case of specific individuals, one does not.[37]

The power of rules to constrain is thus not dependent on some

[37] The distinction that I have drawn between constraint by specific individuals and constraint by rules is largely based upon George Herbert Mead's concept of the generalized other. See Mead, *Mind, Self, and Society* (Chicago: University of Chicago Press, 1962), pp. 154–56.

mysterious social ontology that attributes to rules an existence in some Platonic heaven having a reality independent of the world of concrete individuals. Rules can exercise their power only through particular individuals. But when rules constrain, those particular individuals are thought of in a way that abstracts from their particularity.

This approach to the phenomenon of constraint exercised by rules undercuts ultra-theory. It understands rules so that the constraints they exercise over individuals operate through the same mechanisms that operate in the kinds of constraint that the ultra-theorist is prepared to acknowledge. This undercuts any effort to save ultra-theory by arguing for an account of constraint designed to show that constraint by specific individuals is real but that constraint by social rules is illusory. Any account of constraint by specific individuals can, given the powers of abstraction, easily be turned into an account of constraint by social rules.

The Structure of the Law

The rule of law requires more than that social rules be capable of exercising constraint over a population of individuals. It also requires that the mass of rules that constitute the law have some kind of objective structure. There is thus some truth in Alan Freeman's remark that "the continuing impulse to save the Idea of the Rule of Law . . . must to some extent imagine Law as a 'thing' with an objective referent structure."[38] Insofar as Freeman is suggesting that the idea of the rule of law requires an ontology that regards law as having a reality independent of the thoughts and actions of human individuals (i.e., as being a "thing"), he is wrong, as I hope to have shown in the previous section. But he is right insofar as he is suggesting that the rule of law requires that the mass of legal rules have some kind of objective structure that is independent of the way any particular individual happens to think of the rules as organized. What, then, determines the structure of legal doctrine? On what grounds can one say that a person who thinks of the structure in a radically different way is wrong?

The structure of the group of norms having legal authority is as much a matter of convention as is the legal authority of any particular norm within that group. Just as certain rules carry legal au-

[38] Alan Freeman, "Truth and Mystification in Legal Scholarship," *Yale Law Journal* 90 (1981): 1232.

thority by virtue of what most people in the relevant population conventionally think and do, the structure of those rules is determined by such conventions. Just as it is possible for a given individual to be mistaken about whether a certain rule has legal authority, it is possible for a given individual to be mistaken about the structure of the authoritative rules. Ignorance of what is conventionally accepted or misapplication of the conventional criteria can lead to mistakes in either case. The structure of legal doctrine, just like its content, is a matter of what most people in the relevant population conventionally think and do.

What is the relevant population for determining legal structure? The answer varies from society to society. In contemporary liberal societies, legal officials are the crucial element in that population, though some place should be reserved for lawyers, police, wardens, and even ordinary citizens. Legal officials must be placed at the apex of the relevant population in contemporary liberal states because most people, most of the time, act and think in a way that creates a social rule giving such officials the final say on the meaning of the law. The decisions of such officials usually—though not always—trump what ordinary citizens, wardens, police, and lawyers have to say. If there was a social rule establishing popular tribunals to pass final judgment on the meaning of the law, we would have a different relevant population for determining the structure of legal doctrine. But contemporary liberal states do not run that way.

The structure of legal doctrine in our system of law is not specified with full precision. There is some disagreement among legal officials over the relative centrality of the various rules that constitute the different departments of doctrine. Such disagreement leads to dissenting opinions, reversals of lower court rulings, and the like. However, this disagreement takes place against the backdrop of substantial agreement on the structure of doctrine. Judges may disagree about whether there is a "special relationship" between a psychiatrist and a person against whom one of his patients makes threats in the course of therapy. But most agree that the special-relationship rule is a relatively marginal exception to the central common law rule that there is no duty to act in aid of a person to whom one has no contractual or statutory duty of aid. It is not that most judges agree on the structure of tort doctrine in this regard because the structure has some kind of ontological status apart from the thoughts and actions of judges. Rather, tort doctrine has that structure because of the conventions of reasoning and decision adopted by judges.

Many CLS authors are willing to concede that there is a high degree of uniformity and predictability among judges and other legal officials in our system of law. They argue, however, that this is not due to the determinacy of law or the fact that doctrine has a structure independent of the way any particular person happens to think. Rather, the CLS argument is that it is due to the fact that judges tend to have similar socioeconomic backgrounds and so share similar political and ethical positions. It is these shared background normative principles, rather than some supposed objective doctrinal structure, that lead to the uniformity and predictability. In this regard, Kairys writes:

> The shared backgrounds, socialization, and experience of our judges . . . yield definite patterns in the ways they categorize, approach, and resolve social and political conflicts. Moreover, some rules and results are relatively uncontroversial and predictable in a particular historical context, not based on *stare decisis* or any other legal principle but because of widely shared social and political assumptions characteristic of that context.[39]

In a similar vein, Joseph Singer contends that there is a set of background conventions that give sufficient structure and determinacy to the mass of legal norms to enable reliable predictions to be made about legal outcomes: "Convention, rather than logic, tells us that judges will not interpret the Constitution to require socialism."[40]

In replying to Singer's claims, John Stick has argued that these background conventions are part of the law and not, as Singer presupposes, some set of extraneous factors introduced by judges because the law itself has an insufficiently determinate structure.[41] But why are such background conventions part of the law? The reason is suggested by my account of the ontology of law: because the content and structure of law are determined by the conventions accepted by legal officials. The structure of law, then, is not

[39] Kairys, "Legal Reasoning," p. 15.

[40] Joseph Singer, "The Player and the Cards: Nihilism and Legal Theory," *Yale Law Journal* 94 (1984): 22.

[41] John Stick, "Can Nihilism Be Pragmatic?" *Harvard Law Review* 100 (1986): 354–55.

objectively indeterminate but determined by norms whose authority is, like that of all legal norms, ultimately rooted in convention.

Law and Politics

The CLS reply to the foregoing argument is likely to be that a determinate structure for the law has been bought at a price that the liberal cannot afford—the breakdown of the law-politics distinction. If the background norms that determine the structure of doctrine are class-biased or otherwise unfairly tilted against certain normative conceptions, controversial ethical or political beliefs will taint legal reasoning, and the law-politics distinction will break down. The CLS claim will be that such norms are indeed unfairly tilted against certain viewpoints, especially egalitarian ones.

Note that this CLS argument shifts the issue from the question of whether the law has an objective structure to the question of whether the distinction between law and politics holds. The argument tacitly concedes that there is an objective structure to the law and proceeds to contend that the structure is normatively tilted in an unfair manner and so violates the law-politics distinction.

However, the argument rests on a confusion of two distinct issues. One issue is whether legal reasoning can proceed without any fresh assessment of the substantive merits of the normative views that contend in our political arena. This is an aspect of the issue whether law can be kept separate from politics. Quite distinct is the issue whether our politics are unfairly tilted against (or in favor of) certain normative viewpoints. The CLS argument fallaciously infers the breakdown of the separation of law and politics from the premise that our politics are unfairly tilted against certain normative views. Even if the unfairness charge is conceded, nothing follows for the law-politics distinction.

Thus, let us concede that the conventions that constitute the structure of doctrine are tilted against egalitarian views. It does not follow that an individual judge in reasoning about a case needs to make any fresh assessment of the normative views whose clash led to the establishment of those conventions. Her legal duty is to accept the conventions and do her legal reasoning from there, not to make a fresh assessment of the merits of the conventions and the values that underlie them. Even for the strictest liberal versions of the distinction between law and politics, the distinction holds if legal reasoning proceeds without such assessments. And whether legal reasoning can so proceed is, as a conceptual matter, independent of whether politics are unfairly biased.

CLS scholars will be quick to argue that judges often create the conventions that constitute the structure (and content) of doctrine. This is "judicial legislation," and according to CLS, it amounts to a clear violation of the law-politics distinction.

In response to this CLS claim, it must be said that any theory which allows for a significant degree of indeterminacy in our legal system will concede that judges sometimes go beyond what the law says in reaching a decision and that in doing so, they rely on political judgments. In chapter 2, I conceded the existence of a significant degree of indeterminacy in our system of law and agreed that there was a reliance on normative political judgments in deciding some cases. However, it would be too quick to infer from these concessions that CLS is correct in its charge that the law-politics distinction does not hold in our legal system. The premise that normative political judgments play a role in legal reasoning does not by itself entail that there is no real distinction between law and politics. The inference fails for two reasons. First, it may still be true that in the bulk of cases, legal reasoning can proceed without any fresh assessment of the merits of the normative views that contend with one another in the political arena. Second, even in cases where the law fails to dictate a determinate outcome, where political judgments play a role, legal reasoning might be required to operate under constraints that clearly distinguish it from the sorts of arguments found in the political arena.

In chapter 2, I argued that the dominant convention in our legal culture requires legal decisions and reasoning having maximum coherence with the conventionally accepted body of decisions, doctrines, and rules. The bulk of cases is governed by this convention, and on that account, judges typically make no fresh political assessments in rendering a decision. The decision is usually based on grounds of logical fit with the settled law, not on grounds of its political or moral soundness.

The dominant legal convention sometimes breaks down, as I argued in chapter 2. However, even when there is such a breakdown, judges are not free to render whatever decision they think best on moral or political grounds. There is still a convention operating that demands that the decision and the reasoning supporting it cohere with a substantial portion of the settled law. To be sure, this backup convention allows plenty of room for political judgment to operate, since there will often be a number of competing potential principles of decision that have substantial coherence with the settled law. Nonetheless, legal reasoning is still operating under a convention that demands a substantial degree of fit with the settled law, even under these relatively unconstrained conditions. Legal reasoning always operates under a "fit" requirement: either the "maximum-fit" requirement of the dominant convention or the "substantial-fit" requirement that operates when the dominant convention breaks down.

Political argument, on the other hand, operates under no fit requirements. It is free to invoke and defend principles that would prove incompatible with a far wider range of currently authoritative norms than the conventions of legal reasoning would allow. And the legislation that comes out of such argument may demand major restructuring in whole areas of law, far more restructuring than would be consistent with the demands of legal reasoning in our legal culture.

Legal reasoning can thus be clearly distinguished from the relatively unconstrained modes of argument and deliberation characteristic of political or ideological debate. Even where the law is indeterminate, legal reasoning proceeds under constraints that distinguish it from the sorts of arguments found in the political arena. A significant distinction between law and politics survives the admission that political judgments play some role in legal reasoning.[42]

The CLS radical will reject this claim by contending that the fit requirements impose no true constraints on legal reasoning; any norm can be understood as fitting the settled law as well as any other. But we have seen that this contention rests on a conception of language and social reality that is indefensible. Once it is conceded that the fit requirements have real teeth, there is no good reason to deny that there is a genuine distinction between law and politics in our political culture.

The Fundamental Contradiction

Thus far in this chapter, I have argued that social rules can control power by constraining and channeling behavior and thought and that the law of liberal states is a body of rules with an objective structure, capable of yielding determinate legal outcomes. The

[42] Cf. Kent Greenawalt, "Discretion and Judicial Decision: The Elusive Quest for the Fetters That Bind Judges," *Columbia Law Review* 75 (1975): 382.

radical wing of CLS, invoking ultra-theory, denies that rules, as opposed to individuals, can constrain and that law can have any objective structure. I have attempted to show that ultra-theory relies on an indefensible conception of rules and social reality and that an adequate conception reveals that the law can have an objective structure and control individual behavior. I have also argued that there is a genuine distinction between law and politics in our political culture, even though it must be conceded that there is some infiltration of political judgment into legal reasoning. But there is a line of thinking within the CLS literature holding that even granting my arguments to this point, it would be a mistake to accept the liberal claim that we should rely on the law to control power and protect people from oppression and persecution. This line of thinking centers upon Duncan Kennedy's account of "the fundamental contradiction."[43]

The fundamental contradiction, as Kennedy explains it, involves an insoluble dilemma concerning the relations between the self and the other. The dilemma hinges on the fact that the individual needs others in order to affirm his sense of identity and self-worth but that the others who are thus needed pose a simultaneous threat to the individual's sense of identity and self-worth. Only they can affirm what the individual needs to be affirmed, but they can also destroy it. The dilemma an individual faces, then, is how to order his relationships with others so as to receive what he needs from them without running the undue risk that they will not only fail to give it but will destroy what he needs to be affirmed. To say that the individual's relations with others is plagued by the fundamental contradiction is to say that there is such a dilemma but that there is no adequate solution to it.

As more than one commentator has pointed out, the fundamental contradiction is not a contradiction in the logical sense.[44] There is certainly no inconsistency in asserting that others are both needed by the individual and a threat to him. Nor is there any inconsistency in asserting that there is no adequate solution to the dilemma that stems from this double-edged fact about the relation of the self to the other. The statement of the fundamental contra-

[43] Duncan Kennedy, "The Structure of Blackstone's Commentaries," *Buffalo Law Review* 28 (1979): 211–21.

[44] See, e.g., Phillip Johnson, "Do You Sincerely Want to Be Radical?" *Stanford Law Review* 36 (1984): 257, and Jeffrey Reiman, "Law, Rights, Community, and the Structure of Liberal Legal Justification," in *Justification: Nomos XXVIII*, ed. J. R. Pennock and J. W. Chapman (New York: New York University Press, 1986), pp. 190–91.

diction consists of the perfectly coherent conjunction of those two assertions. Perhaps it would be less misleading to speak of the "fundamental dilemma" in our relations with others, but we need not get entangled with terminology here.

What is the connection between the fundamental contradiction and the law? Kennedy claims that liberal legal theory is committed to the idea that the rule of law is capable of solving the fundamental dilemma: "The liberal mode [of legal thought] was ultimately dependent on mediation [of the fundamental contradiction] through the rule of law."[45] The rule of law allegedly accomplishes this mediation or resolution of the dilemma by sorting out those interactions that are bad for the individual from those that are good, disallowing the former and permitting the latter. The law, if properly formulated and organized, will protect the individual from the threats while freeing him to engage in those relations that can affirm his sense of identity and self-worth.

Kennedy and his CLS followers, of course, vigorously attack the idea that the law is capable of providing a solution to the fundamental contradiction. They regard such an attack as part of an internal critique of liberal legal theory, showing that it cannot meet the requirements it sets for itself. Thus, Clare Dalton says that liberal theory relies on the notion that legal rules can provide "clear guidelines as to what are positive and what are negative interactions" and can "prevent the state from overstepping its proper boundaries."[46] However, no such rules can be provided because of "our inability to decide how we should conceive relationships between people, how we should understand and police the boundary between self and other."[47] Thus, "the liberal system fails to live up to its expectations of itself. The flaw is measured against internal, not external, standards."[48] In the wake of this internal critique of liberalism, Dalton and her CLS colleagues conclude that it would be a mistake to follow liberal advice and rely on the rule of law in order to confine and regulate power.

This CLS argument against liberalism, largely a straw-man argument, rests on a confusion between two quite different claims. One is that the rule of law can solve the fundamental dilemma in our relations with others. Perhaps there is some liberal theorist

[45] Kennedy, "Blackstone's Commentaries," p. 353.

[46] Clare Dalton, "An Essay in the Deconstruction of Contract Doctrine," *Yale Law Journal* 94 (1985): 1006.

[47] Ibid.

[48] Ibid., 1006, n. 12.

who has made such a claim, though I doubt it. But even if there is such a theorist, there is no reason to regard his view on the matter as essential to liberal legal theory. The soundest liberal theories hold not the rather implausible claim that the rule of law solves the dilemma but the quite different claim that the establishment of the rule of law is a better way to respond to the problem than a response that would leave public and private power unconfined and unregulated by law.[49]

Of course the law cannot eliminate the risk that the relations in which a person finds himself will oppress rather than affirm him. Of course the law cannot guarantee that as long as it is obeyed, individuals will involve themselves in only self-affirming relations. It would be preposterous to think otherwise. But no interesting issue between liberalism and CLS hinges on whether the law can accomplish those ends. The issue is whether the rule of law is a better way than the alternatives for handling problems of persecution, prejudice, and oppression. Perhaps the law really is not effective to any significant degree when it seeks to regulate and contain the forces of persecution, prejudice, and oppression. Perhaps some alternative means of control would be better. I explore these issues in the next two sections. The point here is that they are not decided by pointing out that the law is incapable of guaranteeing that the individual will be protected from others who may subvert his sense of identity and self-worth.

Abstraction and the Law

CLS writers often condemn the law for treating, or attempting to treat, people as abstractions. For example, Karl Klare claims that one of the "enormous problems" with liberal theory is its "erroneous belief that it is possible to treat the individual as an abstraction, apart from the entire texture of his or her social life."[50]

The difficulty with Klare's contention is that it wholly ignores

[49] Cf. Don Herzog, "As Many as Six Impossible Things before Breakfast," *California Law Review* 75 (1987): 627.

[50] Karl Klare, "Labor Law as Ideology," *Industrial Relations Law Journal* 4 (1981): 479. As far as I can see, Klare's claim here is utterly inconsistent with his assertion elsewhere that "legalism must be viewed as a great human achievement." Klare, "Law-Making as Praxis," *Telos* 40 (1979): 133. Legalism would be impossible to achieve if it were not possible to treat persons in ways that abstracted from their concrete particularity. Moreover, the assertion about legalism is inconsistent with Klare's efforts to discredit the law-politics distinction. Klare, "The Law School Curriculum in the 1980's: What's Left?" *Journal of Legal Education* 32 (1982): 339.

the fact that all social rules treat individuals as abstractions. It is not only possible for individuals to be treated in that way; it is essential to human social life. Where there are social rules, people must regard themselves and others as "just anybody" or "no one special," to borrow Sartre's suggestive term.[51] This is because rules require behavioral regularities simple enough to be cognized (in relatively short order) by the normal mind. If there were no behavioral regularities, there could perhaps be ideals, but no rules. If the regularities were not cognizable, it would be senseless to adopt a critical internal attitude toward them; that is, it would be senseless to regard the rules as action-guiding. And if there are to be action-guiding behavioral regularities that are cognized by most people in a population, such regularities must be formulated in relatively abstract terms. This is just another way of saying that the people in the relevant population must abstract from their particularity: if they were unable to do so, they could have no action-guiding rules.

Perhaps Klare really means to claim that it is undesirable to treat the individual as an abstraction. This is suggested by his invocation of the romantic young Marx who believed that treating different people in the same way was both essential to law and morally objectionable.[52] But it is simply not tenable to argue that individuals should never be treated in ways that abstract from their particularity. The position requires the belief that all human relation-

[51] See Peter Caws, *Sartre* (London: Routledge and Kegan Paul, 1979), pp. 24, 97, 110, 121, 198. Cf. Mead, *Mind, Self and Society*, pp. 154–56.

[52] Klare cites Marx when he writes of liberal law as treating people as abstractions. Klare, "Labor Law as Ideology," 479 n. 115. The invocation of the stridently antilegalistic views of the young Marx here is difficult to reconcile with Klare's claim from an earlier piece that the idea of a society without law is "a dangerous fantasy which . . . can lead only to the arbitrary tyranny of Stalinism." See Klare, "Law-Making as Praxis," p. 135.

Peter Gabel is also very confusing in his assertions regarding the future of law. On the one hand, he advocates a social movement directed toward "the delegitimation of the law altogether, which is to say the delegitimation of the notion that social life is created and enforced by imaginary ideas." Gabel, "Reification in Legal Reasoning," *Research in Law and Sociology* 3 (1980): 46. I take this statement to be a reflection of Gabel's view that such terms as *law* and *state* have no objective referents. But he adds in a footnote that his claims about the delegitimation of law "should not be taken to imply that there would be 'no law' in a future and more humane society." He attempts to clarify this by saying that in a society such as he envisions there would "develop provisional forms of moral consensus that are externalized and communicated as part of a 'constitutive' politics" (50, n. 11). The only sense that I can make of these rather opaque assertions is that Gabel believes that there would be authoritative norms in the future society but that these norms would not be identified, applied, and altered by Hart-like secondary rules, so the situation would be prelegal in Hart's sense.

ships should be transformed into relations of the deepest intimacy. For only a relationship of such intimacy could overcome completely the tendency to treat others as abstractions. Indeed, Kierkegaard believed that only the individual's relation to God could completely liberate him from being seen as an abstraction; relations with other humans could never be close enough to accomplish it.

We need not go as far as Kierkegaard, though, to recognize that it requires an extraordinary degree of intimacy to remove even most traces of abstraction from one's relations with another. It may well be that such a degree of intimacy is something to be cherished. However, it is preposterous to think that it must be the model of all social relations, and one need not be a liberal individualist to make such an assertion. The most communitarian of human cultures still have social rules, and all social rules involve treating people as "just anybodies," as the abstractions called for by the rules. There is simply no such thing as a human culture without social rules, and there is no good reason to hold that such a culture would be more desirable for human beings were it possible to create one.[53]

Some CLS thinkers suggest that the problem is not abstraction per se, but the relatively high level of abstraction at which law, especially liberal law, operates. It is law that should be eliminated, not all social rules.[54] Clare Dalton expresses this line of thinking in the course of describing the purpose of her critique of law: "Imagine critique as a powerful device for stripping away from us, if we

[53] The assertion that rules are found in all cultures must not be misinterpreted to deny the anthropological evidence that in all cultures rules are often bent, broken, and evaded. There are always rules, but, as Malinowski well puts it, the rules "cannot be rigid, since they act rather as elastic forces of which the tension decreases or increases." See Malinowski, "Introduction," in *Law and Order in Polynesia*, ed. H. I. Hogbin (Hamden, Conn.: Shoe String Press, 1961), p. xxviii. The elasticity of all rules has some important implications for the liberal idea that legal rules can effectively protect people from oppression and intolerance. See the final section in this chapter, "Law as Protector."

[54] Not all CLS authors advocate relinquishing formal legal institutions in favor of nonlegal modes of social regulation. See note 57. Several CLS authors suggest that law needs not so much to be jettisoned as to be made more intelligible to the layperson, so that the contrast between legal expert and layperson can be softened. See Roberto Unger, *Critical Legal Studies*, p. 111, and William Simon, "The Ideology of Advocacy," *Wisconsin Law Review* 1978 (1978): 129–44. This suggestion is wholly consistent with the fundamental principles of liberal legal theory. Indeed, CLS authors would find a useful ally on this issue in the great liberal Jeremy Bentham, who strongly advocated reconstruction of the English legal system to reduce greatly the role played by lawyers. See Frederick Rosen, *Jeremy Bentham and Representative Democracy* (New York: Oxford University Press, 1983), p. 158.

choose, the legal abstractions by which we order our perceptions, leaving us groping to be sure, but forced to deploy whatever *other* means of decision are available to us."[55] I take Dalton to be suggesting that law itself be jettisoned, not merely the particular set of legal categories that reign at present.

Let it be conceded that law typically operates at a higher level of abstraction than other social rules, at least in a liberal society that exhibits moral, religious, and political pluralism. The law there will often exclude considerations that would be viewed as relevant from the perspective of a certain ethical system, religious doctrine, or political morality. If it did not, legal reasoning could not be clearly distinguished from unconstrained moral inquiry and political choice. Moreover, the liberal conception of the rule of law requires that public and private power be regulated by norms that are generalizable across situations and can be applied in a regularized, predictable manner. This again requires that certain aspects of a case be deliberately disregarded in the name of predictability. Where institutions cannot presuppose that all officials share the same set of background moral, religious, and political ideas, the authoritative norms that they lay down cannot regularly call for highly context-sensitive judgments without threatening the regularity, predictability, and perhaps even the stability of the system.

Liberal law, then, does require a high level of abstraction, in the sense that it sometimes prescribes a deliberate disregard for certain particulars of a case that could be quite relevant to a decision if one were involved in more context-sensitive moral or political deliberation. Thus, the liberal should concede that legal reasoning will often take place at a significantly higher level of abstraction than context-sensitive normative deliberation. But he will contend that there are two very good arguments for institutions that regulate power in accordance with reasoning that proceeds at a relatively high level of abstraction, given a context of moral, religious, and political pluralism. First, it settles the terms of social life in a way that allows us to avoid reopening fundamental questions about society and human life every time a conflict or dispute breaks out. This liberates our energies from constant moral and ideological battles and enables us to pursue vigorously other aims: commercial, scientific, artistic, and so forth. Second, legal abstraction can materially assist in protecting people from intolerance and preju-

[55] Clare Dalton, "Review of Kairys, *The Politics of Law*," *Harvard Woman's Law Journal* 6 (1983): 241.

dice: When the Jew, the black, or the homosexual is regarded as "just anybody" by the existing system of legal rules, he or she is protected from the inclinations of intolerance and prejudice that could well play a role in more context-sensitive modes for regulating public and private power. Let us examine the CLS response to each of these liberal arguments.

Many CLS thinkers will see in the first liberal defense of the abstractness of law a characteristic liberal effort to demobilize energies that could be used to reconstruct society. The liberal aims to channel those energies into private pursuits that leave the existing structures of power and privilege unchallenged. Critics object to such rechanneling, not only because they find current social arrangements pervaded by illegitimate hierarchies of power and privilege but also because they believe that the best form of human social life is one that has, in Unger's word, a high degree of *plasticity*.[56] Existing liberal democracies are condemned because they are suffused with oppression and domination and excessively rigidified against the potentially transformative effects of political action.

The extent to which the basic terms of social life should be open to transformative political action and the degree to which energies should be channeled into political or nonpolitical realms are among the fundamental issues that divide liberal political morality from that of CLS. I do not intend to delve into the profound questions about human life that these issues implicate. I will limit myself to two main points.

First, reasoning about the extent to which society should be open to political transformation requires judgments about the worth of political activity relative to other human endeavors. Some liberals suggest that one can remain neutral on this issue of relative worth, but they are wrong. They typically argue that as long as institutional arrangements provide people with the opportunity for both political and nonpolitical activity, leaving the choice to the individual, then the system is neutral on the question of the worth of those activities. But such an argument misses the crucial point that even when arrangements provide opportunity for such choice, different sets of institutional arrangements provide different levels of incentive for people to engage in political activity. Roughly speaking, the more that is at stake in politics and the more that can be accomplished through normal political activity

[56] Unger, *Social Theory*, p. 59.

under a given set of arrangements, the greater the incentive the system provides for people to engage in political action.

Which set of arrangements should be chosen? Arrangements such as liberal democracy, in which many important issues are insulated from politics? Arrangements such as empowered democracy, in which much more is at stake in the course of normal politics? One's judgment about the worth of political activity is quite pertinent to the choice; other things being equal, the higher one rates the relative worth of political activity, the more reason one will have to choose arrangements, such as empowered democracy, that provide greater motivation to engage in politics. Unger defends empowered over liberal democracy in part because he has a higher estimation of the relative worth of political activity than liberals typically do. His higher estimation of its worth is rooted in his view that political activity is a primary form of activity in which humans can display their context-transcending capacity, and he cherishes that human capacity.

Ordinary liberals have a somewhat lower estimation of the human context-transcending capacity, as Galston's criticisms of Unger make abundantly clear, and so a somewhat lower estimation of the inherent worth of transformative politics. Unger does not try to hide the judgments of worth that lie behind his superliberalism; unlike many of his fellow liberals, Galston does not try to hide the competing judgments that lie behind his liberalism. Both are right to see that a political philosophy cannot remain neutral on the vital question of the worth of different forms of human activity.

My second point regarding the worth of politics is that those CLS thinkers who believe that making social life substantially more plastic to political activity requires jettisoning law are wrong. There are no grounds for thinking that any system of law necessarily rigidifies social life at least as much as the law of existing liberal democracies does. As Unger understood in formulating the principles of empowered democracy, the CLS position should not be to eliminate all law but to eliminate those elements of law that freeze too solidly the terms of social life. Systems of law that make social life more malleable to political activity may well need to contain authoritative norms formulated at very high levels of abstraction.

The second liberal argument in favor of legal abstraction is that it can materially assist in the protection of people against whom there is some significant level of illegitimate social hostility. The abstractness of law can require official decision makers to disregard those features of a person that might otherwise lead the decision maker to act on intolerant or prejudicial impulses. For example, if a Jew is trying to recover damages for breach of contract, the rules of contract law will prohibit the judge from taking into account his religion and holding it against him.[57]

CLS thinkers who advocate that we give up on law entirely may contend that legal rules will fail to be effective at protecting those who need protection. Where there is anti-Semitism, they will fail effectively to protect Jews; where there is racism, they will fail effectively to protect blacks, and so forth. Legal rules may have some power to constrain individual conduct, but, the argument goes, they will lack the power to constrain effectively those forms of conduct that issue from religious prejudice, racial hatred, and the like. Thus, we must turn away from the law and legal institutions if our aim is to protect the weak, the despised, and the outcast from oppression.

This CLS-style argument contains the outlines of some very serious limitations on the power of law to promote justice, limitations that liberal legal philosophers must acknowledge. I put off until the next section a detailed discussion of those limitations and how the soundest versions of liberal theory will deal with them. Let me grant for the moment that law will fail effectively to protect those who need protection. Two immediate questions remain. Is there any reason to think that alternative institutional arrangements that fully replace law and legal institutions will be more effective? Is there any reason to think that such alternatives will actually exacerbate intolerance and oppression, given a context of moral, religious, and political pluralism?

These two questions lead to ones about institutional arrangements. How will nonlegal modes of conflict resolution and social regulation operate in a society in which there are fundamental conflicts over the good, the right, the just, and the sacred? How will those modes protect people with unpopular conceptions of

[57] Nancy Rosenblum has nicely captured the general value of legal abstractions in a pluralist context:

> Thinking of oneself and others as if they are simply "persons" bearing rights promotes conduct that supports civil society and constitutional democracy. Liberalism requires people to inhibit the full range and force of their personal judgments and affective ties. In a heterogeneous society cooperation depends on indirectness and impartiality.

Rosenblum, *Another Liberalism* (Cambridge: Harvard University Press, 1987), p. 161.

the good or the sacred? Dalton's remarks about our "groping" for answers once law is jettisoned appear to reveal that she has no clear idea of what the answers to these institutional questions are, and lacking even a sketch of such answers, it is difficult to see how she can conclude that eliminating law is the preferable alternative.[58] Why not conclude instead that things will be just as bad were law to be eliminated? Or why not conclude that things may well be worse? For the antinomian argument to do more than just win a stalemate, these questions must be addressed.

The central problem with the antinomian view, however, is its disregard for the contribution that law can make to the taming of intolerance and prejudice. In the next section, my aim will be to show just how such a contribution is possible.

Law as Protector

In the course of a conversation with Horatio, Hamlet belittles those who would seek protection in the law from being victimized by injustice. The two men are discussing the kinds of parchment on which the laws are written:

> HAMLET: Is not parchment made of sheepskins?
> HORATIO: Ay, my lord, and of calves' skins too.
> HAMLET: They are sheep and calves which seek out assurance in that . . .
>
> (*Hamlet* 5.1.114–17)

Are those who rely on the protection of law indeed sheep and calves, unknowingly vulnerable to slaughter? Can the law really protect individuals from the state and from each other? Can scratches on parchment really exercise a power to protect people?

If the law consisted merely of inscriptions on parchment, words on paper, it would surely lack any such power. I have argued, however, that the law is more than that. Law is not merely, or even primarily, on parchment and paper. It is in the minds and

[58] Critical theorist Richard Abel is much more cautious and prudent than Dalton in drawing conclusions about the desirability of replacing law with informal modes of social regulation. After recounting some of the virtues and vices of formal legal institutions and suggesting that the final moral verdict on them is uncertain, Abel writes, "If the bottom line of the balance sheet on formalism is uncertain, so is the verdict on informalism, with which we have much less experience." See Abel, "Introduction," in *The Politics of Informal Justice*, ed. Abel (New York: Academic Press, 1982) vol. 1, p. 11. Abel goes on to mention some of the ways in which informal institutions tend to increase oppression and illegitimate domination.

the actions of human beings. Like any other element of social reality, it consists of certain patterns of thinking and acting, and as such, it does have the power to exercise constraint over individuals and to regulate and limit human power and action. Yet we may still wonder if law can protect individuals in just those ways that the liberal tradition has regarded as crucially important: protecting persons from religious persecution, racial intolerance, and all the other forms of irrational and immoral hatred and fear that infect social life. It is one thing for law to regulate commercial transactions, the making of contracts, the sale of land. There the law can serve as a kind of coordination device that overcomes Prisoner's Dilemma situations and enables all involved to pursue their goals more effectively. The liberal legal tradition has certainly taken such coordination to be an important virtue of law. But can the law limit and regulate power and action when it comes to the various forms of invidious discrimination, irrational fear, and oppressive intolerance from which humankind has had the misfortune to suffer? Can it limit the expression of religious prejudice or racial hatred? Can it protect the outcast, the despised, or the weak? Can it protect those who dissent from those who would suppress their message and oppress their person?

There is an argument deserving serious consideration that claims that law cannot defeat the human impulses toward intolerance, oppression, and persecution, not because social rules are inherently unable to constrain conduct but because such impulses will overwhelm the law's formal efforts to regulate them. At least, the impulses will overwhelm the law if they are as powerful as liberalism typically regards them.

There is this important element of truth to the argument that, given the liberal picture of human beings, law will prove incapable of effectively confining the impulses of intolerance, oppression, and persecution: Legal rules and procedures cannot, by themselves and in opposition to the force of powerful norms and mores in society, defeat the urge to oppress, persecute, and degrade some disfavored group. Perhaps there are some liberals who have thought that the law could by itself counteract the force of custom and the power of culture, but they are wrong. If a social situation is seething with a deeply rooted, pervasive, and violent anti-Semitism, then it is not likely that the rule of law will be an effective tool to prevent the maltreatment of Jews. More likely, there will be laws that license such maltreatment and/or informal mechanisms that protect anyone who persecutes Jews in some manner prohibited or unauthorized by law. Legal rules cannot accomplish the task of confining the oppressive exercise of power if they must labor alone in the teeth of powerful nonlegal norms that operate in a culture. They need assistance from at least some other social norms. Of course, among the additional auxiliary norms must be one that mandates respect for the rule of law itself, but more than that would be required in the face of powerful counternorms.

Perhaps the most famous proponent of the general point that I am advocating here is Tocqueville. After surveying American culture and law, he concludes, "The laws and customs of the Anglo-Americans are therefore that special and predominant cause of their greatness."[59] But Tocqueville quickly qualifies his claim and leaves no doubt that he believes that our customs are much more important than our laws and would defeat the operation of any set of laws that opposed their basic purposes:

> I am convinced that the most advantageous situation and the best possible laws cannot maintain a constitution in spite of the customs of a country; while the latter may turn to some advantage the most unfavorable positions and the worst laws. The importance of customs is a common truth to which study and experience incessantly direct our attention.[60]

To be sure, not all liberals would go as far as Tocqueville in attributing primary importance to nonlegal social rules and only secondary importance to the law. A recent expositor of Tocqueville has even characterized his version of liberalism as "strange," in part because of the overwhelming importance that the French thinker attaches to nonlegal social rules.[61] But any liberal who would believe that legal rules can by themselves operate effectively in the teeth of all other relevant social norms has wildly exaggerated the power of law. The soundest versions of liberal legal philosophy can and should allow that nonlegal social norms can often defeat the operation of formal legal rules and procedures.[62]

[59] Alexis de Tocqueville, *Democracy in America* (New York: Vintage, 1945), vol. 1, p. 332.

[60] Ibid., p. 334.

[61] Roger Boescher, *The Strange Liberalism of Alexis de Tocqueville* (Ithaca, N.Y.: Cornell University Press, 1987), pp. 177–85.

[62] Owen Fiss is one contemporary legal liberal who insists that law cannot do its liberal job of protecting people without assistance from norms that are part of the general culture. He writes, "Law has been threatened by the disintegration of public values in the larger society. . . . In order to save the law, we must look beyond the law." Fiss, "The Death of Law?" *Cornell Law Review* 72 (1986): 14. Whether or not Fiss's view that law is under threat is accurate, it is clear that he understands

Liberal legal philosophers can go further than the historically nonspecific claim that law needs the assistance of other social norms in order to effectively protect people from intolerance, prejudice, and oppression. They can agree with critical theorists such as David Trubek who argue that contemporary liberal democracies fall far short of meeting the ideals of equality and freedom for all that are embedded in the traditions of our political thought. And they can agree with Trubek in rejecting "the delusion that changes in law and legal institutions alone—without changes in other aspects of society—can resolve the tensions or eliminate the gaps" that arise from the pervasive discrepancy between our political ideals and the political reality.[63] It is perfectly consistent with the soundest versions of liberal legal theory to argue that in contemporary liberal democracies, there are pervasive injustices that cannot be uprooted solely by means of law. The legal liberal would and should insist, however, that such injustices cannot be eliminated in any secure and lasting way without the assistance of law.

If the argument against the effectiveness of law in protecting people from the impulses of intolerance and oppression is to join the issue with the soundest versions of legal liberalism, then it must claim that legal rules are always either redundant or useless in the following way: The rules work to constrain oppressive impulses only when they are not needed because other social norms will do so, and when they are needed because other norms are insufficiently strong, legal rules will not work at all. However, such a position is implausible for several reasons.

Once it is conceded that social rules can constrain conduct, there is no reason to think that legal rules are incapable of exercising some independent constraining influence. And once such an independent influence is granted, there is no reason to deny that legal rules can make a contribution to the restraint of oppressive power.

In addition to exerting a power of their own, legal rules interact with other social norms and can help to change them. The law can be part of a process that creates a culture more deeply imbued with the spirit of toleration and mutual respect. Perhaps the end point

---

that law is dependent on the rest of culture. He also understands that the dependence is a mutual one, a point that no legal liberal should neglect to make. See "The Death of Law?" p. 15.

[63] David Trubek, "Complexity and Contradiction in the Legal Order: Balbus and the Challenge of Critical Social Thought about Law," *Law and Society Review* 11 (1977): 545.

of this process is a situation where legal protections against oppressive inclinations and exercises of power are superfluous. Perhaps such an end point is an unrealistic fantasy. But even if it is not fantasy, even if someday that end point will be reached, for now and the foreseeable future, we are and will be at a stage where law is far from a superfluity.[64]

In the course of criticizing liberal legal philosophy, Robert Gordon has argued against "the kind of rule fetishism that supposes salvation comes through rules, rather than through the social practices that the rulemakers try to symbolize and crystallize."[65] It should now be apparent that Gordon's criticism of liberalism in this regard rests on several misconceptions. First, liberal theory does not promise salvation through legal rules; what it promises is a society that does a better job of protecting people from intolerance, prejudice, and oppression than it would if law was dispensed with. Second, Gordon poses a false dichotomy: Protection must be attempted either through rules (presumably he has legal rules in mind) or through the nonlegal practices of society. The soundest version of liberal theory will reject this dichotomy and argue that protection from intolerance, prejudice, and oppression requires both legal rules and at least some complementary social practices.

Morton Horwitz has correctly pointed out that the rule of law can constrain not only oppressive and misguided uses of power but also benevolent and beneficial ones.[66] Whether the rule of law is to be prized, then, hinges on the question of whether there is a greater need to confine through the rule of law the intolerant and oppressive impulses of humans or to liberate the tolerant and benevolent impulses from the constraints of legality. I do not believe that there is an *a priori* answer to this question. To that extent, Horwitz is quite right to say that it is a mistake to characterize the

[64] It is instructive that many minority legal scholars, while welcoming CLS attacks on the racism, sexism, and economic exploitation endemic in contemporary liberal democracies, reject the radical CLS view that legal rights and rules can provide no genuine protection for individuals and should be scrapped. Richard Delgado describes the attack on rights and rules as "the most problematic aspect of the CLS program." Delgado, "The Ethereal Scholar: Does Critical Legal Studies Have What Minorities Want?" *Harvard Civil Rights–Civil Liberties Law Review* 22 (1987): 304. See also Patricia Williams, "Alchemical Notes: Reconstructing Ideals from Deconstructed Rights," *Harvard Civil Rights–Civil Liberties Law Review* 22 (1987): 423–24.

[65] Robert Gordon, "Unfreezing Legal Reality: Critical Approaches to Law," *Florida State Law Review* 15 (1987): 219.

[66] Morton Horwitz, "The Rule of Law: An Unqualified Human Good?" *Yale Law Journal* 86 (1977): 566.

rule of law as an "unqualified human good," a characterization made by E. P. Thompson.[67] However, the sorry human history of persecution, prejudice, and intolerance over the past several centuries makes one conclusion inescapable: Within the context of the nation-state and over the foreseeable future, the need to confine the impulses of intolerance and oppression with the requirements of legality will continue to be far greater than the need to liberate the impulses of tolerance and benevolence from the restrictions of the rule of law.[68]

There are undoubtedly elements of the liberal tradition which exaggerate the extent to which the law alone gives contemporary liberal societies the degree of humanity and decency they have. There are undoubtedly elements of the liberal tradition which exaggerate the power of law to work its will against the entrenched customs and traditions of a culture. We would be wise to keep in mind Tocqueville's lesson about the failures of law in cultural settings where it has tried to operate in opposition to pervasive and deep-seated social norms. But it would be equally wrong to dismiss the protections offered by the law as superfluous or useless. Between the area in which law is useless because it receives insufficient support from the rest of the culture and the area in which law is superfluous because the rest of the culture provides all of the protections we can reasonably ask for, there is a wide expanse of territory. It is within the borders of that territory that law can and does make a difference. It is within the borders of that territory that legal rights can and do work to protect people from the evils of intolerance, prejudice, and oppression. This is the heart of the liberal tradition in legal philosophy. It is a tradition worthy of allegiance.

[67] Ibid. See E. P. Thompson, *Whigs and Hunters: The Origins of the Black Act* (New York: Pantheon, 1975), p. 266.

[68] Don Herzog drastically overstates the liberal case when he sarcastically argues: "No one has ever had to fear that the rule of law prevents the benevolent exercise of power: State functionaries are hardly poised waiting to do us splendid good deeds that alas! they're forbidden by law from doing." See Herzog, "As Many as Six Impossible Things before Breakfast," p. 619. Herzog's statement displays an extraordinary disregard for one of the central issues of twentieth-century jurisprudence, viz., whether the administrative-welfare state is compatible with the rule of law. See chapter 2. Of course, critical theorists would not defend the welfare state as an agent of good. Yet, many liberals would defend it as an agent of good, and those who do certainly should be concerned to address with some care the claim that the observance of the rule of law would hamstring the activity of the welfare state, even if such liberals do not have to conclude that the claim is accurate.

INDEX

INDEX